HILARY OF POITIERS' ROLE
IN THE ARIAN STRUGGLE

KERKHISTORISCHE STUDIËN

BEHORENDE BIJ HET

NEDERLANDS ARCHIEF VOOR KERKGESCHIEDENIS

ONDER REDACTIE VAN

Dr. J. N. BAKHUIZEN VAN DEN BRINK, Dr. C. C. DE BRUIN

Dr. W. F. DANKBAAR

DEEL XII

HILARY OF POITIERS' ROLE
IN THE ARIAN STRUGGLE

door

DR. C. F. A. BORCHARDT

'S-GRAVENHAGE

MARTINUS NIJHOFF

1966

Dr. C. F. A. BORCHARDT

HILARY OF POITIERS' ROLE
IN THE ARIAN STRUGGLE

THE HAGUE
MARTINUS NIJHOFF
1966

PRINTED IN THE NETHERLANDS

To
Sanet and
my parents

INTRODUCTION

Every struggle brings great men into prominence, because the slumbering powers inert in them are aroused to action. The truth of this statement is proved in the Arian struggle and among the many great men the figures of Athanasius in the East, and Hilary, the bishop of Poitiers, in the West, rise above their contemporaries.[1] One German scholar called them the two pillars of the Church in the East and the West.[2] Of the two, Hilary is less known, yet well-known by the epithet which the historian K. Hase gave to him, namely "durch Thaten, Leiden und Schriften der Athanasius des Abendlandes."[3]

Scholars agree that in words and deeds he did not play such an important part in the history of the Church as Athanasius, although he did occupy an important place among the secondary figures in the Arian dispute, but in "depth of earnestness and massive strength of intellect he is a match for Athanasius himself, and in powers of orderly arrangement decidedly superior."[4] Smulders maintains that in the formation of doctrine his place is certainly near to that of Athanasius and Basil.[5] Another scholar holds the view that as a thinker he surpassed the Alexandrian.[6] Harnack thought that he was "bei aller Abhängigkeit von Athanasius ein eigenthümlicher Denker, der den alexandrinischen Bischof als Theologe übertroffen hat."[7]

Loofs saw in Hilary a true "disciple of the truth," as he called himself in his *Contra Const.* 12, an enemy of all the many false men in the Church

---

[1] M. Schanz, *Geschichte der römischen Litteratur bis zum Gesetzgebungswerk des Kaisers Justinian*, München, 1914², Vol. IV.1, p. 296.

[2] J. H. Reinkens, *Hilarius von Poitiers*, Schaffhausen, 1864, Vorwort p. viii.

[3] K. Hase, *Kirchengeschichte*, Leipzig, 1836², p. 137. As the first edition was not available, it is not known whether Hase referred thus to Hilary in the first edition of his work.

[4] H. M. Gwatkin, *Studies of Arianism*, Cambridge, 1900², p. 154.

[5] P. Smulders, *La doctrine trinitaire de S. Hilaire de Poitiers*, Rome, 1944, p. 11.

[6] O. Bardenhewer, *Geschichte der altkirchlichen Literatur*, Freiburg im Breisgau, 1912, Vol. III, p. 366.

[7] A. von Harnack, *Lehrbuch der Dogmengeschichte*, Tübingen, 1909⁴, Vol. II, p. 252 n.1.

of his day.[8] He had a powerful personality and where he appeared he dominated those around him.[9]

Many reasons are given for the fact that Hilary is less known and studied than some of the other fathers of the Western Church. He suffered "partly from a certain obscurity in his style of writing, partly from the difficulty of the thoughts which he attempted to convey."[10] Another important reason is that since Hilary was a pioneer in speculative theology in the West, he has been succeeded by greater writers, for example Augustine.[11] Hilary was quite overshadowed by this great Church Father[12] and the brilliancy of Augustine as a theologian and religious writer drew away the attention of mediaeval Christendom from the splendid work of this "first of Western theologians."[13] This is even the case in modern times. The fact is that the publication of Augustine's great work of the same title, only a generation later, caused Hilary's *De Trinitate* almost to be forgotten.

Hilary was one of the few theologians of the fourth century who knew the theology of the East just as well as that of his own West and who tried to combine the two.[14] The role he played as an intermediary between these two, has been accredited as one of his greatest merits.[15] And yet, like many great men, his contemporaries did not value him at his true worth. Watson says that "certainly no firmer purpose or more convinced faith, perhaps no keener intellect has devoted itself to the defence and elucidation of truth than that of Hilary."[16] It is the purpose of this study to determine the part he played in the Arian struggle.

As a writer Hilary has also been praised for his eloquence, forcefulness and beauty of thought, but on the other hand his method of expression has also been censured for its obscurity and complexity. It has been pointed out, quite rightly, that both views have a degree of justifiability and it would be counter to the facts to accept one judgement to the ex-

---

[8] F. Loofs, "Hilarius von Poitiers," *RE*, Leipzig, 1900³, Vol. VIII, p. 67.
[9] Schanz, *op. cit.*, p. 296.
[10] E. W. Watson, "Introduction Ch. I, The life and writings of St. Hilary of Poitiers," *NPNF*, Second Series, Vol. IX, Grand Rapids-Michigan, 1955 (= New York, 1908), p. i.
[11] J. E. Emmenegger, *The Functions of Faith and Reason in the Theology of Saint Hilary of Poitiers*, Washington, 1947, pp. 29–30.
[12] P. Galtier, *Saint Hilaire de Poitiers*, Paris, 1960, p. 170.
[13] T. S. Holmes, *The Origin and Development of the Christian Church in Gaul*, London, 1911, p. 183.
[14] P. Löffler, "Die Trinitätslehre des Bischofs Hilarius von Poitiers zwischen Ost und West," *ZKG*, Vol. 71 (1960), p. 27.
[15] Emmenegger, *op. cit.*, p. 32; Galtier, *op. cit.*, p. 5.
[16] Watson, *op. cit.*, p. lvii.

clusion of the other.[17] Bardenhewer says that he holds the attention by his individuality and originality[18] and it has also been said that Hilary wrote as he fought: as a bishop and pastor of souls.[19]

The main source for the study of Hilary's life is from his own works, although it is true that he was too involved and occupied in the struggle, to give us much detail of his life. We have to be content with fragmentary information gleaned from his works. There is an early biography extant on Hilary by Venantius Fortunatus.[20]

The different sources and biographies of Hilary are enumerated by Reinkens.[21] Although the study of Hilary has always been neglected it may fortunately be stated that in the last two decades numerous books and articles on diverse aspects of Hilary's life and theology have been published, but it is a sad fact that the best comprehensive biography of the bishop of Poitiers, that of Reinkens, was written more than a century ago.

In this study the Benedictine edition of Hilary's works (PL 9 and 10) is used. Reference is also made to his works which have so far appeared in the Corpus Scriptorum Ecclesiasticorum Latinorum, viz. *Tractatus super Psalmos* (CV 22) and *Collectanea Antiariana Parisina* and *Ad Constantium Imperatorem* (CV 65).

---

[17] Emmenegger, *op. cit.*, p. 24.
[18] Bardenhewer, *op. cit.*, p. 368.
[19] Galtier, *op. cit.*, p. 8.
[20] Venantius Fortunatus, *Vita S. Hilarii* (PL 88). A. Viehhauser, *Hilarius Pictaviensis geschildert in seinem Kampfe gegen den Arianismus*, Klagenfurt, 1860, pp. 5–9, argued that the first book of this biography had been written by a pupil of Hilary and only the second book by Venantius Fortunatus. According to Viehhauser the first book therefore is of much more value than if it had been written by Venantius Fortunatus, two centuries after Hilary had lived. Viehhauser's view is however rejected by modern scholars.
[21] Reinkens, *op. cit.*, pp. xiv–xxiv. T. Förster, "Zur Theologie des Hilarius," *Theologische Studien und Kritiken*, Vol. 61 (1888), p. 651, said that the picture of Hilary painted by Reinkens is very much like the old panegyric biographies. Reading Reinkens' work, pesecially pp. 100–103, we may agree with Förster to some extent.

CONTENTS

ABBREVIATIONS

AbhB – Abhandlungen der Preussischen Akademie der Wissenschaften, Phil.-hist. Klasse, Berlin.
BKV² – Bibliothek der Kirchenväter, Zweite Reihe.
CV – Corpus Scriptorum Ecclesiasticorum Latinorum.
DCB – A Dictionary of Christian Biography and Literature.
DThC – Dictionnaire de Théologie catholique.
DACL – Dictionnaire d'archéologie chrétienne et de liturgie.
GCS – Die griechischen christlichen Schriftsteller der ersten drei Jahrhunderte.
Nachr. Gött. Ges. – Nachrichten von der Königl. Gesellschaft der Wissenschaften zu Göttingen. Phil.-hist. Klasse.
NPNF – A Select Library of Nicene and Post-Nicene Fathers of the Christian Church.
PG – J. P. Migne, Patrologiae Cursus Completus, Series Graeca.
PL – J. P. Migne, Patrologiae Cursus Completus, Series Latina.
PWK – Paulys Real-encyclopädie der classischen Altertumswissenschaft.
RB – Revue Bénédictine.
RGG – Die Religion in Geschichte und Gegenwart.
RE – Realencyklopädie für protestantische Theologie und Kirche.
RHE – Revue d'histoire ecclésiastique.
SbW – Sitzungsberichte der Kais. Akademie der Wissenschaften in Wien, Phil.-hist. Klasse.
ZkTh – Zeitschrift für katholische Theologie.
ZKG – Zeitschrift für Kirchengeschichte.

Ad Const. (I) – The so-called ad Constantium liber primus.
Ad Const. (II) – The so-called ad Constantium liber secundus.
Coll. ant. Par. – Collectanea antiariana Parisina.
C. Aux. – Liber contra Arianos vel Auxentium Mediolanensem.
C. Const. – Contra Constantium Imperatorem.

De Syn. – De Synodis.
De Trin. – De Trinitate.
Fragm. – Fragmenta historica.
In Matt. – Commentarius in Matthaeum.
Or. Syn. Sard. – Oratio Synodi Sardicensis ad Constantium Imperatorem.
Text. narr. – Textus narratiuus (= ad Const. (I) 6–8).
Tract. in Ps. – Tractatus in Psalmos.

CHAPTER I

HILARY'S LIFE BEFORE HIS PUBLIC APPEARANCE

Hilary was born in Limonum or Pictavi, as it was later called, in Aquitania, the present Poitiers.[1] The date of his birth, like that of many of the men who played an important part in church history and the doctrinal struggle of the fourth century, is unknown.

A few scholars put his birth at about the beginning of the fourth century.[2] While Viehhauser and Griffe do not offer any proof for their statement, Watson endeavours to substantiate his. In the so-called first letter to Constantius, which was written about 355 according to Watson, Valens and Ursacius are called "ignorant and unprincipled youths."[3] Watson argues that Hilary had found these words either in some of Athanasius' writings or in the records of the council of Sardica and borrowed them without enquiry. "He could not have done so had he been only some thirty-five years of age; at fifty-five they are natural enough."[4]

It is generally accepted today, that the so-called first letter to Constantius was in fact not a letter written to the emperor by Hilary, but that it is part of the first book of Hilary's historical work, consisting of different historical documents with his own comments on them, probably called *Adversus Valentem et Ursacium* and written in 356. The above-mentioned phrase was used by the council of Sardica in a letter to the emperor and Hilary quotes the letter unaltered in his work. Valens and Ursacius were still "youths" in 343. The phrase, however, does not help us in any way to solve the problem of Hilary's date of birth. Watson's conclusion is wrong because he was under the impression that the first part of the so-called first letter to Constantius was an authentic work by Hilary.[5]

---

[1] Jerome, *Comment. in ep. ad Gal.* II 3 (PL 26.380C); Venantius Fortunatus, *Carmina Miscellanea* II 19 (PL 88.109B); VIII 1 (PL 88.261C). Cf. H. Leclercq, "Poitiers," *DACL*, Paris, 1939, Vol. XIV.1, col. 1255, 1278.

[2] Viehhauser, *op. cit.*, p. 10; Watson, *op. cit.*, p. ii; E. Griffe, *La Gaule chrétienne à l'époque romaine*, I. *Des origines chrétiennes à la fin du IVe siècle*, Paris-Toulouse, 1947, p. 156.

[3] *Oratio Synodi Sardicensis ad Constantium Imperatorem* 5 (CV 65.184; *ad. Const.* (I) 5 PL 10.560A).

[4] Watson, *op. cit.*, p. ii n. 3.

[5] The whole question concerning this work of Hilary, is discussed later on.

Reinkens put Hilary's birth in the second decade of the fourth century. He cites Hilary's words which were written at about the end of 359 or the beginning of 360. Hilary wrote to Emperor Constantius, saying that if he had done anything unworthy not only of the sanctity of a bishop but even of the integrity of a layman, he would "grow old in penitence as a lay-man."[6] According to Reinkens these words would only have made sense if Hilary had, at that stage, been younger than fifty years of age, because they were meant as a very strong assurance of his innocence. If a man of sixty had written these words, they would not have been such an assurance of his innocence.[7] This same text in Hilary's work was used by another scholar, F. Loofs, when he stated that Hilary was about 40 years old when the council of Milan (355) was held.[8] It seems probable, as the majority of scholars think, that Hilary was born between 310-320 A.D.[9]

It is a much debated question whether Hilary's parents were Christians or not. Antweiler admits that we do not have an absolutely explicit statement which confirms the one possibility to the exclusion of the other.[10]

The view that Hilary grew up in a Christian home and therefore became acquainted with the Christian faith at an early age, is largely based upon the report in the biography of Hilary by Venantius Fortunatus which reads: "a cunabulis tanta sapientia primitiva lactabatur infantia, ut jam tunc potuisset intelligi Christum in suis causis, pro obtinenda victoria, necessarium sibi jussisse militem propagari."[11] Coustant thought that it meant that Hilary put on Christ from his infancy and drank the Christian doctrine with his milk.[12] Elsewhere he states that Hilary nowhere mentions the fact that he left the error of paganism,[13] and his conclusion is that it is uncertain whether Hilary was ever devoted to idolatry and it is just as probable that he was subject to the law of Christ from childhood.[14]

Viehhauser thought that much importance should be attached to the account of Hilary's life by Venantius Fortunatus and that Hilary's parents were therefore Christians. It is conceivable according to Viehhauser, that through the study of the heathen classics and philosophy, the youthful

[6] *Ad Const.* (II) 2 (CV 65.198; PL 10.565A–B).
[7] Reinkens, *op. cit.*, pp. 3–4.
[8] Loofs, *art. cit.*, p. 58.
[9] Bardenhewer, *op. cit.*, p. 369; X. Le Bachelet, "Hilaire," *DThC*, Paris, 1947, Vol. VI.2, col. 2388; A. Antweiler, "Des heiligen Bischofs Hilarius von Poitiers zwölf Bücher über die Dreieinigkeit," (*BKV²*, Vol. V), München, 1933, Vol. I, p. 20; G. Giamberardini, *S. Ilario di Poitiers, e la sua attività apostolica e letteraria*, Cairo, 1956, p. 9.
[10] Antweiler, *op. cit.*, p. 17.
[11] Venantius Fortunatus, *Vita S. Hilarii* I 3 (PL 88.441A–B).
[12] P. Coustant, *Vita Sancti Hilarii* c. I 5 (PL 9.127C).
[13] *Loc. cit.* (PL 9.127D).
[14] *Ibid.* c. I 7 (PL 9.128C–D).

Hilary developed one-sidedly and that he attached too much value to these ideas and that his enthusiasm for the Christian faith gradually died down, until, after a thorough study of the holy Scriptures, it flared up again. Viehhauser assumes that a man who found the abstract words "sum qui sum" clarifying on the divine being, must have had a religious Christian background.[15]

On the other hand Dormagen thought that this passage by Venantius Fortunatus was obscure and its evidence not quite indisputable. Dormagen found that in these words "nous ne voyons rien là qui ne puisse se dire même d'un païen."[16] Giamberardini thought that this passage in Venantius Fortunatus should be interpreted in a sense of predestination in the faith rather than actual faith.[17]

It is generally accepted today that Hilary was not born of Christian parents. Most scholars quite rightly, point to the first chapters in the first book of Hilary's De Trinitate to prove their contention that Hilary was converted to Christianity when he had already attained manhood.[18] In these chapters Hilary describes how he was led to the Christian faith. He wanted to know the God who gave us life, and finding no satisfactory answer in pagan philosophy, he searched the Scriptures. He learnt about God the Father, and the Son, the incarnate Word, who died for our sins so that we may awaken to immortality with Him. In this way Hilary found peace and rest.

Reinkens expressed the opinion that the first book of the De Trinitate should not be interpreted in a figurative sense only, because chapter 14 where Hilary speaks about the episcopate which has been conferred upon him, is written in the same tone as the previous chapters.[19] Galtier thinks that because there are so few indications of a personal step by Hilary, it could be that the whole account was "un procédé littéraire," and that the description of his conversion therefore did not have the character of a personal experience, but was only used to bring the reader up to the level of this work.[20]

[15] Viehhauser, op. cit., pp. 10–11. Cf. Hilary, De Trin. I 5 (PL 10.28C).

[16] E. Dormagen, Saint Hilaire de Poitiers et l'Arianisme, Saint-Cloud, 1864, p. 24.

[17] Giamberardini, op. cit., p. 10 n. 5.

[18] Reinkens, op. cit., p. 28; Dormagen, op. cit., p. 24; Watson, op. cit., p. v; C. Jullian, Histoire de la Gaule, Vol. VII, Paris, 1926, p. 177; Holmes, op. cit., p. 148; Antweiler, op. cit., p. 19; Smulders, op. cit., p. 37; Griffe, op. cit., p. 157; Galtier, op. cit., p. 9; Leclercq, art. cit., col. 1313; A. L. Feder, "Kulturgeschichtliches in den Werken des hl. Hilarius von Poitiers," Stimmen aus Maria – Laach, Vol. 81 (1911), p. 33.

[19] Reinkens, op. cit., p. 28 n. 1. Le Bachelet, art. cit., col. 2389, states that it is difficult to see book 1 of the De Trinitate simply as literary fiction. H. Lietzmann, "Hilarius, Bischof von Poitiers," PWK, Stuttgart, 1913, Vol. VIII, col. 1601, mentions but apparently dismisses the possibility that the first part of book 1 of the De Trinitate could be literary scheme.

[20] Galtier, op. cit., pp. 9–10.

On the other hand Smulders thinks it to be unlikely that Hilary gave a description of the exact way in which he came to the faith because it is given too systematically. But we do, however, have a certain part of his personal experience given in the sketch of his conversion, according to Smulders.[21] It is true that we do find religious truths and ideas in some of the opening chapters of book I, which were far too advanced for someone who had only just been converted,[22] but there is no reason why we cannot agree with Smulders that in the first part of book I we find a description of at least some part of his way to the Christian faith. The fact that Hilary knew the New Testament so well and quoted so many parallel texts when he read the words "sum qui sum," is no proof that Hilary was imbued with the Christian faith from his childhood and that he only had a new dedication to God later on in his life,[23] but it only confirms the view that the first book of his *De Trinitate* does not give us an exact description of his conversion. When he wrote his *De Trinitate* he could quote all the parallel texts but that does not have to imply that he could have quoted them all when he became converted. The knowledge of the Scriptures displayed in the beginning of his book was the result of years of Scripture study, but his first book does nevertheless offer us some of the main points of his search for spiritual light.

A passage in one of Jerome's works, where Cyprian and Hilary are described as formerly being noble trees in the world, may be interpreted as implying that Hilary, like Cyprian, was only converted to Christianity later on in his life.[24] A passage in one of Hilary's own works[25] is sometimes quoted as an indication that his parents were pagan. The words however, are vague and it is uncertain whether the difference between a baptized and unbaptized person is being stressed or whether the conversion of a heathen to the Christian faith is to be understood.[26] Another passage, found in the works of Augustine,[27] is also no definite indication that

---

[21] Smulders, *op. cit.*, p. 37 n. 96.

[22] Galtier, *op. cit.*, p. 10.

[23] As Viehhauser, *op. cit.*, p. 11, stated.

[24] Jerome, *Comm. in Isaiam prophetam*, XVII 60 (PL 24.617D): Ac ne longo sermone sensum traham, vir sanctus et eloquentissimus martyr Cyprianus, et nostri temporis confessor Hilarius, nonne tibi videntur excelsae quondam in saeculo arbores, aedificasse Ecclesiam Dei? Cf. Dormagen, *op. cit.*, p. 25; Le Bachelet, *art. cit.*, col. 2389.

[25] *Tract. in Ps.* 146, 12 (CV 22.853, 9–10; PL 9.874C): nos enim uel ceteri ante nos ex inpudentibus et procacibus et inmundis et cruentis geniti atque nati. Cf. Loofs, *art. cit.*, p. 58; P. de Labriolle, *Histoire de la littérature latine chrétienne*, Troisième édition revue et augmentée par G. Bardy, Paris, 1947, Vol. I, p. 345 n. 2.

[26] Antweiler, *op. cit.*, p. 19; Lietzmann, *art. cit.*, col. 1601. The same can be said of the passage *Tract. in Ps.* 61,2 which is quoted by Le Bachelet, *art. cit.*, col. 2389, as cited by some scholars to prove that Hilary was not born from Christian parents.

[27] *De doctrina christiana* II 40 (PL 34.63): Nonne aspicimus quanto auro et argento

Hilary was born as a heathen. It is possible that not the superstitious cult of Egypt is meant, but the worldly doctrine.[28] All these passages usually cited by scholars as indications that Hilary was only converted to Christianity rather late in his life, are therefore vague and do not satisfactorily prove the point. And yet it is likely that Hilary was converted to the Christian faith as an adult and the way in which he came to the faith is described, to a certain extent, in the beginning of his *De Trinitate*. Jullian's surmise that Hilary was converted or led to Christianity by Maximinus of Trèves, the brother of Maxentius, who might possibly have been the bishop of Poitiers before Hilary,[29] is mere speculation.

It is also uncertain when Hilary was baptized. Giamberardini puts the date of his baptism at 345,[30] but he does not advance any evidence from our sources to substantiate his claim. Other scholars deduced from a passage in one of Hilary's works[31] that he was an adult when he was baptized. This passage however, does not prove their point. Hilary states that he had only learnt about these heretics after he had been regenerated, but, for the sake of argument, he could have been a Christian for quite a number of years, before he learnt of the doctrines of the Arians.

Viehhauser again, cited a passage in his *De Synodis*[32] as an indication that Hilary was probably only baptized at a mature age. This passage, however, offers no conclusive proof to the problem of when Hilary was baptized. All we can say is that according to this passage a notable interval of time elapsed between his baptism and his elevation to the episcopate.[33]

It is, however, likely that Hilary was baptized at a mature age, because he was only then converted to Christianity. But if this is true, this fact in itself does not, on the other hand, in any way confirm the view that he was born from pagan parents,[34] because in those days the baptism was often deferred until late in life.

The report by Venantius Fortunatus[35] that Hilary's parents belonged

et veste suffarcinatus exierit de Aegypto Cyprianus doctor suavissimus et martyr beatissimus? quanto Lactantius? quanto Victorinus, Optatus, Hilarius.

[28] Coustant, *Vita S. Hilarii* c. I 6 (PL 9.128B–C); Viehhauser, *op. cit.*, pp. 10–11.

[29] Jullian, *op. cit.*, p. 177.

[30] Giamberardini, *op. cit.*, p. 12.

[31] *De Trin.* VI 21 (PL 10.173A): Inauditis ego his nominibus (=heretics) in te ita credidi, per te ita renatus sum; et exinde tuus ita sum. Cf. Le Bachelet, *art. cit.*, col. 2389; S. McKenna, "Saint Hilary of Poitiers—The Trinity," *The Fathers of the Church*, Vol. XXV, New York, 1954, Introduction, p. v n. 2; Emmenegger, *op. cit.*, p. 3.

[32] *De Syn.* 91 (PL 10.545A): Regeneratus pridem et in episcopatu aliquantisper manens, fidem Nicaenam numquam nisi exsulaturus audivi. Cf. Viehhauser, *op. cit.*, p. 13.

[33] Coustant, *Vita S. Hil.* c. II 11 (PL 9.130); Reinkens, *op. cit.*, p. 29; Galtier, *op. cit.*, p. 9.

[34] As McKenna, *op. cit.*, p. v, and Le Bachelet, *art. cit.*, col. 2389 seem to think.

[35] *Vita S. Hil.* I 3 (PL 88.441A).

to one of the eminent families in the country seems credible. The passages where Hilary warns against worldly riches, the ordinary vanities of life, the theatre and circus shows, seem to suggest that he had grown up in a well-to-do home and that he himself had once indulged in these pleasures.[36]

We may assume that Hilary had a good school education especially if his parents were well-off as we suggested above, but his writings too are evidence that their author was well qualified for the task. Jerome says that education in Gaul flourished at that time.[37] Since the first century A.D. most of the important cities in Gaul had had their own schools[38] and Poitiers would have had one too,[39] although it probably could not offer quite the same facilities and was not as renowned as the schools in Autun and Burdigala (Bordeaux), which were both within Hilary's reach.[40] The province of Aquitania was the most distinguished in Gaul and its most famous city, Bordeaux, was the intellectual capital of Gaul during the fourth century. When it arose again from the ruins which had been left after its destruction in 276 or 277 by the barbarians, its people were no longer concerned with the extension of their trade with other cities but they devoted themselves to the pursuit of knowledge and learning.[41]

It has been asserted that Hilary spent ten years in schools in Rome and Greece,[42] but this view has to be rejected because it is not supported by any evidence from our original sources.[43] This hypothesis probably originated through some scholars being unaware of the fact that in the fourth century one could receive a good education in Greek in Gaul.

There are scholars who hold the view that it is unlikely that Hilary had acquired "a good knowledge" of Greek during his early training and that he only learnt Greek during his sojourn as an exile in the East.[44] Jerome says that Hilary had only a little knowledge of Greek.[45] Tillemont sug-

---

[36] *Tract. in Ps.* 118 HE 14; *in Ps.* 118 NUN 9; *in Ps.* 138:34. Cf. Reinkens, *op. cit.*, p. 7 n. 3; Antweiler, *op. cit.*, p. 21.

[37] Jerome, *Ep.* 125,6 (CV 56.123).

[38] T. Haarhoff, *Schools of Gaul*, Oxford, 1920, p. 34.

[39] Feder, *art. cit.*, p. 37 n. 2. He refers to Ausonius, *Commemoratio professorum Burdigalensium*, 11,46-8 (Monumenta Germaniae Historica, Auct. Ant. V 64).

[40] Reinkens, *op. cit.*, p. 7; Galtier, *op. cit.*, p. 7.

[41] Haarhoff, *op. cit.*, pp. 46–7.

[42] *Acta Sanctorum*, collegit, digessit, notis illustravit Joannes Bollandus, Antverpiae, MDCXLIII, s.v. XIII Januarii § III 23 (p. 785). Dormagen also thought so, although he admitted that from Jerome, *Ep.* 34 it could be deduced that the sojourn in Greece was only of a short duration, *op. cit.*, p. 24 n. 2.

[43] Reinkens, *op. cit.*, p. 8 n. 3; Holmes, *op. cit.*, p. 149 n. 2; Le Bachelet, *art. cit.*, col. 2388.

[44] Loofs, *art. cit.*, p. 59; H. Chadwick, "Hilarius von Poitiers," *RGG*, Tübingen, 1959³, Vol. III, col. 317; Labriolle, *op. cit.*, p. 360.

[45] *Ep.* 34,3 (CV 54.262,12–17): nisi quod non eius (= Hilary) culpae adscribendum est, qui Hebraei sermonis ignarus fuit, Graecarum quoque litterarum quandam aurulam ceperat, sed Heliodori presbyteri, quo ille familiariter usus ea, quae intellegere non poterat, quomodo ab Origene essent dicta, quaerebat.

gested that Jerome said so because he did not want to attribute certain mistakes to Hilary, but wanted to put the blame on Heliodorus who helped Hilary.[46] Watson thought that Jerome's words could not be employed to prove Hilary's defective Greek. "Heliodorus knew Hebrew, and Hilary for want of Hebrew found Origen's notes on the Hebrew text difficult to understand, and for this reason, according to Jerome, used to consult his friend; not because he was unfamiliar with Greek."[47] While it is true that the account of Jerome, a contemporary of Hilary, and one who knew Hilary's writings well, must be taken into account,[48] the fact is that when Hilary wrote his commentary on the Psalms, after his return from the East and in the last years of his life, he then knew Greek very well, and therefore Jerome's report cannot be taken too literally.

A view put forward by some scholars, is that he must have known Greek very well because he made such a thorough study of Origen's works.[49] But he could have only acquired his thorough knowledge of Greek during the time of his exile and this argument does not therefore afford any proof for the view that he had learnt Greek in his early youth. The same can be said of the view that because Hilary had translated Origen's commentary on Job[50] he must have had a very good knowledge of Greek and have learnt it early in his life. This work by Hilary is lost and we do not know whether he wrote it before his exile.

It is, however, likely that Hilary did learn Greek during his school years. If he did have a good education, as seems likely, he would have had to learn Greek as well as Latin.[51] Among the upper classes Latin supplanted Greek in the fourth and fifth centuries, but tradition was strongly upheld and, especially in Aquitania, there were very strong ties with Greece.[52] Bardy also holds the view that Hilary learnt Greek at school, but he adds that he did it, like everybody else, in a way "assez livresque et plutôt superficielle."[53] It is true that Hilary, after his exile, was a complete master of the Greek language, and it is probable that he achieved this mastery during his stay in the East where he was introduced to the Greek

[46] M. Lenain de Tillemont, *Mémoires pour servir à l'histoire ecclésiastique des six premiers siècles*, Bruxelles, MDCCXXXII², Vol. VII, p. 352 n. 3.
[47] Watson, *op. cit.*, p. ii n. 4.
[48] Dormagen, *op. cit.*, p. 24.
[49] Viehhauser, *op. cit.*, p. 13.
[50] Reinkens, *op. cit.*, p. 8.
[51] Haarhoff, *op. cit.*, p. 56, states that the authors which were mostly read in schools were Vergil, Homer and Varro. Haarhoff also says that the children sometimes started learning Greek at the age of five, *op. cit.*, p. 224–231.
[52] Haarhoff, *op. cit.*, p. 220.
[53] G. Bardy, "Un humaniste chrétien: saint Hilaire de Poitiers," *Revue d'histoire de l'église de France*, Paris, Vol. 27 (1941), p. 7. Smulders, *op. cit.*, p. 37, claims that by 356 Hilary was "instruit des lettres latines et grecques." Cf. Watson, *op. cit.*, p. ii.

Christian literature,[54] but it must also be remembered that before he went into exile he knew of the Arian heresy and wrote a historical-polemical book in which he translated creeds and documents which were written in Greek. Before he went into exile he therefore must have had a reasonable knowledge of Greek.

We do not know for which vocation Hilary prepared himself, but judging by his works it is evident that he had had a good literary education.[55] Smulders thought that, judging by the way he handled matters, he appeared to have had a training as a magistrate,[56] but this is only conjecture because our primary sources do not give us any indication of what Hilary did before he was elected bishop.

Hilary was married but we do not know whether the marriage took place before or after his conversion to Christianity. Neither do we know how many children Hilary had. Venantius Fortunatus mentions a daughter named Abra[57] and this tradition has never been contradicted. Fortunatus also mentions a letter by Hilary to his daughter and among the works ascribed to Hilary, there is such a letter, but in its present form it is certainly by a later scribe although it possibly contains a genuine core.[58]

We have already seen that Hilary's own words indicate that quite an interval of time elapsed between his baptism and his election as bishop.[59] Without substantiating his claim Giamberardini states that Hilary was baptized in 345[60] but this is only conjecture on his part. According to Venantius Fortunatus, Hilary led such an admirable life as an ordinary layman, that even bishops aspired to imitate him[61]. Although Reinkens apparently accepts this statement because it was not contradicted in Fortunatus' time,[62] and although we must also remember Hilary's own statement,[63] the statement by Fortunatus seems a rhetorical exaggeration.

It is not known whether Hilary held any church office during the time between his baptism and his election to the episcopate. Bouchet evidently

[54] Feder, art. cit., p. 37; Giamberardini, op. cit., p. 14; Labriolle, op. cit., p. 347.
[55] Griffe, op. cit., pp. 156–7.
[56] Smulders, op. cit., p. 38.
[57] Venantius Fortunatus, Vita S. Hil. I 6 (PL 88.442C).
[58] Bardenhewer, op. cit., p. 387; Bardy, art. cit., p. 9. A. L. Feder, "Studien zu Hilarius von Poitiers III," SbW 169,5, Wien, 1912, p. 52, says that the outline of the contents of the letter as given by Venantius Fortunatus formed the basis of the letter which a later writer composed and which was handed down to us.
[59] See page 5 note 32 and 33 above.
[60] Giamberardini, op. cit., p. 12.
[61] Vita S. Hil. I 3 (PL 88.441C): o quam perfectissimum laicum, cujus imitatores ipsi etiam esse desiderant sacerdotes.
[62] Reinkens, op. cit., p. 32.
[63] Ad Const. (II) 2. See page 2 note 6 above.

thought so[64] and it may be implied by the words found in the biography of Hilary.[65] This passage, however, is obscure and these words may refer to the fact that Hilary was, according to Fortunatus, predestined to become bishop because he was imbued with the faith from his birth. Seeing that Fortunatus describes Hilary as a perfect layman in such glowing terms and then directly passes over to his election as bishop,[66] we might justifiably expect a word or two about the time Hilary occupied another office in the church, if he really did. In view of this, it seems unlikely that Hilary performed any function in the church before he was elected bishop, the more so because he himself does not mention anything to that effect in any of his extant works.

Fortunatus says that Hilary was unanimously elected bishop by the people or rather by the Spirit of God.[67] In those days it often happened that the people took a hand in the election of bishops, but it does not have to mean that Hilary was elected by the people against the wishes of the other bishops.

According to Lupus of Ferrara, Maxentius, the brother of Maximinus of Trèves, was a bishop in Poitiers before Hilary.[68] According to the list of bishops of Poitiers which was generally accepted in Poitiers in the twelfth century, Hilary was only the ninth bishop while Maxentius was the fourteenth. After a thorough examination of the list and all the evidence we have about the different names appearing on the list, it is clear that Nectarius, who heads the list, never was a bishop of Poitiers. There are objections to some of the names on the list of bishops before the sixth century but after the sixth century the names are well attested. The authors of Gallia Christiana began their list with Hilary and the conclusion reached by Duchesne is "sans affirmer que le célèbre docteur ait été le fondateur de son église, on est cependant obligé de reconnaître que la liste épiscopale ne fournit pas un argument décisif pour remonter plus haut."[69]

We do not know when Hilary was elected bishop. The only indication

[64] J. Bouchet, Les Annales d'Aquitaine, augmentees et recueillies par A. Mounin, édition dernière et nouvelle, Poictiers, MDCXXXXIIII, p. 25.

[65] Venantius Fortunatus, Vita S. Hil. I 4 (PL 88.441D–442A): concordante favore populi, ... vir olim mysteriis deputatus, aliquando sacris altaribus sacerdos electus est. Cf. Viehhauser, op. cit., p. 14.

[66] Venantius Fortunatus, Vita S. Hil. I 3–4 (PL 88.441C–D).

[67] Ibid. I 4 (PL 88.441D–442A): concordante favore populi, aut potius Dei Spiritu proclamante, ... sacerdos electus est.

[68] Lupus, Vita S. Maximini I (PL 119.668B). Jullian, op. cit., p. 177 n. 2, apparently accepts this report while Le Bachelet, art. cit., col. 2389, thinks it is probable.

[69] L. Duchesne, Fastes épiscopaux de l'ancienne Gaule, Paris, 1900, Vol. II, pp. 77–82; Leclercq, art. cit., col. 1270–1, 1273–6; Holmes, op. cit., p. 149 n. 7.

we have in this connection, is the phrase we quoted above[70] where Hilary says that he had been chosen as bishop for some time before he was exiled. Most scholars therefore put his consecration as bishop at about the year 350.[71] Le Bachelet however, thinks that the "aliquantisper" is in contrast with "pridem regeneratus" and must be understood as a limited lapse of time. According to him it is possible that this generally accepted date (350), somewhat anticipates the event.[72]

Without giving any reason for his opinion, Cazenove put Hilary's election as bishop at 353.[73] Jullian put Hilary's elevation to the episcopate at the time when the synod at Arles took place (353), because he argued that Hilary would have acted vigorously if he had, by then, already been a bishop for some time.[74] Leclercq even puts his election as bishop at 355.[75] It is clear that we do not know the exact date of Hilary's election as bishop of Poitiers. The most we can say is that it must have taken place a few years before 355, because by then he must have been well-known as a bishop. We only have to recall the decree which was promulgated after the council of Milan by some bishops on the initiative of Hilary. His election therefore probably took place in about 350.

From the foregoing it is evident how little we know of the early part of the life of the man who was destined to play such an important part in the struggle against the Arians. He was a brave leader who never shrank from the struggle in which he was engaged and he exerted all his strength for the cause which he thought was right. As Jullian put it: "Il sut trouver pour les âmes timorées de ses frères en épiscopat, les sentiments qui groupent les hommes, les formules qui fixent le dogme, les oeuvres qui favorisent les résistances. La Gaule chrétienne recevait enfin, un siècle et demi après Irénée, le nouveau chef qui ranimerait sa vie. Hilaire était, au surplus, de la tradition d'Irénée, comme lui théologien, polémiste, apologiste, à la fois orateur, écrivain et organisateur, mais d'abord et en toutes choses homme d'action et de combat."[76]

Hilary held the office of bishop in high esteem. According to him the

[70] De Syn. 91 (PL 10.545A): Regeneratus pridem, et in episcopatu aliquantisper manens, fidem Nicaenam numquam nisi exsulaturus audivi. See p. 5 n. 32 above.
[71] Tillemont, op. cit., p. 198; Reinkens, op. cit., p. 33; Watson, op. cit., p. ix; Holmes, op. cit., p. 149; Griffe, op. cit., p. 159; Galtier, op. cit., p. 9; Bardy, art. cit., p. 9; Smulders, op. cit., p. 38; Giamberardini, op. cit., p. 12.
[72] Le Bachelet, art. cit., col. 2389.
[73] J. G. Cazenove, "Hilarius Pictaviensis," DCB, London, 1911, p. 474. McKenna, op. cit., p. v, puts it at 353 or 354.
[74] Jullian, op. cit., p. 177 n. 5. The question whether Hilary attended this synod or not, is discussed later on.
[75] Leclercq, art. cit., col. 1313.
[76] Jullian, op. cit., p. 177.

apostles were the eyes of the church, i.e. the body of Christ.[77] The bishops took over the office of the apostles and they had to reveal the deeply hidden secrets of the Gospel by apostolic preaching.[78] The bishop had to lead a sinless life but he also had to have the knowledge: "for an innocent minister is profitable to himself alone, unless he is instructed also, while he that is instructed has no authority to support his teaching, unless he is innocent."[79] The words used by Hilary in his so-called *Ad Constantium Augustum* (II) 2: "episcopus ego sum ...," must not however, be interpreted as if Hilary wanted to commend himself to the emperor as someone worthy of every respect, as Coustant thought.[80] With these words Hilary only wanted to introduce himself to the emperor as a bishop who was still in communion with the bishops in Gaul.

To reveal the secrets of the Bible to his people, Hilary made a thorough study of the Scriptures. Today we have his *Commentarius in Matthaei Evangelium* as a result of his pastoral work. In some manuscripts the work is called *Tractatus super Matthaeum*, while in others it is known as *Expositio super Matthaeum*.[81] Jerome refers to it as *Commentarium in Matthaeum*[82] and this is in accordance with Hilary's own words: "De orationis autem sacramento ... commentandi Cyprianus ... liberavit."[83] Hilary also refers to this work of his as a book.[84]

Some scholars think that the work was a compilation of original homilies, especially as only certain passages of the Gospel are treated.[85] Other scholars, again, noting the fact that Hilary himself speaks of the work as a commentary, think that it is a commentary.[86] It is correct to state that although the echoes of homilies preached by the bishop to his flock may be found in the work, it is a carefully composed book,[87] and thus a commentary, although it is not a commentary in the absolute strict sense of the word because not all the verses in the Gospel are treated.

Another problem which gave rise to a difference of opinion is the question of whether Origen had any influence on Hilary in this work of his. The account given by Jerome in his *De viris illustribus* is ambiguous and

---

[77] *Tract. in Ps.* 138,34 (CV 22.768,11–12; PL 9.810A).
[78] *Comm. in Matt.* 10,17 (PL 9.972C).
[79] *De Trin.* VIII 1 (PL 10.236B).
[80] *Vita S. Hil.* c. III 22 (PL 9.134C).
[81] *In Evangelium Matthaei Admonitio* VIII (PL 9.912A).
[82] Jerome, *de viris illustribus* c. 100 (PL 23.739A).
[83] *Comm. in Matt.* 5,1 (PL 9.943A).
[84] *Ibid.* 19,11: sed in primordio libri ... (PL 9.1027B).
[85] Coustant, *Vita S. Hil.* c. III 24 (PL 9.135); Le Bachelet, *art. cit.*, col. 2400; Giamberardini, *op. cit.*, p. 20.
[86] Reinkens, *op. cit.*, p. 61; Watson, *op. cit.*, p. vii. Galtier, *op. cit.*, p. 15, says that it is more like a catechism which explains the profound sense of the divine teachings.
[87] Griffe, *op. cit.*, p. 159; Bardy, *art. cit.*, p. 10; Watson, *op. cit.*, pp. vii-viii.

may mean that the commentary on Matthew and the treatise on Job, or only the treatise on Job were translated from the Greek of Origen. The Benedictines compared this account with other passages found in the works of Jerome[88] where he only speaks of Origen's influence on Hilary's works on the Psalms and Job and no mention is made of any influence by Origen on Hilary's work on the Gospel of Matthew. Modern scholars consider it to be unlikely that Origen's work was used by Hilary when he wrote this work.[89]

Watson however, claims that although Hilary is not dependent upon Origen in this work in the same way as in his homilies on the Psalms and the lost work upon Job, "yet if he is not in this work the translator, or editor, of Origen, he is manifestly his disciple. We cannot account for the resemblance otherwise. Hilary is independently working out Origen's thoughts on Origen's lines."[90] On the other hand Reinkens thought that any resemblance between Origen and Hilary in this work, would be due to the fact that the results of the Alexandrian in the exposition of Scripture were common knowledge in the literature of the fourth century, and that many of his ideas would be known without someone actually having read his works and that two commentaries on the same book must always agree to some extent and especially in the case of the Gospels. Reinkens therefore ruled out the possibility that Hilary had read Origen's commentary when he wrote his.[91] Bardy who examined Jerome's account, mentioned above, found, after comparing Origen's and Hilary's works, that in his work on the Psalms Hilary adapted Origen's work and did not merely translate it. He also thought that Hilary probably wrote his *Commentary on Matthew* before he knew the works of the Greek exegetes and those of Origen in particular and that in his work Hilary showed that he could expound the Scriptures quite interesting enough without having to refer to a model. Later on he did not hesitate to draw inspiration from Origen because he found that many of the Alexandrian's ideas pleased him.[92] It is therefore unlikely that Hilary used Origen's commentary on Matthew and neither did he compare the Latin text of the Gospel with a Greek version[93] as he did in his later works, especially the *De Trinitate*

---

[88] *Ep.* 61,2 (CV 54.577); *Apologia adv. libros Rufini* I 2 (PL 23.417B). Cf. *In Evang. Matt. Admonitio* II–III (PL 9.910A–C).

[89] Loofs, *art. cit.*, p. 59; Bardenhewer, *op. cit.*, p. 372; Bardy, *art. cit.*, p. 11; Griffe, *op. cit.*, p. 160.

[90] Watson, *op. cit.*, p. viii.

[91] Reinkens, *op. cit.*, p. 71.

[92] G. Bardy, "Traducteurs et adaptateurs au IVe siècle," *Recherches de Science Religieuse*, Vol. 30 (1940), p. 273.

[93] Reinkens, *op. cit.*, p. 60; Bardenhewer, *op. cit.*, p. 371; Loofs, *art. cit.*, p. 59; Schanz, *op. cit.*, p. 281.

and *Tractatus in Psalmos* where he often refers to the Greek text.

We do not know in which year Hilary wrote this commentary. Watson thought it was evidently the earliest of his extant works and probably the earliest of all, "as it gives no sign of being written by a Bishop."[94] There is, however, no reason why Hilary could not have written this book while he was a bishop. On the contrary it seems very likely that he rewrote his homilies in this form and that he saw it as his duty as a bishop, to enlighten his flock and to reveal to them the secrets of the inner meaning of the Scriptures.

The consensus opinionum of scholars up to a few decades ago, was that Hilary made no reference to the Arian dispute in his *Commentary on Matthew* and that it therefore must have been written before his first public appearance in this struggle.[95]

The Benedictines thought that Hilary's treatment of the subject in ch. II 6 and XVI 6 was, "quasi Arianos non cognovisset."[96] Reinkens agreed with this view and added that in this work Hilary opposed those who denied the divinity of Christ. Hilary therefore opposed the Jews more than the heretics and the latter, moreover, as if they were already defeated. According to Reinkens the technical expressions used by the Arians in their doctrine on Christ and those which Hilary repeatedly used later on in his *De Trinitate* and *Commentary on the Psalms*, are not to be found in this early work of his. In any case, Hilary did not use the allegorical method of exegesis when he defended the divinity of Christ against the Arians but the grammatical-historical, but here the allegorical method is used.[97] Other scholars thought that it was because Hilary still stood outside the Arian dispute that he was careless in the use of some expressions.[98] Other scholars failed to find a trace of any influence of the Nicene Creed or any of the doctrinal phrases of the day in this Commentary.[99] According to Watson there is no clear sign that Hilary knew of the existence of Arianism. He did however, know that there were heresies which impugned the Godhead of Christ, but Hilary discussed many texts which were used in the Arian dispute, without alluding to that burning question, according to Watson.[100]

[94] Watson, *op. cit.*, p. vii.
[95] *Admonitio in Evang. Matt.* XV (PL 9.914C–D); Reinkens, *op. cit.*, p. 59; Watson, *op. cit.*, p. viii; Bardenhewer, *op. cit.*, p. 371; Schanz, *op. cit.*, p. 280; Griffe, *op. cit.*, p. 160; Bardy, "Humaniste," p. 11.
[96] *Admon.*, loc. cit.
[97] Reinkens, *op. cit.*, pp. 59–60,62.
[98] Dormagen, *op. cit.*, p. 33; Griffe, *op. cit.*, p. 160 n. 21, quotes ch. 31,3 as an example of carelessness.
[99] Loofs, *art. cit.*, p. 59; Labriolle, *op. cit.*, p. 346.
[100] Watson, *op. cit.*, p. viii.

All the above-mentioned scholars were probably influenced to some extent by Hilary's own words in *De Synodis* 91: "Regeneratus pridem, et in episcopatu aliquantisper manens, fidem Nicaenam numquam nisi exsulaturus audivi." These words however, do not necessarily imply that Hilary knew nothing about the doctrinal issues until he was about to go into exile. In his book *Adversus Valentem et Ursacium liber I* which was written before he actually went into exile, he discusses the Nicene creed. The way in which he reacted to the events at the council of Milan and the reason he gives for writing his *Adversus Valentem et Ursacium*—viz. because he saw that while the action of the Arians was nominally directed against Athanasius, it was actually an attack upon the orthodox faith— proves that he knew what the real issue at stake was.

The problem of the interpretation of the above-mentioned words by Hilary, however, remains. Antweiler thought that this meant that until 355 Hilary had not heard of ὁμοούσιος and ὁμοιούσιος.[101] Galtier states that the above-mentioned text speaks of the Nicene faith only in its specific formula, with, in particular, the word ὁμοούσιος and it does not mean that he should have gone into exile to hear about it. This formula imposed itself on his attention when the prospect of exile lay before him, and this possibility had emerged since the council of Milan in 355. Hilary must have known precisely what had passed at Milan where Eusebius of Vercelli wanted all those present to sign the Nicene creed,[102] and thus Hilary must have known about this creed and ὁμοούσιος at least since the council of Milan. Smulders even thinks that this was the case after the synod of Arles in 353.[103]

Despite Reinkens' view as described above,[104] elsewhere in his book he thought that Hilary did oppose the Anti-trinitarians and the Arians in his *Commentary on Matthew*.[105] Hilary did not however, first give his opponents' view and refute it, but he simply stated the orthodox Christology and condemned those who denied it. That indicated, according to Reinkens, that these opponents and their attacks did not directly confront Hilary's congregation. Arianism with Sabellianism and all heresy against the Trinity had in the view of Hilary, already been defeated and belonged to historical antiquity.[106] Reinkens thus contradicts himself.

Contrary to the general opinion, Smulders, followed by Galtier, held

[101] Antweiler, *op. cit.*, pp. 16–17.
[102] Galtier, *op. cit.*, pp. 22–23,25.
[103] Smulders, *op. cit.*, p. 38.
[104] See p. 13 note 97.
[105] Viz. *in Matt.*, 8,2; 11,12; 12,17–18; 26,5; 31,3. Cf. Reinkens, *op. cit.*, p. 75 n. 4.
[106] Reinkens, *op. cit.*, p. 76.

the view that although Hilary never mentioned Arius by name, he never-theless was not wholly ignorant of the Arian heresy but made allusions to these theories.[107]

In his *Commentary on Matthew* Hilary states that Jesus Christ is God, the Son of God, eternal, His eternal birth is mentioned and His works are called the works of God.[108] It may not, however, be assumed that with these statements Hilary necessarily attacks the doctrine of the Arians. It has been pointed out that Hilary considered the main theme of this Gospel to be the unbelief and rejection of the Jewish people and the elec-tion of the heathens.[109] The Jews were rejected because they did not be-lieve in Christ's words or the miracles which He performed to prove His divine authority and mission.[110] Hilary considered it to be a sin against the Holy Spirit to deny the divinity of Christ; and those who thus denied Him would receive no remission for this sin.[111] In one of the passages Hilary expressly mentioned the Pharisees who denied the divinity of Christ; and it is therefore clear that with the emphasis Hilary places on the fact that the man Jesus, was also the Son of God and therefore God, he attacks all who denied the divinity of Christ, Jews just as well as the Arians.

Smulders however, did find a few examples in Hilary's work, from which it appears that the Arian doctrine was known to Hilary. In the footnotes of the Benedictine edition of Hilary's works, the opinion is expressed that in two instances Hilary made allusions to Arian doctrine in his *Commentary on Matthew*. Hilary wrote that those who maintain that Christ did not exist from eternity nor came forth from the infinity of the substance of the Father, but that He was made from nothing by Him Who created all things, ascribed fear of death to the Son of God. These people asserted that one who could fear death, could also die, and one who could die, could not be eternal. If these people had been receptive to the Gospels, they would have known that the Word was in the begin-ning God, and from the beginning with God and born of Him Who existed.[112] Arius in his *Thalia* said: "God was not always a Father, for

---

[107] Smulders, *op. cit.*, p. 39; Galtier, *op. cit.*, p. 22.

[108] Inter alia God 3,3; 4,14; 8,6; 12,18; Son of God 2,6; 7,10; 16,5 & 7; eternal 1,1; 5,15; eternal birth 1,2; works of God 8,2.

[109] Smulders, *op. cit.*, p. 73.

[110] Cf. *in Matt.* 12,8 (PL 9.986B); 9,8 (PL 9.965A).

[111] *In Matt.* 12,17 (PL 9.989A–B); 12,18 (PL 9.990B); 5,15 (PL 9.950C).

[112] *In Matt.* 31,3 (PL 9.1066D–1067A): Sed eorum omnis hic sensus est, ut opinen-tur metum mortis in Dei filium incidisse qui asserunt non de aeternitate esse prolatum neque de infinitate paternae substantiae exstitisse, sed ex nullo per eum qui omnia creavit effectum: ut assumptus ex nihilo sit, et coeptus ex opere, et confirmatus ex tempore. Et ideo in eo doloris anxietas, ideo Spiritus passio cum corporis passione,

there was a time when God was alone and not yet a Father, but afterwards He became a Father. The Son was not always; for whereas all things were made out of nothing, and all existing creatures and works were made, so the Word of God Himself was made out of nothing and once He was not and He was not before He was made but he had an origin of creation."[113]

Elsewhere Hilary wrote that while some things are attributed to Christ, the most important things are denied Him. He is honoured as God, but robbed of communion with God. Because of His great deeds, people would not dare to deny Him the name of God, but malevolently they detract from His excellence, which they are forced to confess nominally, by denying Him communion of substance with the Father.[114]

Arius taught that: "The Word is not true God. Though He is called God, yet He is not truly God but by participation of grace, He, as all the others, is called God only in name."[115] Smulders also pointed out that in the passage where Hilary spoke of Christ as the Wisdom Himself and not merely a work of the Wisdom, Hilary refers to the Arian doctrine.[116]

It is true that in Hilary's work we find traces of the old Western (Tertullian) Novatian Christology. Loofs said that when Hilary uses the phrases "communio paternae substantiae" (8,8 and 12,18) and "eadem utriusque substantia" (11,12) it does not necessarily mean that he got it from the Nicene tradition, but it came from the Tertullian-Novatian tradition.[117] On the other hand, Galtier rightly pointed out that in the passage 12,18 Hilary opposes the Arians who honour Christ as God, while they deny Him the communion of substance with God.[118]

It is therefore evident that Hilary did know of the Arian doctrine when he wrote his *Commentary on Matthew*. Smulders rightly states that in this

---

ideo metus mortis: ut qui mortem timere potuit, et mori possit; qui vero mori potuit, licet in futurum erit, non tamen per eum qui se genuit ex praeterito sit aeternus. Qui si per fidem vitaeque probitatem capaces Evangeliorum esse potuissent, scirent Verbum in principio Deum, et hoc a principio apud Deum, et natum esse ex eo qui erat, et hoc in eo esse qui natus est ... Cf. Benedictine footnote, PL 9.1067 n. c; Smulders, *op. cit.*, p. 39 n. 102.

[113] Athanasius, *Oratio contra Arianos* I 5 (PG 26.21).

[114] *In Matt.* 12,18 (PL 9.990B): Caeterum medium se agere, et Christo aliqua deferre, negare quae maxima sunt; venerari tamquam Deum, Dei communione spoliare, haec blasphemia Spiritus est: ut cum per admirationem operum tantorum Dei nomen detrahere non audeas; per malevolentiam mentis et sensus, generositatem ejus, quam confiteri es coactus in nomine, abnegata paternae substantiae communione decerpas. Cf. Benedictine footnote, PL 9.990 n. e; Smulders, *op. cit.*, p. 39 n. 102.

[115] Athanasius, *Or. c. Ar.* I 6 (PG 26.21-2).

[116] Cf. *in Matt.* 11,9 (PL 9.982B–983A); Smulders, *op. cit.*, p. 39 n. 102.

[117] Loofs, *art. cit.*, p. 59. Cf. Novatian, *de Trin.* XXXI 192 (ed. Weyer p. 204); XXIV 140 (ed. Weyer p. 160).

[118] Galtier, *op. cit.*, p. 26.

book we find a reaction of the ancient Latin theology against the first manifestations of the heresy.[119] On the other hand this point must not be overemphasized. Galtier is wrong in causing it to appear as though Hilary positively refutes the Arian doctrine in his work.[120] It would rather seem as though Hilary was not directly confronted by his opponents, and their attacks therefore did not directly affect his congregation.[121] Hilary did not involve himself in a controversy with the heretics, but calmly wrote a commentary on the Gospel. In it he positively expounded the orthodox doctrine where occasion demanded it. The fact that he frequently mentioned the lack of faith of the Jews and their rejection of Christ must be borne in mind when the purpose for writing this book is being established. His theology presents a certain affinity to that of Tertullian and Novatian but he is not quite free from Greek influence.[122]

Though we have established that Hilary did know of the Arian heresy when he wrote this book, this is no reason to reject the accepted opinion that the work was written before his exile, probably between 353-355.[123] If he had written it later, he would have refuted the Arians whenever the opportunity presented itself. In character this work differs completely from his polemical works in which he constantly attacked the Arians. In his polemical works Hilary employed the grammatical-historical exegesis, while in this early work of his, he used the allegorical method.

---

[119] Smulders, *op. cit.*, p. 39.
[120] Galtier, *op. cit.*, pp. 26–33.
[121] Reinkens, *op. cit.*, p. 76.
[122] Smulders, *op. cit.*, p. 88, pointed to his use of theoteta in *in Matt.* 16,4 and 26,5. F. Loofs said that there were Greek influences, independent of Hilary, in the West since about 350, *Leitfaden zum Studium der Dogmengeschichte*, ed. by K. Aland, Pt. 1 and 2, Tübingen, 1959⁶, p. 200 (§ 34,3b).
[123] Bardenhewer, *op. cit.*, p. 371; Giamberardini, *op. cit.*, p. 20; Bardy, "Humaniste," p. 11.

CHAPTER II

HILARY'S PUBLIC APPEARANCE AND BANISHMENT

1. EVENTS PRECEDING HIS OPPOSITION TO THE ARIANS

The Arian struggle began when Arius, a presbyter in Alexandria, began to publish his conclusions about the nature of the Word in 318. Arius has been very harshly dealt with by modern critics. One scholar spoke of the wretchedness of the Arian Christology. The Arian Christ was "ein leidens-fähiger Halbgott, der weder die ἀψθαρσία, noch die rechte Gotteserkennt-nis zu vermitteln vermag."[1] Another scholar said: "But as a system, Arianism was utterly illogical and unspiritual, a clear step back to heathen-ism, and a plain anachronism even for its own time."[2] The Christology of Arius has been called the worst Christology we know of.[3] According to Harnack a very serious deficiency in the system of Arius is that he fails to show "wie durch Christus die Gemeinschaft mit Gott zu Stande ge-kommen ist. ... den Eindruck hat man schlechterdings nirgends, dass es Arius und seinen Freunden auf Gemeinschaft mit Gott in ihrer Theologie angekommen ist."[4]

But despite deficiencies in his doctrine and these damning opinions by modern historians, Arius commanded considerable support among the populace of his day. He even succeeded in gaining the support of some influential bishops, the most notable among them being Eusebius of Nicomedia and Eusebius of Caesarea. It is probable that Arius gained this support when in putting his case to the bishops, he emphasized some of Alexander's extreme views, thus causing it to appear as though he himself held to the current doctrine of the Church.[5] The attraction of the Arian system may have been that "it seemed simpler than orthodoxy, and was more symmetrical than Semi-arianism, more human than Sabellian-ism, while to the heathen it sounded very Christian,"[6] and Harnack saw its mission in the fact that "die Arianer haben den Massen der Gebildeten

---

[1] Loofs, *Dogmengeschichte*, p. 185 (§ 32,1c).
[2] Gwatkin, *op. cit.*, p. 2.
[3] R. Seeberg, *Lehrbuch der Dogmengeschichte*, Darmstadt, 1959 (= 3 ed., Leipzig, 1923), Vol. II, p. 27.
[4] Harnack, *op. cit.*, p. 222.
[5] H. Berkhof, *Die Theologie des Eusebius von Caesarea*, Amsterdam, 1939, pp. 164–5.
[6] Gwatkin, *loc. cit.*

und Halbgebildeten, die die Politik Konstantins in die Kirche führte, den Uebergang erleichtert."[7]

After various synods had been held by the different groups and after Ossius of Cordova, trusted counsellor of the emperor, had failed in his mission to appease the opposing parties in Egypt, Emperor Constantine convened a general council at Nicaea. A creed was drafted in which at the express wish of the emperor, it was stated that the Son was ὁμοούσιον τῷ πατρί.[8] Arianism was condemned and Arius and a few sympathizers were banished. This however, was not the end of the struggle, as the emperor had hoped, but only the beginning. In the ensuing struggle the policy of the Eusebians, named after their leader, Eusebius of Nicomedia, was, not to attack, but to undermine the Nicene decisions. They did this by procuring the recall of Arius and the other banished leaders, and in their turn, engineering the deposition and exile of their principal opponents. The Arian struggle afforded an opportunity which many bishops seized, to further personal interests and secure their own positions. Athanasius was not only the leader of the orthodox party but since 328 also the bishop of the metropolis Alexandria, and personal envy and enmity on the part of his opponents were also behind the drive to oust him from his seat.

The above-mentioned policy of the Eusebians was successful, for when Constantine died in 337 all the leaders of the orthodox party in the East had been driven into exile: Eustathius of Antioch in 330; Athanasius in 335, condemned by the synod of Tyre and eventually exiled by the emperor; and Marcellus of Ancyra in 336. The three sons of Constantine divided the empire among them and although Constantius was favourable to the Eusebian cause, he could do nothing to prevent the return of Athanasius to Alexandria in November 337. The Eusebians changed their tactics and in a letter in which they repeated their accusations against Athanasius, they appealed to Julius, the bishop of Rome and stated that Athanasius was no longer the rightful bishop of Alexandria. Thus for the first time the West, that had had only a few representatives at Nicaea, was now truly drawn into the struggle which had more or less only been a struggle of the East.[9]

Athanasius was again condemned at a synod held at Antioch in the beginning of 339 and he fled to Rome. A synod was held at Rome in 340 but the Eusebians declined Julius' invitation to attend. Athanasius and Marcellus were both declared fully vindicated of the charges brought

[7] Harnack, *op. cit.*, p. 223.
[8] The different interpretations which were given of this phrase and the theological contents of this and other creeds, will be treated when Hilary's *de Synodis* is discussed.
[9] K. Müller, *Kirchengeschichte*, Tübingen, 1929², Vol. I.1, pp. 416–7.

against them by their opponents. The Eusebians reacted with a synod at Antioch in 341 and a new phase was introduced into the struggle when a new creed was drafted. Thus "begins the long series of attempts to raise some other formulary to the rank of the Nicene creed, and so to depose the ὁμοούσιον from its position as an oecumenical test."[10]

The two Emperors, Constans and Constantius, decided that a general council was to be held at Sardica (Sophia), to try and unite the two sections of the Church. The Eusebians (Eusebius their leader had died soon after the synod at Antioch) would not meet with the orthodox group but held their discussions separately and departed to Philippopolis. Both sections excommunicated the leaders of the opposing group and Christendom was more divided after the council of Sardica than before. The preoccupation of Constantius, at first with the Persian (343–50) and then with the Civil War (351), also left events free to take their course. After this synod the question concerning the faith received prominence above the personal one and the West, formerly ignorant, progressively came to know the Arian doctrine.[11] About this time Constans sent a letter to his brother which might have influenced Constantius to change his church policy. On the death of Gregory in June 345, Athanasius was allowed to return to his see. Ursacius of Singidunum (Belgrade), and Valens of Mursa (Esseg), sensing the change of events, wrote to Julius requesting to be received into his church communion again, and this request was granted by a synod in Milan 347. It seemed as though peace would be restored to the Church at last. But then an unexpected event changed the whole situation.

In January 350 Magnentius was proclaimed emperor in Autun and the unpopular Emperor Constans was killed while fleeing. The army of the usurper however, was defeated in September 351 in a decisive battle at Mursa, by the troops of Constantius. Although Magnentius escaped he could only afford little resistance and Constantius was practically the absolute monarch of the Roman Empire. In the summer 353 the last battle was fought and the revolt of Magnentius finally ended with his suicide in August 353.

After his imperical court had been moved to Sirmium, Constantius was strongly influenced by the two Pannonian Bishops Valens and Ursacius. The emperor decided that the time had come to force his will upon the Western Church and to eliminate Athanasius, which was, in the words

---

[10] B. J. Kidd, *A History of the Church to A.D. 461*, Oxford, 1922, Vol. II, pp. 78–9.
[11] G. Bardy, "L'Occident en face de la crise arienne," *Irénikon*, Vol. 16 (1939), p. 412.

of Gibbon "an enemy more odious to him than the vanquished tyrant of Gaul."[12]

Meanwhile a synod had been held in Rome in May 353,[13] where Athanasius was acquitted of the charges against him. Liberius, who succeeded Julius, now wanted a general council to be held in Aquileia to overcome the differences between the East and the West. The emperor, who had been in Arles since October 353, convened a provincial synod there instead. A condemnatory decree against Athanasius was submitted to the assembled bishops for their approval. Liberius' envoys and a number of the bishops wanted to discuss matters of faith, but they were not allowed to do so. After the death of Magnentius the emperor was now in an exultant and victorious mood and he did not wish to unnecessarily prolong the synod.[14] Only Paulinus of Trèves refused to sign the condemnation of Athanasius and he was subsequently exiled. Jullian apparently wanted to exonerate the bishops of Gaul of blame by stating that the synod had signed the condemnation of Athanasius "peut-être sans s'apercevoir qu'il reniait ainsi la foi traditionnelle de l'Église." He attributes the opposition of Paulinus of Trèves "à la rivalité des deux villes se mêlait la lutte de leurs deux évêques."[15] There is however, no reason to doubt that Paulinus resisted because of the fundamental issues which were at stake, and not purely because of rivalry between the two cities and their bishops.

It is impossible to establish without any doubt that Hilary had attended the synod of Arles. Some historians believe that Hilary did not attend.[16] Watson however, inclines to believe that he did. "It is not probable that he was absent: and his ignorance, even later, on important points in the dispute shews that he may well have given an honest verdict against Athanasius. The new ruler's word had been given that he was guilty; nothing can yet have been known against Constantius and much must have been hoped from him."[17] Jullian, as stated above,[18] ascribes the date of Hilary's elevation to the episcopate to the time when the synod at Arles was held. "Il a dû être fait évêque au temps du concile d'Arles de 353: car je doute qu'il n'y eût pas agi, et vigoureusement, s'il avait été évêque

---

[12] E. Gibbon, *The History of the decline and fall of the Roman Empire*, ed. by J. B. Bury, London, 1909, Vol. II, p. 393.

[13] M. Goemans, *Het Algemeen Concilie in de Vierde Eeuw*, Nijmegen-Utrecht, 1945, p. 120.

[14] H. Lietzmann, *Geschichte der alten Kirche*, Berlin, 1953², Vol. III, p. 212.

[15] Jullian, *op. cit.*, p. 158.

[16] Loofs, "Hilarius," p. 60; Antweiler, *op. cit.*, p. 22; McKenna, *op. cit.*, p. vi; Bardy, "Humaniste," p. 12.

[17] Watson, *op. cit.*, pp. x–xi.

[18] See page 10, note 74.

depuis plusieurs années."[19] According to him Hilary thus could have attended the synod, but having only been a bishop for a short while, he therefore did not oppose the emperor's wishes.

Neither Watson nor Jullian could give reasons why Hilary would not have attended a synod held in Gaul, so they had to seek for explanations to the problem. It would, of course, be difficult to explain why Hilary, who, as we assume, had by 353 already been a bishop for a few years, would not have attended the synod at Arles. On the other hand, we do not find any evidence to the contrary. Even if Hilary had only newly been elected bishop, as Jullian thought, or even if he had been convinced of Athanasius' guilt, as Watson surmised, then it still seems strange that he did not refer to this fact even later in life. When he described the events which led to the banishment of Paulinus of Trèves, and the events at the council of Milan (355),[20] one would suppose that he would have mentioned having been present at Arles. Hilary, even if he had been ignorant at the time of the synod of Arles, did after Milan (355), know the truth about the condemnation of Athanasius, and would have mentioned that he had been a signatory at Arles and his enemies would surely have exploited this fact. Had he opposed the wishes of the emperor, he would have shared the same fate as Paulinus of Trèves. Many unsolved problems remain, whichever view we hold as to Hilary's attendance or absence at Arles, but it does seem improbable that Hilary could have attended and participated with the majority, in condemning Athanasius.

Liberius was very upset by his legates' submission to the wishes of Constantius at Arles and he gladly accepted when Lucifer of Calaris (Cagliari) offered to go to the emperor and request him to convene a new council. At the request of Liberius a few other bishops joined Lucifer, amongst whom was Eusebius of Vercelli. In his letter, which the delegation delivered to Constantius, Liberius begs that the council should not only concern itself with the case of Athanasius, but also with many other matters, and above all that that of faith should be diligently investigated.[21] Liberius also thought that if all would agree with the exposition of faith as established at Nicaea, it would prove a good example for the future.[22]

Constantius granted the request and summoned the bishops to a council. During the summer of 355 a number of bishops,[23] mainly from the

---

[19] Jullian, *op. cit.*, p. 177 n. 5.
[20] *Textus narratiuus* 3 (CV 65.186–7; *ad Const.* (I) 8 PL 10.562B–564A).
[21] Hilary, *Coll. ant. Par.* Ser. A VII 1 (CV 65.89–90; *fragm.* V 1 PL 10.682B–683A).
[22] *Ibid.* 6 (CV 65.93; *fragm.* V 6 PL 10.686A).
[23] Modern scholars consider that the number of bishops who attended, estimated at over three hundred by Socrates, *h.e.* II 36 and Sozomenus, *h.e.* IV 9, is exaggerated. Griffe, *op. cit.*, p. 155; Goemans, *op. cit.*, p. 122. V. C. de Clercq, *Ossius of Cordova,*

West, assembled in Milan. Eusebius of Vercelli was not present, but after receiving letters from the council and Emperor Constantius, he decided to attend the sessions. There he produced a copy of the *Nicaenum* and proposed that all those present should sign it, because he suspected some of the bishops of heresy. This was the first time that the orthodox party directly appealed to the Nicene creed.[24] Valens however, intervened just as the local bishop, Dionysius, was about to sign and halted the proceedings. Consequently the council meetings were no longer held in the church but in the imperial palace where the emperor himself took part in the discussions. He demanded that all sign the condemnation of Athanasius and when some of the bishops pointed out that such an act would be a violation of the laws of the Church, he uttered the well-known words: "... but whatever I wish must be considered church law. The bishops of Syria allow me to speak thus. Either obey or go into banishment."[25] Most of the bishops yielded and the few who refused were banished, among them Dionysius of Milan, Eusebius of Vercelli and Lucifer of Cagliari. Hilary later referred to this council as a "malignantium synagoga."[26]

History does not record whether Hilary took part in this council. Coustant suspected that for the same reason that Eusebius of Vercelli did not, at first, go to Milan, Hilary also might have absented himself; or if he was present, "forte etiam ei praesenti pepercit Constantius, ne Gallorum animos exasperet."[27] This last remark may seem possible, but it is improbable in view of the events at Arles. At the time when the council was held at Milan there may have been some rumours of danger but the unrest in Gaul caused by the German invasions in the autumn of 355, and the insurrection of Silvanus, the magister militum in Cologne, only took place after the council of Milan.[28] It seems most unlikely that Constantius would have shown any such consideration to Hilary or Gaul, as Coustant suspected.

Washington, 1954, pp. 431-2, points out that if so many (300) bishops had signed at the council there would have been no need for the violent pressure exerted on the provinces in the period following the council. Constantius himself, in his letter to Eusebius of Vercelli, states "venientes pauci de provinciis singulis" (PL 13.565A).

[24] H. Berkhof, *De Kerk en de Keizer*, Amsterdam, 1946, pp. 97-8. This step taken by Eusebius might have been prompted by the statement by Liberius in his abovementioned letter to Constantius. See note 22.

[25] Athanasius, *Historia Arianorum* 33 (PG 25.732C). Gwatkin, *op. cit.*, p. 152 n. 1, holds the view that "the language ascribed to Constantius is no unfair account of his conduct from the Nicene point of view; but he cannot have used it himself."

[26] *Textus narratiuus* 3 (CV 65.187,3; *ad Const.* (I) 8 PL 10.562B).

[27] *Vita S. Hil.* c. IV 27 (PL 9.136D).

[28] For the German invasions see Jullian, *op. cit.*, pp. 170-176. For Silvanus see Gibbon, *op. cit.*, p. 275. Silvanus died in September 355, only eight days after his uprising began, Jullian, *op. cit.*, p. 169 n. 5.

There is no evidence in any of our sources that Hilary did attend this council of Milan. We may presume that by 355 Hilary would have taken up a strong decision in connection with the question of Athanasius and the matters of faith, and we may also presume that no friend of Athanasius would have been spared at the council, but Hilary's name is not found among those who were banished. The complete silence concerning his presence at the council, if he did attend, would be inexplicable.[29] Scholars therefore assume that Hilary did not attend this council.[30]

2. HIS RESISTANCE AND BANISHMENT

After the council, the emperor sent emissaries all over the Western provinces to extort the signatures of those who had not attended the council. Those who refused to sign were banished. Terror and confusion reigned everywhere.[31] But at this stage the orthodox elements in Gaul were grouped around Hilary of Poitiers, a courageous and able man, who became one of the leaders of the Church in the West in the struggle against the Arians.

Hilary's first move was the issuing of a decree whereby all signatories severed communion with Saturninus, Valens and Ursacius and whereby an opportunity for repentance was given to their followers. These three leaders and those who persevered in their erroneous ways, were, as Hilary put it, cut off from communion with the Church so that the whole body of the Church would not be corrupted.[32] We may assume that Hilary was the author of this decree because the synod which was later held at Béziers, specifically aimed at deposing Hilary as bishop.[33]

We do not know how many bishops supported Hilary in this measure against Saturninus. Watson thought it improbable that many would have followed him in so bold a venture. Even men of like mind as himself, might have thought it unwise "for this was not the constitutional action

---

[29] Reinkens, *op. cit.*, p. 107 n. 1; Watson, *op. cit.*, p. xi.

[30] Loofs, "Hilarius," p. 60; Holmes, *op. cit.*, p. 151; Antweiler, *op. cit.*, p. 22; C. J. Hefele–H. Leclercq, *Histoire des Conciles*, Paris, 1907, Vol. I.2, p. 872 n. 4; Bardy, "Humaniste," p. 12. Galtier, *op. cit.*, p. 22, admits that we do not know whether Hilary attended or not, but he points out that Hilary knew very well what had happened there, as we can see from his account in *Textus narratiuus* 3 (CV 65.186–7; *ad Const.* (I)8 PL 10.562B–564A). Hilary of course, did not necessarily have to attend the council to know what had expired there.

[31] Athanasius, *Historia Arianorum* 31–32; Hilary, *Coll. ant. Par.* Ser. B I 4 (CV 65.101; *fragm.* I 4 PL 10.630A–B).

[32] *C. Const.* 2 (PL 10.578D–579A).

[33] Coustant, *Vita S. Hil.* c. IV 29 (PL 9.137D). Cf. Facundus of Hermiana, *Lib. contra Mocianum* (PL 67.858C): quod cum suis collegis Hilarius fecit.

of a synod but the private venture of Hilary and his allies. However righteous and necessary ... their conduct may have seemed to them, to Constantius and his advisers it must have appeared an act of defiance to the law, both of Church and State."[34] Another historian thought that Hilary even succeeded in causing the bishops who had yielded to the pressure of Constantius at Arles, to change their opinion.[35] Other scholars state that a great number of bishops supported Hilary,[36] but all these opinions are mere assumptions as no further details on this point are to be obtained from our sources. Watson's view however seems the more probable one, because if a great number of bishops had supported Hilary, some of them would surely have suffered the same fate as Hilary at the synod of Béziers.

Neither do we know how this decree was brought about and promulgated. Reinkens pointed out that Hilary was no metropolitan and could not convene a synod. The circumstances at that time were not favourable either for holding a synod which condemned the advisers of the emperor. Reinkens therefore thought that the signing of the decree could have taken place by means of confidential correspondence.[37] An objection which could be raised against this view, is the shortage of time in which to bring this about, viz. after the council at Milan which took place in the summer of 355 and before the synod of Béziers which was held early in 356, unless only a few neighbouring bishops followed Hilary's lead.

Nevertheless there are scholars who hold the view that Hilary held a meeting of bishops where the decree was promulgated.[38] Some even think that a council or synod was held.[39] We have already pointed out that Hilary could not convene such a synod, but it could have been done by a metropolitan who was well-disposed to Hilary. But in that case, such a metropolitan would surely have been banished by the subsequent synod of Béziers. Thus, whatever the case, we do not know what the actual circumstances were under which the decree was brought about or whether Hilary found wide support for it or not.

The general opinion among the older scholars was that Hilary at this stage addressed a letter to Constantius (about the end of 355), the so-called

[34] Watson, op. cit., p. xii. Cf. Kidd, op. cit., p. 129.
[35] Goemans, op. cit., p. 124.
[36] Viehhauser, op. cit., p. 18; Hefele–Leclercq, op. cit., p. 884.
[37] Reinkens, op. cit., p. 114 n. 2. C. Douais, L'Église des Gaules et le conciliabule de Béziers, Poitiers–Paris–Montpellier, 1875, p. 39, thought that Hilary had written a pastoral letter, signed by some bishops, in which Saturninus cum suis was excommunicated.
[38] Jullian, op. cit., p. 179 n. 3; Antweiler, op. cit., p. 22.
[39] Dormagen, op. cit., pp. 33–4; Le Bachelet, art. cit., col. 2390, thought that a synod was held probably in Paris, by the end of 355.

Ad Constantium Augustum liber I.[40] Since the articles by Wilmart and Feder[41] we know that this work is part of the records of the Synod of Sardica (343), to which Hilary added his own comments as well as a short report of the events at Arles (353) and Milan (355).

As could be expected, Saturninus did not wait long before he reacted to this deed of excommunication by Hilary and his friends. A synod was called to Biterrae (Béziers). It is not known when it was held but it probably took place during the first months of 356.[42] It is not quite clear why Béziers was chosen as the meeting place. It may be that it was on the way from Arles to the west and from Toulouse and Aquitania to the south-east. Béziers may have been an important city in those times.[43]

We do not even know who the local bishop was at the time, nor how many bishops attended the meeting. Griffe thought that those present were mostly from the Narbonensis, which was strongly under the influence of Saturninus, although Griffe added that according to Hilary's own words[44] it was evident that the other provinces were also represented at this synod. From this same passage by Hilary, Reinkens, on the other hand, deduced that only a few bishops outside of the so-called seven provinces attended the synod.[45] It is not clear how Reinkens reached this conclusion. The *De Synodis* is addressed to the bishops of Germania 1 and 2, Belgica 1 and 2, Lugdunensis 1 and 2 and Britannia, while only four of the so-called seven provinces are mentioned by Hilary in his address, viz. the province of Aquitania (1 and 2), the province of Novempopulana and Tolosa in Narbonensis. It could be that Hilary did not address his letter to the other three provinces as none of his supporters lived there. All we can deduce from the above quoted passage in the *De Synodis* 2, is that some of the bishops in the provinces to whom Hilary's letter *De Synodis* was addressed, were present at Béziers. It may be that some of those who did attend the synod were not included among the addressees of *De Synodis*, but we cannot substantiate this supposition.

[40] *Admonitio* V–VI (PL 10.556A–B); Reinkens, *op. cit.*, p. 116; Watson, *op. cit.*, p. xii; Loofs, "Hilarius," p. 60; Holmes, *op. cit.*, p. 151; Hefele–Leclercq, *op. cit.*, p. 884.
[41] A. Wilmart, "L'Ad Constantium liber primus de Saint Hilaire de Poitiers et les Fragments historiques," *RB*, Vol. 24 (1907), pp. 149–179, 291–317; "Les Fragments historiques et le Synode de Béziers en 356," *RB*, Vol. 25 (1908), pp. 225–229; A. L. Feder, "Studien zu Hilarius von Poitiers I," *SbW* 162,4, Wien, 1910. The question concerning this work is treated more fully later.
[42] Hefele–Leclercq, *op. cit.*, p. 885; Watson, *op. cit.*, p. xiv; Griffe, *op. cit.*, p. 161; Holmes, *op. cit.*, p. 154; Antweiler, *op. cit.*, p. 22.
[43] Douais, *op. cit.*, pp. 48–9; Holmes, *op. cit.*, p. 155.
[44] *De Syn.* 2 (PL 10.481B–482A): Patronos hujus haereseos ingerendae quibusdam vobis testibus denuntiaveram. Griffe, *op. cit.*, p. 162.
[45] Reinkens, *op. cit.*, p. 119 n. 3.

Douais devoted many pages of his book trying to work out which of the bishops would have attended the assembly in Béziers. His conclusion was that eighteen bishops from the whole of Gaul would have attended and that only eight of these were Arians. The rest must have been timid and passive and that is why only Hilary and Rhodanius of Tolosa (Toulouse) had been brave enough to resist the Arians.[46] All this is only speculation and it is not drawn from accepted historical facts. We know that Hilary, Rhodanius and Saturninus did attend, while Phoebadius of Agen probably did not, for he would have taken his stand with Hilary and Rhodanius, but even this remains conjecture.

Hilary was apparently unwilling to go to Béziers. A likely reason for this is the fact of his severance of communion with Saturninus and that he no longer acknowledged Saturninus; but he was compelled to attend the assembly of bishops.[47] Of what the compulsion consisted we do not know. He may just have been summoned to attend, and could not without loss of dignity have refused, knowing that charges would be brought against him,[48] or he could have been explicitly commanded to attend by the emperor, who was always well-disposed to granting the wishes of the Arians.[49]

Of the proceedings of the synod very little is known except for a few relevant remarks gleaned from some of Hilary's works. Hilary was ready to expose the Arian heresy,[50] and fearlessly he denounced its supporters.[51] Just as at Arles and Milan, it was probably requested at Béziers that matters of faith should be discussed and settled before the case of Athanasius be presented.[52] From a passage in one of Hilary's works it may be deduced that he very hurriedly said a few words.[53] Griffe thought this to mean that "the error hurriedly sneaked amongst us,"[54] i.e. that the proceedings were hurriedly brought to a close forcing the error on the meeting as a surprise. This interpretation is possible because, as we shall see, the synod did not wish to give Hilary a hearing. Another interpretation however, is that in the context of this fragment, which is probably the

---

[46] Douais, *op. cit.*, pp. 52–76.
[47] *C. Const.* 2 (PL 10.579A): per factionem eorum pseudoapostolorum ad Biterrensem synodum compulsus.
[48] Watson, *op. cit.*, p. xiv.
[49] Dormagen, *op. cit.*, p. 37.
[50] *C.Const.* 2 (PL 10.579A): cognitionem demonstrandae hujus haereseos obtuli.
[51] *De Syn.* 2. See p. 26 n. 44 above.
[52] Sulpicius Severus, *Chron.* II 39,2 (CV 1.92,12–15).
[53] *Coll. ant. Par.* Ser. B I 5 (CV 65.102,2–4; *fragm.* I 5 PL 10.630C–631A): raptim enim tunc haec per nos ingerebantur, corruptio euangeliorum, deprauatio fidei et simulata Christi nominis blasphema confessio.
[54] Griffe, *op. cit.*, p. 162: "c'est à la hâte que l'erreur se glissait parmi nous."

preface to his historical work, Hilary in this passage wanted to explain why he found it necessary to write this book. At Béziers Hilary only briefly remarked on the "corruption of the gospels, the perverting of the faith and the blasphemous, simulated confession of Christ" by the heretics. He himself declares that his speech was "over-hasty, disordered and confused,"[55] and it was for this reason that he wanted to explain the whole case in a book.[56]

His opponents however, were not inclined to listen to him.[57] It is clear that he was afforded an opportunity to say something,[58] but not the chance to state his case in full. He says that the more he sought a hearing, the more he was opposed,[59] so that he was forced to terminate his speech. Hilary did not yield to their wishes and the synod decided to banish him, but to effect this the imperial power had to be called in and they thus turned to the newly elected Caesar, Julian.

Julian however, was not at all as inimical to Hilary as might have been expected of him. Hilary later wrote that he had had an important witness in Caesar Julian, who suffered more from abuse by Hilary's enemies than Hilary himself from the injustice done to him by his banishment.[60] From this passage in Hilary's work, Coustant wrongly inferred that Julian was either at Béziers or in the vicinity when the synod was held.[61] Because Julian is mentioned in connection with the proceedings leading to Hilary's exile, it does not have to mean that Julian attended the synod, as Reinkens[62] supposed. This contact between the synod and Julian could have been by means of correspondence. Douais also thought that Julian attended the synod to authorize it by his presence.[63]

[55] *Coll. ant. Par.* Ser. B I 5 (CV 65.102,4–5; *fragm.* I 5 PL 10.631A): et necesse fuit in eo sermone omnia esse praepropera, inconposita, confusa.

[56] *Loc. cit.* (CV 65.102,1–2; *fragm.* I 5 PL 10.630C): tamen propensiore cura rem omnem hoc uolumine placuit exponere.

[57] *C.Const.* 2 (PL 10.579A): Sed hi timentes publicae conscientiae, audire ingesta a me noluerunt.

[58] See note 53 (ingerebantur) and 55 (sermone).

[59] *Coll. ant. Par.* Ser. B I 5 (CV 65.102,5–7; *fragm.* I 5 PL 10.631A): quanto nos inpensiore cura audientiam quaereremus, tanto illi pertinaciore studio audientiae contrairent. Feder, "Studien I," p. 82, thought that this meant: "Er hatte gehofft, die Angelegenheit in einer Audienz beim Kaiser vorlegen zu können, aber diese war von seinen Gegnern hintertrieben worden." Cf. *in fragmenta praefatio* IV (PL 10.620D) where the opinion is expressed that Hilary sought an audience with the emperor to convince him of the true faith. This specific meaning does not necessarily have to be given to "audientiam" here, but it could merely mean that the synod did not want to listen to Hilary. This is clear from the words quoted in note 57 above.

[60] *Ad Const.* (II) 2 (CV 65.198,5–7; PL 10.565A): nec leuem habeo querellae meae testem dominum meum religiosum Caesarem tuum Iulianum, qui plus in exilio meo contumeliae a malis, quam ego iniuriae, pertulit.

[61] *Vita S. Hil.* c. V 38 (PL 9.142A).

[62] Reinkens, *op. cit.*, p. 120.

[63] Douais, *op. cit.*, p. 51.

Julian was appointed caesar in November 355 and on 1 December 355 left Milan for Vienne. After spending the winter there, he went further northwards and reached Autun on 24 June.[64] It would thus have been far out of his way for Julian to journey to Béziers from Vienne and bearing in mind the fact that he certainly did not have much interest in the doctrinal struggle of the Church and that he was occupied with preparations for his military campaign, it seems very unlikely that he did attend the synod or that he was anywhere in the vicinity of Béziers at the time. Indeed, if he had been at Vienne and the contact between the bishops at the synod and Julian and the emperor had been by means of correspondance, then quite some time must have elapsed before the order of banishment by the emperor could have been served on Hilary and his actually going into exile.

Reinkens enumerates a few reasons why Julian would not want to intervene in the case: Julian did not have much interest in Arianism and the doctrinal struggle; the young ruler wished to appear lenient and would not want to issue decrees of banishment in cases which seemed to him very dubious; he would not have been hostile to Hilary because he saw in the bishop of Poitiers a rhetor who, through his classical training and high morals, was far superior to his adversaries; the preparations for his forthcoming military campaign also demanded all his attention so that he could not consider Hilary's case in detail.[65]

Watson thought that Julian probably took no action because he felt that the matter was too serious for him to decide without referring it first to the emperor; and also, that he had no wish to outrage the dominant church feeling of Gaul and alienate the sympathies which he might need in the future.[66] The latter thought appears to somewhat anticipate the events of 361. While it is true generally that the newly elected caesar would not want to alienate sympathies unnecessarily, it is questionable whether "the dominant church feeling of Gaul" was in sympathy with Hilary and if this was the case, how could Julian in any case have known that Hilary represented the dominant Church feeling of Gaul when at the last few councils, i.e. Arles, Milan and Béziers, all, with the exception of but a few bishops, had subscribed to the emperor's wish. The first reason given by Watson however, seems a very likely one, especially if we bear in mind that in the first period of his caesarship, Julian had very little power, and as Bidez pointed out, he was not

[64] Ammianus Marcellinus, *Res gestae*, XV 8,18 and 21; XVI 2,1–2.
[65] Reinkens, *op. cit.*, pp. 119–120.
[66] Watson, *op. cit.*, p. xiv. Cf. Kidd, *op. cit.*, p. 130.

sent to Gaul as a sovereign ruler, but rather as an ordinary deputy.[67]

The above-mentioned opinions are all mere suppositions, although also probabilities, as it will never be known what Julian's motive was in acting as he did. In any case, he refused to pass a sentence which he must have known would be in accordance with the emperor's desire.[68] The statement by Bidez that Julian was obliged to send Hilary into exile,[69] is only correct if it meant that he merely approved the emperor's verdict. But Julian did not, according to Hilary, sentence him in the first place, for Hilary would not have referred to Julian as a witness if the latter had been hostile towards him.

The report by the synod was then sent to the emperor in Milan, but unfortunately its contents are not known. Hilary later declared it to be false and he thus wanted to dispute it with Saturninus in the presence of the emperor in 360 in Constantinople.[70] Coustant had suggested that it would have been easy at that time for Hilary's enemies to bring suspicion on his faith and political integrity, because of the turbulent state of Gaul.[71] Coustant's authority for his statement that Hilary was exiled because of political suspicions,[72] only mentions that the report was false and that the emperor was deceived by it. Feder too, although he admits that the contents of the false report which led to Hilary's banishment are nowhere expressly given, supposes that they were partly of a political nature.[73] Quite wrongly Chadwick supposes that Hilary rose in revolt against Constantius because of the opportunity offered by the revolt of Silvanus, and another statement by Chadwick,[74] viz. that Hilary was convicted of treason, is to be doubted. Hilary opposed the emperor, not because of the revolt of Silvanus, but rebelled against his enforcing his will upon the Church in demanding the condemnation of Athanasius. By this time Hilary had also realized that the whole case was not just the condemnation of a person (Athanasius), but that this condemnation also entailed

---

[67] J. Bidez, *La vie de l'empereur Julien*, Paris, 1930, pp. 133–4.

[68] Watson, *loc. cit.*

[69] Bidez, *op. cit.*, p. 141.

[70] *Ad Const.* (II) 2 (CV 65.198,2–12; PL 10.564D–565A): exulo autem non crimine, sed factione et falsis nuntiis synodi ad te imperatorem pium, non ob aliquam criminum meorum conscientiam per impios homines delatus. ... in promtu enim sunt pietatis uestrae litterae. falsa autem eorum omnia, qui in exilium meum procurauerunt, non in obscuro sunt. ipse quoque (Saturninus) uel minister uel auctor gestorum omnium intra hanc urbem (Constantinople 360) est. circumuentum te Augustum inlusumque Caesarem tuum ea confidens conscientiae meae condicione patefaciam.

[71] *Vita S. Hil.* c. V 37 (PL 9.141D).

[72] Hilary, *ad Const.* (II) 2. See n. 70 above.

[73] Feder, "Studien III," p. 15. Cf. Le Bachelet, *art. cit.*, col. 2390.

[74] Chadwick, *art. cit.*, col. 317. Gwatkin who admits that we do not know what the charge against Hilary was, thinks that it may have been one of immorality, *op. cit.*, p. 154.

the rejection of the Nicene creed.[75] All we can therefore conclude, is that the emperor received false reports from the synod and that he consequently banished Hilary. Rhodanius of Toulouse, inspired by Hilary's example, also stood firm against the threats of the Arians, and likewise suffered the fate of banishment.[76]

Some scholars thought that Hilary was probably banished before June 356.[77] This assumption may be inspired to some extent by the view that Julian was at the synod or in the vicinity of Béziers when it was held, and thus in close contact with the proceedings. We have maintained that this was unlikely but as Julian was appealed to by the synod, this must have taken place before he went on his journey to Autun which he reached on 24 June. Thus the final order of banishment from the emperor must have reached Hilary round about June. Griffe made it even later and thought that Hilary may only have left Gaul in the autumn.[78] We do know that Hilary must have left Gaul before September 356, because when a council was held at Seleucia in September 359, Hilary was already in his fourth year of exile.[79]

Before his departure to the East, Hilary published a historical-polemical work. In the previous century scholars were faced with many unsolved problems in connection with the so-called *Fragmenta historica* and the so-called *Ad Constantium Augustum liber I*. After the brilliant articles by Wilmart, Feder[80] took the matter further, and continuing on the basis laid by Wilmart, he worked out a theory which is generally accepted by modern scholars.

They pointed out that the so-called *Ad Const. I* was not an independent authentic work by Hilary, but a letter from the council of Sardica to Emperor Constantius, to which Hilary added some comments and a description of the events at the council of Milan (355). It was also established that this so-called *Ad Const. I* was not mentioned in the catalogue of Hilary's works given by Jerome. It was further established that the

[75] *Coll. ant. Par.* Ser. B I 5 (CV 65.101–102; *fragm.* I 5 PL 10.630C).
[76] Sulpicius Severus, *Chron.* II 39,7 (CV 1.93, 3–5). The accounts by the ancient historians do not exactly agree as to who was banished by which synod. Most of the accounts mention the resistance to the Arians by the Western bishops and then give a list of those who were banished without specifying who was exactly banished at each synod. Cf. Socrates, *h.e.* II 36; Sozomenus, *h.e.* IV 9; Athanasius, *historia Arianorum* 76. Hilary however specifies those banished at Arles and Milan, *Textus narr.* 3 (*ad Const.* (I) 8). From the account by Sulpicius Severus it may be deduced that Rhodanius was banished by the synod of Béziers.
[77] Hefele–Leclercq, *op. cit.*, p. 885 n. 2; Douais, *op. cit.*, p. 49; Le Bachelet, *art. cit.*, col. 2390.
[78] Griffe, *op. cit.*, p. 163.
[79] Sulpicius Severus, *Chron.* II 42,2 (CV 1.95,19–20).
[80] See p. 26 n. 41.

so-called *Fragmenta historica* could only be part of the work *Liber adversus Valentem et Ursacium* mentioned by Jerome, but his qualification of this work as "historiam Ariminensis et Seleuciensis synodi continens,"[81] deceived all the scholars through the centuries. He probably arrived at this qualification after a superficial glance at it, for it does not apply to the whole work, but only to part of it. The so-called *Ad Const. I* was originally also part of the *Liber adversus Valentem et Ursacium*, but was separated from the complete work before the end of the fourth century, because Sulpicius Severus knew it in its separate independent form. Someone, noticing that it was a letter to Constantius, and knowing that it was part of a work by Hilary, bearing in mind the known letter of Hilary to Constantius, named them respectively *Ad Const. I* and *Ad Const. II*. Jerome only knew of the one *Ad Const.*, (the so-called *Ad Const. II*) and the *Contra Const.*

One part of the *Adversus Valentem et Ursacium* was well-known in Gaul and probably used by Phoebadius of Agen in his work *Liber contra Arianos* (357/8) and by Gregory of Elvira in his *De fide orthodoxa contra Arianos* (358). The first fragment, probably the introduction of Hilary's historical work, could have been written just after the synod of Béziers was held, for there is evidence that Hilary had not yet departed on exile. Wilmart and Feder therefore thought it probable that the *Adversus Valentem et Ursacium* was composed of three books of which the first was published in 356, the second, fitting Jerome's qualification,[82] in 359/360 and the third book in 366/7.

As stated above, there must have been some correspondence after the synod of Béziers between the bishops, Julian and Constantius, and some time must have elapsed before Hilary was finally sent into exile.[83] Hilary could have completed and published his work during the time he awaited the emperor's verdict. He may have collected these documents before the synod was held and it is probable that this historical work was the material which he brought to Béziers to use in the dispute with his opponents. As he was not given the opportunity to state his case in full at the synod, he therefore edited his notes and published them afterwards under the title *Adversus Valentem et Ursacium*. After the councils of Rimini and Seleucia he again published some documents as book II of his work *Adversus Valentem et Ursacium*. The work published in 356 therefore acquired the title *Adv. Val. et Urs. liber I*. Griffe however, thought that this

---

[81] Jerome, *de viris illustribus* c. 100 (PL 23.739A).
[82] See the previous note.
[83] See p. 29.

first book by Hilary was written in the beginning of his exile.[84] In a later work of his, Hilary declares that during his exile he did not write or say anything against the Church.[85] He did not consider his *De Trinitate* and *De Synodis* as polemical works.[86] But this fact would confirm the idea that the first book of this historical-polemical work was written before he went into exile. This view is generally accepted by scholars today.[87]

Feder did away with the name *Fragmenta historica* which it had casually acquired. Because of its heterogeneous origin he thought it could be characterized by the title "Collectanea Antiariana" and because the most important codex is the "codex Parisinus Armamentarium," he thought an applicable title would be *Collectanea antiariana Parisina (Coll. ant. Par.).*[88] Feder restored the order of the documents as they appeared in the oldest manuscripts, i.e. first the anonymous series and then the series which the title attributed to Hilary,[89] whereas Le Fevré placed the second series first in his edition (published in 1598). Coustant had arranged the documents in a chronological order up to fifteen. That is why the numbers of the documents in the present edition edited by Feder (CV) differ from those in the Migne series which followed Coustant's order.

In the introduction of the book[90] which Hilary wrote in 356, he re-

---

[84] Griffe, *op. cit.*, p. 168.

[85] *C. Const.* 2 (PL 10.579B): denique exinde nihil in tempora maledictum, nihil in eam, quae tum se Christi ecclesiam mentiebatur, nunc autem antichristi est synagoga, famosum ac dignum ipsorum impietate scripsi, aut locutus sum.

[86] Wilmart, *RB*, Vol. 24 (1907), p. 305. E. Schwartz, "Zur Geschichte des Athanasius II," *Nachr. Gött. Ges.*, Göttingen, 1904, p. 390, thought that the fragments should have been named *polemica*, rather than *historica*.

[87] Smulders, *op. cit.*, p. 40; Bardenhewer, *op. cit.*, p. 381; Schanz, *op. cit.*, p. 289; Lietzmann, "Hilarius," col. 1603; Bardy, "Traducteurs," p. 260. Unfortunately the book by J. Fleming, *Commentary on the so-called Opus Historicum of Hilary of Poitiers*, (Thesis Durham 1951) was not available. Jullian, *op. cit.*, p. 178 n. 2, hesitated to renounce the traditional opinion that the *ad Const. I* was a letter by Hilary to Constantius written about 355. He argued that Sulpicius Severus knew the *ad Const. I* in its present form, as a separate work, and Sulpicius Severus must have known the truth about Hilary's works, as he lived in Gaul and was acquainted with Martin of Tours, a friend of Hilary, cf. *Chron. II* 45,3: "tribus libellis publice datis audientiam poposcit." The scholars, even Wilmart, *RB*, Vol. 24 (1907), p. 155 and Feder, "Studien I," p. 136, accepted that with these letters the so-called *ad Const.* (*I*), *ad Const.* (*II*) and *contra Const.* were meant, but this is quite inaccurate because Hilary requested an audience with the Emperor in the *ad Const.* (*II*) only. The fact that Sulpicius Severus knew the *ad Const.* (*I*) in its present form, may prove that this work had already been separated from the complete work, *adversus Valentem et Ursacium*, by the year 403. It is likely that Sulpicius Severus only knew Hilary's work in its present fragmentary form and not as a complete book. Feder, "Studien I," pp. 151, 136.

[88] Feder, "Studien I," p. 5.

[89] See Feder, "Studien I," pp. 2–3 and Coustant, PL 10.625–6, for the various ways in which the editors arranged the documents.

[90] *Coll. ant. Par.* Ser. B I (CV 65.98–102; *fragm.* I PL 10.627–631). The reconstruction of the three books as proposed by Feder, is used. Cf. Feder, "Studien I," Anhang 5 and CV 65.191–3.

collects the words of the Apostle Paul about the excellence of faith, hope
and love (1 Cor. 13:13) (§ 1) and that of these love was the greatest (§ 2).
He indicates that he also could have enjoyed the good things of life, including domestic peace and friendship with the emperor, if he had chosen
to corrupt the Gospel-truth by falsehood, and then consoled the guilt of
his conscience with the excuse of ignorance. But the love of which the
apostle wrote, would not tolerate this and he would rather suffer injustice
for the sake of his confession of God, than seek honour by remaining
silent (§ 3). It was a grave and multiplex matter which he was bringing
to the public attention. While peace reigned in imperial matters there was
unrest and anxiety in the Church. Imperial officials were taking action
against bishops and those who did not condemn Athanasius were driven
into exile. Most of the bishops did not deem this worthy of exile (§ 4).

Hilary does not choose to mention the part played by the emperor,
because there were more important matters for attention. From the
course of events at Béziers[91] it was evident that the issue was different to
what it was thought to be, and it seemed necessary to relate the whole case
with care in this book. At Béziers Hilary was not given a fair hearing as
his opponents prevented this (§ 5).

He began by describing the events at Arles when Paulinus of Trèves
was banished so that from this may be understood that it was his profession of faith rather than his favour towards Athanasius which caused his
banishment[92] (§ 6). Finally Hilary appeals to the readers of his work to
diligently and carefully study all the evidence, so that the reader may form
his own opinion and not merely echo that of another (§ 7).

After the letter of the orthodox bishops at Sardica (343) to all the
churches and the synod's letter to Julius, we find some comments by
Hilary. He states that at the council of Sardica the innocence of Athanasius was proved. Hilary enumerates the different accusations brought
against Athanasius and he points out that they are unfounded.[93] He then
addresses the bishops[94] and warns them that they must bear in mind the

[91] The proposal by Duchesne that instead of "ex his, quibusque in terris gesta sint"
the original text might have read "ex aliquibus, quae Biterris gesta sint" (Cf. Wilmart,
RB, Vol. 25 (1908), p. 228), seems probable and most fitting.
[92] *Coll. ant. Par.* Ser. B I 6 (CV 65.102,14–16; *fragm.* I 6 PL 10.631A–B): ut ex his
primum confessio potius fidei quam fauor in hominem intellegatur, ex quibus in eum,
qui adsensus his non est, coepit iniuria. A. (L.) Feder, "Epilegomena zu Hilarius
Pictaviensis," *Wiener Studien*, Vol. 41 (1919), p. 56, pointed out the correct interpretation of these lines: *eum* does not refer to Athanasius, as the Benedictines thought (cf.
PL 10.631 n.b.), but to Paulinus who was mentioned just before this. The reason for
his exile was not his *fauor in hominem*, i.e. *in Athanasium*, but his *confessio fidei*.
[93] *Coll. ant. Par.* Ser. B II 5,1–2 (*fragm.* II 16–17).
[94] It may be the bishops who condemned Athanasius at Arles (Feder, "Studien I,"

future judgement. He refers to Matt. 7:2 where it is said that we will be judged according to our judgement of others. If they should blame bishops for passing sentence on Athanasius, Hilary would remind them that although Valens, Ursacius and Saturninus condemned Athanasius, the other bishops Ossius, Maximinus and Julius received him in their communion. Authority is given to these false bishops, but it is denied to the other true bishops. Athanasius is innocent of all the charges against him.[95]

Then Hilary deals with the cases of Photinus and Marcellus. We are told that Photinus, the bishop of Sirmium had been influenced by Marcellus and that he once served as a deacon under Marcellus. Photinus was corrupted in morals and doctrine and he persisted in confusing the Gospel truth by his new teachings. He was condemned as a heretic by a synod in Milan (345). Hilary also informs us that at another synod in Milan (347) Ursacius and Valens begged to be readmitted to the church communion of Rome, and their request was granted by Julius.[96] After the letters of Ursacius and Valens to Julius and Athanasius respectively, are given, Hilary continues his narrative on Photinus. We are informed that, although he was condemned as a heretic, he was not removed from his see because of the favour of the populace. Hilary also mentions the fact that Athanasius had severed communion with Marcellus. After his book had been read at the council of Sardica, Marcellus had been restored to the episcopate. Athanasius however, had condemned Marcellus not because of his book but because of ambiguous sermons which he had delivered. From the book by Marcellus it had been clear that he was innocent of the charges brought against him by the Arians and he was therefore absolved at Sardica of the condemnation which had been passed by the Arians at Constantinople (336). Hilary thus defends the action of Athanasius in first acquitting Marcellus and then at a later date condemning him.[97] The issue therefore does not involve Athanasius so much as the faith, for while Arian hatred against Athanasius has now been appeased, the movement progresses to an even greater degree of wickedness.[98]

Hilary then discusses part of a creed which reads: "Profitemur enim ita: unum quidem ingenitum esse deum patrem et unum unicum eius

p. 90) but those who signed the condemnation of Athanasius at Milan and at Béziers may also be included (Griffe, *op. cit.*, p. 169).
[95] *Coll. ant. Par.* Ser. B II 5,3 (*fragm.* II 18).
[96] *Ibid.* Ser. B II 5,4 (*fragm.* II 19).
[97] *Ibid.* Ser. B II 9,1–3 (*fragm.* II 21–23).
[98] *Ibid.* Ser. B II 9,3 (CV 65.147,19–22; *fragm.* II 23 PL 10.651D–652A): uerum omnis ista alterius causae et doloris est quaestio. et quamquam conceptis iam diu in Athanasium odiis suis satisfiat, in maiorem tamen sceleris gradum molitio tanta procedit.

filium, deum ex deo, lumen ex lumine, primogenitum omnis creaturae, et tertium addentes spiritum sanctum paracletum."⁹⁹ He comments that behind the phrases "deum ex deo" and "lumen ex lumine" there is the idea that God and light were made by God and not born of God, i.e. that the Son is not from the substance of the eternal Father. The word "primo-genitus" introduces a certain relation of time between the Son's begin-ning and that of the creatures. Thus because the world exists in the dimension of time, Christ, although He is prior to the world, also exists in the dimension of time, and thus, has no eternity before all ages. From the non-existent He received a beginning, born of Mary in the dimension of time.¹⁰⁰ Hilary then treats the phrase "primogenitus omnis creaturae" which, the Arians said, is to be found in Col. 1:15. He points out that the bishops at Sirmium did not take into account the words that preceded and followed the words of this phrase. The image of the invisible God can neither receive its existence out of nothing nor have a beginning in the dimension of time. He is not the firstborn of all creatures which, by their connection with one another, succeed one another. It is also written in Col. 1:16 that "all things were created by Him and in Him." He is therefore not the first in number, in the order of creatures, but by virtue of His creative power He is the first of all the things that would have been created by Him.¹⁰¹ The bishops at Sirmium also used the word "Trinity" but in a false sense because they separated the Son from the Father by different substances and the Spirit was added as third. The true doctrine teaches that the Father is in the Son and the Son in the Father and that the Holy Spirit receives from Both, so that It expresses the unity of this Holy Trinity.¹⁰²

According to Hilary it had always been the concern of the Church to extinguish the perversity of the erring doctrine, by expounding the Gos-pel-truth. The Father is in the Son and the Son is in the Father and therefore Christ said: "I and the Father are one" (John 10:30) and "As thou Father in me and I in thee" (John 17:21). Hilary thought that "neither the ill-will of the Jews nor the hate of the gentiles or the rage of the heretics was excited against us for any other reason than our confes-sion of the Son in the Father." The Arians had taught: "patrem deum instituendi orbis causa genuisse filium et pro potestate sui ex nihilo in

⁹⁹ *Ibid.* Ser. B II 9,4 (CV 65.147,25–29; *fragm.* II 24 PL 10.652A). This is part of a letter from a synod held at Sirmium. It is probably the meeting which was held in 347. Cf. Wilmart, *RB*, Vol. 24 (1907), p. 313.
¹⁰⁰ *Ibid.* Ser. B II 11,2 (CV 65.151–2; *fragm.* II 29 PL 10.655A–C).
¹⁰¹ *Ibid.* Ser. B II 11,3 (CV 65.152; *fragm.* II 30 PL 10.655C–656B).
¹⁰² *Ibid.* Ser. B II 11,4 (CV 65.153; *fragm.* II 31 PL 10.656B–C).

substantiam nouam atque alteram deum nouum alterumque fecisse." This is profane towards the Father to believe that He generated something similar to Himself out of nothing; and blaspheming Christ for depriving Him of the eternity of the Father. They ascribed to our Lord Jesus Christ a beginning in the time and an origin out of nothing.[103]

To check this evil more than three hundred bishops assembled at Nicaea.[104] Hilary calls the Nicene Creed "plena atque perfecta"[105] and "perfectusque sermo ueritatis."[106] In this creed is expressed the faith in one God the Father and in one Son Jesus Christ and Both are one. The Son is true God from true God and the words "begotten not made" refers to the peculiarity of His beginning and origin. He was not made and thus was subject to a beginning from nothing but He was begotten and birth is peculiar to the Father. The Son is of one substance with the Father and thus is similarly eternal. Thus one and the same substance of eternity is in God, the ingenerate, and in God, the begotten.[107] Being the unchangeable Son of God, by His assumption of manhood He brought glory to the corruption of man rather than causing a defect to His eternity.[108]

Finally Hilary tells us that Athanasius was a deacon at the time of the Nicene Council and later bishop of Alexandria where he conquered the Arian heresy and that was the reason why he was persecuted and hated by his enemies.[109]

In his comments on the *Oratio Synodi Sardicensis ad Constantium Imperatorem* (the so-called *Liber I ad Constantium*) he disapproves of the persecution of the orthodox bishops by the Arians. He states that even God does not require a forced confession, but receives those who are willing to come to Him. The Arians compel people not to be Christians, but to become Arians and they even deceive the emperor. To achieve their aim they desire the aid of worldly judges and implore the imperial authority.[110] Hilary then tells of the injustice done to Athanasius[111] and relates the recent events at Arles (353) and Milan (355).[112]

---

[103] *Ibid.* Ser. B II 9,5–6 (CV 65.148–9; *fragm.* II 25–26 PL 10.652B–653B).
[104] *Ibid.* Ser. B II 9,7 (CV 65.149,22–23; *fragm.* II 27 PL 10.653B–654A).
[105] *Ibid.* Ser. B II 11,1 (CV 65.151,3; *fragm.* II 28 PL 10.655A).
[106] *Ibid.* Ser. B II 11,5 (CV 65.153,8–9; *fragm.* II 32 PL 10.656C).
[107] *Ibid.* Ser. B II 11,5 (CV 65.153–4; *fragm.* II 32 PL 10.656C–658A). Cf. Ser. B II 11,1 (CV 65.151; *fragm.* II 28 PL 10.655A).
[108] *Ibid.* Ser. B II 11,5 (CV 65.154; *fragm.* II 32 PL 10.658A).
[109] *Ibid.* Ser. B II 11,6 (CV 65.154; *fragm.* II 33 PL 10.658A–B).
[110] *Textus narratiuus* 1 (CV 65.184–6; *ad Const.* (I) 6 PL 10.560B–561C).
[111] *Ibid.* 2 (CV 65.186; *ad Const.* (I) 7 PL 10.561C–562B).
[112] *Ibid.* 3 (CV 65.186–7; *ad Const.* (I) 8 PL 10.562B–564A).

CHAPTER III

HILARY'S EXILE

1. INTRODUCTION

Hilary arrived sometime before September 356, at his place of exile,[1] which according to some sources was Phrygia.[2] He himself alludes to his place of abode as the East,[3] but also mentions more specifically the ten provinces of Asia,[4] i.e. the diocese Asia which consisted of the province Asia, Hellespontus, Lydia, Phrygia (Phrygia prima or Pacatiana and Phrygia secunda or Salutaris), Caria, Provincia Insularis, Pisidia, Pamphylia and Lycia.[5] The report that Hilary was banished to Phrygia may be correct, as he spent most of the time of his exile in this province,[6] but it is evident that he was, to some extent free to go where he wished, and he certainly visited a number of cities.[7]

As far as is known no other bishop was elected in Hilary's place in Poitiers. Our sources do not record that either the emperor or Saturninus tried to declare the diocese of Poitiers vacant. Contrary to the procedure in other cities, e.g. Milan, where Auxentius was installed as bishop after Dionysius had been banished, Hilary's see remained vacant, without apparent reason. One scholar suggested that because of the false reports that led to his banishment, Hilary's enemies did not have the courage to fill the vacancy,[8] while another thought that Saturninus did name another bishop in Hilary's place but that the other bishops in Gaul were not co-operative in choosing a successor.[9] Yet another scholar held the view that Hilary "was still bishop of Poitiers, recognised as such by the govern-

---

[1] According to Sulpicius Severus, *Chron.* II 42,2 (CV 1.95,19–20) Hilary was in his fourth year of exile when the council was held at Seleucia in September 359. Cf. p. 31 n. 79 above.

[2] Jerome, *de viris illustribus* c. 100; Sulpicius Severus, *loc. cit.*; Venantius Fortunatus, *Vita S. Hil.* I 5 (PL 88.442B).

[3] *De Syn.* 8 (PL 10.485B).

[4] *Ibid.* 63 (PL 10.522C).

[5] W. Ensslin, "Valerius Diocletianus," *PWK*, (Zweite Reihe) Vol. VII, 1948, col. 2457.

[6] Feder, "Studien III," p. 15.

[7] In his *de Syn.* 1 (PL 10.479B–480B) he wrote to his fellow-bishops in Gaul: cum frequenter vobis ex plurimis Romanarum provinciarum urbibus significassem.

[8] Viehhauser, *op. cit.*, p. 20.

[9] Douais, *op. cit.*, p. 95.

ment, which only forbade him, for reasons of state ostensibly not connected with theology, to reside within his diocese."[10] Two incidents seem to
substantiate the view that Hilary was still regarded as bishop. When Hilary later—after his return to Gaul—charged Auxentius with heresy, the
latter retorted that as Hilary had once been condemned by Saturninus,
he was deprived of the authority of a bishop. This objection however was
not upheld.[11] The second incident occurred when the bishops in the East
were commanded to gather in Seleucia for a council and Hilary was also
ordered to attend.[12] Hilary could therefore claim that he remained a
bishop and was in communion with all the churches and bishops of
Gaul.[13] The conditions under which he served his exile were therefore
reasonably favourable, and it is likely that his homeland supported him
not only morally but also financially, thus enabling him to travel about.

2. HIS *DE TRINITATE*

a. Title

During his sojourn in the East, Hilary had the opportunity to become
acquainted with the Eastern bishops and to make a special study of the
current theological questions, thus gaining an insight into the mind of
the East, and of the reasons for their opposition to certain doctrinal
phrases. He then employed this valuable knowledge to the advantage of
the theology of the West. This contact with Eastern theology forced him
to study and analyse the mystery of the Trinity.[1] Carefully he had to re-
consider the texts which were cited in the theological disputes and the
arguments which were advanced by the Arians and their associates.
Because of this acquaintance with all the conflicting doctrines, and as a
result of his renewed study of the Scriptures, he came to write his great
work *De Fide*, known today as *De Trinitate*. Bardenhewer thought that
"eine glänzendere Leistung hat die Geschichte der literarischen Bekämp-
fung des Arianismus überhaupt kaum aufzuweisen."[2] This work was
indeed destined to justify his title of "doctor ecclesiae."[3]

---

[10] Watson, *op. cit.*, p. xvi.
[11] Hilary, *c. Aux.* 7 (PL 10.614A).
[12] Sulpicius Severus, *Chron.* II 42,1–3 (CV 1.95,17–24).
[13] *Ad Const.* (II) 2 (CV 65.197–8; PL 10.564D): episcopus ego sum in omnium
Galliarum ecclesiarum atque episcoporum communione, licet exilio, permanens et
ecclesiae adhuc per presbyteros meos communionem distribuens.
[1] Holmes, *op. cit.*, p. 156; Galtier, *op. cit.*, p. 49.
[2] Bardenhewer, *op. cit.*, p. 379. Cf. Reinkens, *op. cit.*, p. 129.
[3] Galtier, *op. cit.*, p. 6.

The present title *De Trinitate* is probably not the one given by Hilary himself. Some ancient writers quoted this work as "de fide."[4] Reinkens deduced from two passages in Hilary's work[5] that Hilary might have called his book "de fide vera" or "evangelica" or "contra Arianos."[6] The two passages do not prove his point as the words are used in a purely general sense and it cannot be assumed that they refer to the title of the work. Jerome calls the work "against the Arians,"[7] and Augustine apparently concurs by naming Hilary the defender of the Church "adversus haereticos";[8] but this does not necessarily refer to the book, but can be taken generally. The present title *De Trinitate* is found in writings of authors in the sixth century.[9] Modern scholars assume that the original title was probably *De Fide (adversus Arianos)*.[10]

There is some difference of opinion as to when and where the book was written. The data, upon which all the arguments used in the discussion of this question are based, are the following. In the beginning of book IV it is said that the preceding books "jam pridem conscripsimus." In IV 2 there is a reference to the "first book" and indeed I 19 is meant. In V 3 the fifth book is called the second book. In VI 4 there is a reference to book IV as the first book, although in later manuscripts the "primo" is substituted by "quarto"; but in the same line (VI 4) there is a reference to this book as the sixth.[11] This last reference is not mentioned by scholars in their discussions of this problem and therefore no explanation has been attempted. The seventh book is called thus by Hilary (VII 1). To this fact also, no reference has been made by scholars. In X 4 we read the words: "Loquemur enim exsules per hos libros." From the above it is clear that the first three books were written some time before Hilary began with the fourth. Book V is called the second and that implies that

---

[4] E.g. Rufinus, *h.e.* X 32 (GCS 9,2 p. 994,13); Cassian, *de incarnatione Domini contra Nestorium* VII 24 (CV 17.382,20). In the quotations from Socrates, *h.e.* III 10 cited by Antweiler, *op. cit.*, p. 49 and from Sozomenus, *h.e.* III 14,41 cited by Reinkens, *op. cit.*, p. 137 n. 5, there is no proof that reference is made to a title of a work.

[5] *De Trin.* I 16 (PL 10.36B): quidam ita evangelicae fidei corrumpunt sacramentum; *de Trin.* I 17 (PL 10.37C): ut unum in fide nostra sint uterque.

[6] Reinkens, *op. cit.*, p. 137.

[7] Jerome, *de viris ill.* c. 86 and 100: adversus Arianos; *Ep.* 55,3 (CV 54.490,11–13): contra Arrianos. Schanz, *op. cit.*, p. 295, points out that Jerome was very careless with regard to references to titles of works.

[8] *Contra Julianum* I 3,9 (PL 44.645).

[9] Cassiodorus, *de institutione divinarum litterarum* c. xvi (PL 70.1132C); Venantius Fortunatus, *Vita S. Hil.* I 14 (PL 88.447C).

[10] Reinkens, *op. cit.*, p. 138; Watson, *op. cit.*, p. xxx; Bardenhewer, *op. cit.*, p. 377; Schanz, *op. cit.*, p. 295; Giamberardini, *op. cit.*, p. 20 n. 11.

[11] The line reads (PL 10.160A): consequens existimavimus omnem jam in primo (quarto) licet libro editionem hujus haereseos conscriptam, nunc quoque huic sexto inserere.

book IV is the first, a fact which is confirmed by VI 4, although further on in the same line book VI is called the sixth and this again is in accordance with the fact that Hilary names book VII the seventh, while in IV 2 Hilary refers to the "first book" which proves to be a reference to I 19. From X 4 may be deduced that the work, or at least up to and including the tenth, was written in exile.

Some scholars held the view that the first book was written after the others had been completed, because "it is a survey of the accomplished task,"[12] and furnishes a summary of the contents of each of the subsequent books. An objection to this view is that in IV 2 there is a reference to I 19 and in IX 10 to I 13. Watson does not offer any explanation for these references to book I. Smulders, who held the view that the first book was written before the others, did however point out that Hilary used the perfect tense in some paragraphs and the future tense in others and this indicated that the prologue was corrected and augmented after the work was completed.[13] As there is no convincing argument against the assumption that the first book was written first, the majority of scholars hold this view,[14] and indeed "c'est un cas singulier dans toute la littérature patristique, que celui d'un livre élaboré d'après un schéma antérieurement composé."[15]

The Benedictines mentioned the possibility that the first three books, which were written before the rest, could have been written in Gaul before Hilary's banishment.[16] Le Bachelet thought this possible specifically with regard to the second and third books wherein Hilary does not mention the word "homoousios."[17] Watson also thought that these two books comprising a short treatise, complete in itself, were written before Hilary's banishment and that in comparison with the subsequent nine "it suffers ... by a certain want of intensity; ... it is not, as later portions of the work were, forged as a weapon for use in a conflict of life and death."[18] Galtier also thought that in the first three books "se manifeste une diversité de ton et d'allure" to that in the other nine. He pointed out that the last nine were polemical, while in the first three Hilary calmly

---

[12] Watson, op. cit., p. xxxiii; Holmes, op. cit., p. 159. Holmes however is very dependent on Watson for his description of the events concerning Hilary.

[13] Eg. I 30,32,24. Smulders, op. cit., p. 41 n. 113.

[14] Reinkens, op. cit., p. 130; Bardenhewer, op. cit., p. 378; Schanz, op. cit., p. 294; Bardy, "Humaniste," p. 13. Some unsolved problems remain, e.g. that in V 2 the fifth book is called the second book and VI 4 refers to the fourth as the first and yet just after that, the sixth is correctly referred to.

[15] Smulders, op. cit., p. 41.

[16] Praefatio in libros de Trinitate XXIV (PL 10.19B).

[17] Le Bachelet, art. cit., col. 2397; McKenna, op. cit., p. vii.

[18] Watson, op. cit., p. xxxii.

expounds the orthodox doctrine. Galtier concludes: "Rien n'y indique que leur auteur, en les écrivant, ait songé à leur donner une suite."[19] The first three books which were originally published as a separate book, would have been incorporated by Hilary in the greater work, when he decided to defend extensively the true faith.[20] It is possible that the first three books were published separately before the others but the change in tone has a quite feasible explanation. Hilary first wished to instruct the readers of his work in the positive true faith. Having laid this foundation, he could proceed to examine and refute the arguments of the heretics.

The answer to the question as to whether the first three books had been written before his banishment, depends to a large extent on the interpretation which is given to "jam pridem" (IV 1). Galtier thought that this could not mean that Hilary could have written it during his first year of exile, as the whole period of exile did not exceed four years.[21] Reinkens thought that these words alluded to an interruption in the work which could have taken place during his exile. He also surmised that if this interruption had been caused by the banishment, Hilary would have mentioned this fact when he later continued the work during his exile. Finally Reinkens decided that the first three books did not create the impression of having been written before his exile.[22]

According to the majority of scholars the remainder of the book was written and completed during Hilary's years of exile,[23] but Watson and Galtier thought that the work was finalized and published after Hilary's return to Gaul (360).[24] There are however, no decisive arguments in favour of the latter view. We may summarize as follows: the first three books were probably written some time before the rest, probably while Hilary was still in Gaul or during the first year of his exile. After a lapse of time he resumed his work, finishing and publishing it before the end of his exile. Chronologically it therefore may have been published after his

---

[19] Galtier, *op. cit.*, pp. 36,41.

[20] Galtier, *op. cit.*, pp. 41-2; Watson, *op. cit.*, pp. xxxi–xxxiii, surmises that Books 2 and 3 formed a separate work, as well as Books 4–7. Even the remaining books, the eighth to the twelfth were published separately, according to Watson. However, when Hilary began to write Book 8, he had already determined to use his previous minor works. Finally he wrote Book 1 and then published all 12 as a complete book.

[21] *Op. cit.*, pp. 35-6.

[22] Reinkens, *op. cit.*, p. 130. Bardenhewer, *op. cit.*, p. 378; Schanz, *op. cit.*, p. 295; Labriolle, *op. cit.*, p. 347, and Griffe, *op. cit.*, p. 171, also thought that it was written during his exile.

[23] Bardenhewer, *loc. cit.*; Schanz, *op. cit.*, p. 294; Antweiler, *op. cit.*, p. 22; McKenna, *op. cit.*, p. vii; Smulders, *op. cit.*, p. 194. Loofs, "Hilarius," p. 60, thought that it must have been written even before he came to know of the homoeousianism, thus before the synod at Ancyra (358).

[24] Watson, *op. cit.*, p. xxxiii; Galtier, *op. cit.*, pp. 73,75.

De Synodis, but since the greater part was written before this, we treat it first.[25]

b. Purpose

The purpose for the writing of the *De Trinitate* was firstly that Hilary felt compelled and under an obligation to undertake this work. The errors of the heretics forced him to do what was unlawful—to speak of the ineffable.[26] The infidelity of the heretics brought him into the difficult and dangerous position of going beyond the heavenly command and enquiring into celestial and abstruse subjects.[27] Elsewhere he relates that evil-minded men who were false in the profession of faith, imposed on him the necessity of having to contradict them, for under the guise of true religion they instilled their deadly doctrines into the simple minds of their hearers.[28] In addition to the duty of preaching the Gospel, which he as a bishop owed to the Church, he felt a greater urge to write, as the number increased of those who were endangered and possessed by this false belief.[29]

Secondly, Hilary had a burning desire to reply to the insane attacks of the heretics, for it is salutary not only to believe in God, but in God the Father; not only to hope in Christ, but in Christ as the Son of God; and not in a creature, but in God the Creator who was born of God.[30] Hilary knew that it was an arduous task which he set himself and although the consciousness of his own weakness held him back, yet inspired by the ardour of faith, he could not remain silent about these matters of which he dare not speak.[31]

And yet his undertaking was an immense task, and his venture incomprehensible, because he had to speak about God beyond the bounds set by God.[32] He was forced to put a strain on the weakness of words to express thoughts that are ineffable. Because of the errors of others, he

[25] Smulders, *op. cit.*, p. 281 n. 11, thought that *de Trin.* VII was written about the same time as his *de Syn.*, i.e. winter 358-359.

[26] *De Trin.* II 2 (PL 10.51A).

[27] *Ibid.* II 5 (PL 10.53C). According to II 1 the Apostles were commanded by the Lord only to preach the Gospel but the action of the heretics forced Hilary to go beyond this command and investigate the secrets of the divine nature, McKenna, *op. cit.*, p. 38 n. 5. Hilary thought that the so-called baptismal command in Matt. 28:19, 20 was a perfect summary of the knowledge which was necessary for man's salvation. See II 1.

[28] *Ibid.* VIII 2 (PL 10.237B).

[29] *Ibid.* VI 2 (PL 10.158C).

[30] *Ibid.* I 17 (PL 10.37B).

[31] *Ibid.* VII 1 (PL 10.199B).

[32] *Ibid.* II 5 (PL 10.54B).

was also compelled to err: truths that should have been restricted to the pious heart, now had to be expressed in human speech.[33] He would have preferred to preserve in his heart these things about the Father, than have to express them in mere human words which were powerless to convey what must be said.[34] The human language cannot sufficiently express the things of God. The ineffable surpasses the bounds and limits of definition.[35] It was also a dangerous task which he had undertaken. The necessity to contradict the heretics had placed him in the unhappy position where his answer or silence was equally dangerous.[36] There were many snares in Hilary's way and the heretics were waiting on every word of his to find a reason for an accusation against him. There was the constant fear and peril of wandering off the narrow road or stumbling into a pit.[37] Conscious of all this, Hilary concludes the first book by beseeching God to support the first trembling steps of his undertaking and to aid him in a steady progress. He also asks God to grant him the precision of language, the light of understanding, the nobility of diction and faith of the truth; and that God may grant that he confess the things which he believes.[38]

Hilary wanted to produce a work, well arranged and logical.[39] He also employed the method which is followed in every branch of learning—after becoming familiar with the preliminary easy lessons, the student is tested in the subjects in which he has been instructed. The soldier, rhetor and sailor are only allowed to go into their respective fields after they have received the basic training. Hilary therefore first instructed his readers in the simple faith, gradually leading them onwards until they could demolish every plea by the heretics. Then the readers are led into the arena of the great and glorious combat where they, through their study of things divine, may apprehend mysteries which are beyond the ordinary resources of the unaided human reason.[40]

Hilary thus wrote this work because he felt compelled to contradict the heretics who under the guise of religion, poisoned the simple minds of the believers. He also wished to reply to the attacks on the faith by the heretics. Elsewhere he stated that he had a twofold object in refuting the idle talk: to instruct what is holy, perfect and sound and to expose as ridiculous their crafty arguments.[41]

[33] *Ibid.* II 2 (PL 10.51B).
[34] *Ibid.* II 7 (PL 10.56A).
[35] *Ibid.* IV 2 (PL 10.97C).
[36] *Ibid.* V 1 (PL 10.129B–C).
[37] *Ibid.* VII 3 (PL 10.200C–201A).
[38] *Ibid.* I 38 (PL 10.49B–C).
[39] *Ibid.* I 20 (PL 10.39A).
[40] *Ibid.* I 34 (PL 10.47A–B).
[41] *Ibid.* VIII 2 (PL 10.238A).

c. Faculty of reason and function of faith

It has been pointed out that the Arian heresy was not solely a wrong interpretation of the Scriptures, but also that the Arians reached some of their conclusions and rejected the eternal generation of the Word, in the name of Reason. Hilary in his refutation, appealed to the authority of the Scriptures, but he also used the weapons of human logic and speculative reasoning.[42] We therefore have to ascertain what Hilary thought of the faculty of reason and how he proposed that it was to be used in theological study.

Hilary did not underestimate or deem worthless the faculty of human reason. From his own experience he knew that it was just this faculty which fired in him the desire to know more about God.[43] But in his search for this knowledge, he found that God is so far above the power of comprehension, that the more the mind endeavours to encompass Him to any degree, the more the infinity of His boundless eternity exceeds the outstretched mind.[44]

By itself, the human mind cannot attain to the knowledge of celestial things; and even the knowledge of corporeal things cannot assist in understanding the invisible things, for this is beyond the power of the human mind.[45] Hilary points out that we acquire knowledge through our sense of perception. We cannot therefore judge the invisible and our reason can only decide on matters posterior to receiving reason. Our reason cannot project itself into the time when it did not exist. The comprehension of which our minds are capable, cannot conceive either the invisible or the eternal.[46] Elsewhere he states that the human mind is wise only in that which it understands, only believes that which is possible, and regards as possible only what it can see or do.[47]

Hilary therefore did have a positive evaluation of the human reason and realized that it was this faculty in man which was responsible for his urge to seek knowledge of the supernatural and the divine; but he unequivocally pointed out the total inability of the human intellect to comprehend God. Reason can only provide the knowledge that God exists, but not any knowledge about God.

Dormagen thought that Hilary advanced a strong argument against the Arians in the first chapters of his book, by averring that he too, had, as a

---

[42] Dormagen, *op. cit.*, pp. 66–7; Emmenegger, *op. cit.*, p. 70.
[43] *De Trin.* I 3 (PL 10.27B–C); I 7 (PL 10.30A).
[44] *Ibid.* I 6 (PL 10.29C). Cf. X 69 (PL 10.396B).
[45] *Ibid.* IV 14 (PL 10.107B); I 12 (PL 10.33B).
[46] *Ibid.* XI 46 (PL 10.430A–B). Cf. III 18 (PL 10.86C).
[47] *Ibid.* VIII 53 (PL 10.276B).

heathen in the past, relied solely on reason, which had led him nowhere.[48] This is only partly correct because the Arians did appeal to Scripture—although probably only to confirm conclusions reached without its help[49] —whereas Hilary could not, while he was a heathen.

According to Hilary the human mind therefore cannot grasp the divine mystery.[50] But what man cannot conceive is nevertheless possible to God.[51] We cannot say that an event did not happen just because we do not grasp an understanding of the fact, for that would be making our sense perception the limit of reality.[52] The human intellect cannot therefore understand the deeds of God; that God became man, that the Immortal died and that the Eternal was buried.[53]

It is clear that in the above statements Hilary had the Arians in mind and that he ascribed these examples of the abuse of human reason to them. Although, as we have seen above, he maintains the inability of the human reason to comprehend God, the heretics measured the omnipotent nature of God by the feebleness of their own nature. They did not claim that they had risen to an infinite knowledge of infinite things, but that they had enclosed infinite things within the boundaries of their reason.[54] Hilary once even rebuked the Arians for teaching something which was contrary to common sense and reason: they deny to God that which their own human hopes was pleased to expect, so that what God is able to effect in man, He is powerless to achieve in Himself, i.e. He shall grant us the form of His own glorified body and yet be unable to bestow anything more upon His own body than that which is common to us and to Him.[55]

Hilary thought that the correct use of reason must ensure that the actions of God are not treated in accordance with the limited power of reasoning of the human mind, for the Creator must not be judged by those who are the work of His hands. That we may gain wisdom, we must choose foolishness, not in the sense of ignorance, but in the consciousness of our frail human natures. The human mind must become foolish in its own estimation in order to be wise unto God, viz. by learning the poverty of its own reasoning, and then seeking the wisdom of God.[56] Human reason can therefore attain to some avail only if it is con-

[48] Dormagen, *op. cit.*, p. 68.
[49] Gwatkin, *op. cit.*, p. 20.
[50] *De Trin.* III 24 (PL 10.92C); IX 72 (PL 10.338C); X 53 (PL 10.385A); XI 45 (PL 10.429B).
[51] *Ibid.* III 1 (PL 10.76B).
[52] *Ibid.* III 20 (PL 10.89A).
[53] *Ibid.* I 13 (PL 10.35B).
[54] *Ibid.* I 15 (PL 10.36B).
[55] *Ibid.* XI 43 (PL 10.427B–428B).
[56] *Ibid.* III 26 (PL 10.94C–95A); V 1 (PL 10.130A).

scious of its own limitations. Hilary also declares that there is in God something that we can perceive if we are content with what is possible. Just as there is something in the sun which we can see if we are content to see only what is possible. But we lose what we can see if we strive for what is impossible, e.g. if we look directly into the brightness of the sun, we are blinded and lose our sight. We must be content to see only as much as we can bear to see. Likewise there is much in the Divinity which we can understand if we are content with accepting, to the limit of our intellect. But if we aspire beyond what is possible, we lose that which would have been possible.[57]

While our reason cannot lead us to knowledge of God, there is another way which will. Hilary describes his own experience of how he gained this knowledge. He came to recognize God as so great that He cannot be comprehended but only believed.[58] And when someone believes, he finds that God's gift of understanding is the reward of faith and then this weakness of our reason merits the gift of revelation.[59] Faith and reason however, are not opposed to one another, for there is a mutual relationship between the two. Faith and reason must be in harmony with one another. Hilary stated that the apostles did not leave us a faith which is bare and devoid of reason. Although such a bare faith would be very helpful to salvation, yet, unless it is supported by teaching, it will merely be a secure retreat in time of adversity, but it will not hold a secure position for resistance.[60] There is therefore a close relationship between faith and reason. The one is incomplete without the other. This was the case with the heretics, for when they rejected the true faith, they lost the possibility of a correct use of the faculty of reason. Hilary states that when the fear of God, which is the beginning of wisdom, is lacking, then also, is every trace of intelligence.[61] The heretics lacking the true faith, are incapable of knowing the one, true God. The faith and understanding necessary for this confession is beyond the grasp of unbelief.[62] Elsewhere he states that what the dull nature of man cannot grasp, is achieved by faith equipped with reasonable knowledge.[63]

Emmenegger pointed out that Hilary's teaching on the act of faith is that "the act by which one assents to the teachings of faith is an intellectual act, and that the function of the act of faith, even if it be supernatural and

---

[57] *Ibid.* X 53 (PL 10.385B–386A).
[58] *Ibid.* I 8 (PL 10.31A).
[59] *Ibid.* XI 23 (PL 10.416A).
[60] *Ibid.* XII 20 (PL 10.445B).
[61] *Ibid.* V 26 (PL 10.146C).
[62] *Ibid.* V 35 (PL 10.153B).
[63] *Ibid.* I 22 (PL 10.39C).

divinely granted, is nevertheless a function of the intellectual faculty."[64] Hilary states that God reveals divine truths to men through their intelligence, bringing a knowledge of the faith.[65] Human reason does therefore play a necessary part in the act of faith. By direct statements as well as by implication, Hilary gives the power of human reason its due position in the part that he lets it play in theological study. He appreciated the powers and recognized the limits of human understanding.[66]

d. Interpretation of Scripture

Hilary tells us that after God had given him life, He also endowed him with the power of reason and then instructed him in the knowledge of Himself by means of the Scriptures,[67] so that he was able to refute the heretics through the assertions of the prophets and evangelists.[68] He thus constantly appealed to the Scriptures to refute his opponents. His work therefore often lacks an even-flowing continuation and systematical arrangement, and contains much repetition of thought.[69]

The heretics appealed to the same source as did the orthodox bishops in the Church, viz. the Scriptures. According to Hilary the heretics imagined that they could present a reasonable explanation for each of their doctrines, having submitted testimonies from the Scriptures as proof of their assertions; but with these distortions of the true meaning they could offer but a mere semblance of truth.[70]

The Church and the heretics offer a different interpretation of the same text. In his refutation of the heretics Hilary uses the same texts as they did, but with totally different results. Hilary once stated that they could be refuted by the very passages which they adduced,[71] as they interpreted the Scripture in their own arbitrary way. Hilary very clearly states that "heresy does not come from Scripture, but from the interpretation of it, and the exposition, not the text, is to blame."[72] The heretic adapts what he reads, to his own view, rather than submit his view to what he has read.[73]

---

[64] Op. cit., p. 135.
[65] De Trin. VI 16 (PL 10.169C).
[66] Emmenegger, op. cit., p. 67.
[67] De Trin. VI 19 (PL 10.171B).
[68] Ibid. I 17 (PL 10.37B).
[69] Antweiler, op. cit., p. 30.
[70] De Trin. IV 7 (PL 10.100B–C).
[71] Ibid. VIII 6 (PL 10.241B).
[72] Ibid. II 3 (PL 10.51B–52A): De intelligentia enim haeresis, non de Scriptura est: et sensus, non sermo fit crimen.
[73] Ibid. VII 4 (PL 10.202B).

The heretic thus reads the Scriptures with a preconceived opinion. They understand the words in their own arbitrary manner, interpreting them in a sense which the force of the words did not warrant, e.g. when the name father is heard, sonship is involved in that name; thus by stripping the Son of His sonship, they deprive the Father of His fatherhood.[74] Another error committed by the heretics was to quote isolated texts without explaining the context in which they appear. The meaning of the words was to be deduced from the reasons for using them, because the words are subordinated to the circumstances, not the circumstances to the words.[75] Words which were spoken in one context and for one purpose were so arranged by the heretics as to be understood in a different context for a different purpose.[76]

Another problem was the replacing of objective fact with wishful thinking. When subjective desire dominates objective truth, controversy is inevitable. If the will did not precede reason and could be used to will what is true, the word of truth would not meet with opposition. The heretics however compiled a doctrine that suited their own desires and they gathered about them teachers who would only tell them what they wished to hear.[77] Hilary also describes how the unbeliever "dashes against truth itself and rushes headlong to destroy the power of God." Were it possible he would raise his hands and body against heaven, upset the sun and other stars, disturb the ebb and flow of the ocean, and rage with fury against all the works of God. Fortunately the limitations of our body confine us within modest bounds; we are only free in one respect, i.e. freedom of thought, and thus the unbeliever distorts the truth and declares war upon the word of God,[78] even to placing the Gospels and Prophets in contradiction to each other. According to these "correctors of the apostolic faith," Solomon called us to the worship of a creature (for they regarded Wisdom in Prov. 8:22 as a creature), while Paul convicts those who serve a creature.[79]

Hilary declared that in the struggle against the heretics, it is the Church who preaches the truth, which acquires strength through being attacked. And this is characteristic of the Church: that she is triumphant when being assailed, understood when she is blamed and gains when she is deserted. The heretics mutually conquer themselves and

---

[74] *Ibid.* II 3 (PL 10.51B–52A).
[75] *Ibid.* IV 14 (PL 10.107C).
[76] *Ibid.* IX 2 (PL 10.281B,282B).
[77] *Ibid.* X 1–2 (PL 10.344C–345C).
[78] *Ibid.* III 21 (PL 10.89A–90A).
[79] *Ibid.* XII 3 (PL 10.435B).

50   EXILE

though they all rise up against the Church, she conquers all of them.[80]

The correct exposition of Scripture is firstly, that there must be no preconceived ideas in the reader's mind but that the words, as they are recorded, be allowed to speak. Hilary points out that God is the best witness about Himself. We must learn from God what we are to think of God, for He is the only source of knowledge about Himself.[81] Secondly, Hilary admonishes that the context in which a word is used, be carefully studied to ascertain the meaning of the word in that particular context.[82] Thirdly, that the meaning of a word be not altered. Hilary mentions the example of the Arians who talk of "God" and "not true God." Hilary points out that if someone should say that "this is fire but not true fire" or "this is water but not true water," his words would be senseless. If something is fire, it is true fire as long as it retains the properties of fire. The moment it loses these attributes, it ceases to be fire. We do not refer to "not true fire."[83] Finally he warns against the over-emphasizing of any one text, to the exclusion of others. A typical example of this is the Arian interpretation of Deut. 6:4 in which is excluded the possibility of another God (Christ).[84]

Although the Scriptures constitute the revelation of God and deal with divine matters, they are written in words comprehensible to the human understanding. Hilary discovered this when he, in his search for God, chanced to read them.[85] The use of illustrations in interpreting the divine truths may be profitable, but Hilary reminds us that it could be dangerous. He emphasizes that there can be no comparison between earthly things and God. He justifies the use of human analogies to explain the mysteries of the divine power. The weakness of our understanding forces us to search for resemblances in inferior things, as though they were manifestations of higher things. Any comparison must be regarded as profitable to man rather than as appropriate to God.[86] The outward appearance of visible things therefore throws some light upon the invisible things.[87]

Hilary was cautious with regard to the role of the human reason in the interpretation of the Scriptures. He avers that although the conclusions

[80] *Ibid.* VII 4 (PL 10.202A–C).
[81] *Ibid.* I 18 (PL 10.38B); IV 14 (PL 10.107B); V 21 (PL 10.143B); VII 30 (PL 10.225B), 38 (PL 10.231B).
[82] *Ibid.* IV 14 (PL 10.107C).
[83] *Ibid.* V 14 (PL 10.137A–B).
[84] *Ibid.* V 1 (PL 10.129B–130C). Athanasius thought that there were three points which had to be considered when expounding a text, viz. καιρὸν, καὶ τὸ πρόσωπον, κὰι τὸ πρᾶγμα, *Or. c. Ar.* I 54 (PG 26.124B).
[85] *Ibid.* I 5 (PL 10.28C). Cf. IX 40 (PL 10.312B–C).
[86] *Ibid.* I 19 (PL 10.38B–C); VI 9 (PL 10.163B); VIII 16 (PL 10.248B).
[87] *Ibid.* IV 2 (PL 10.98A); VII 30 (PL 10.225B).

of the understanding of Scripture may coincide with the conclusions of ordinary reason, they must still be confirmed by the actual words of the Lord so that we, with our arbitrary interpretations, do not contradict God's testimony about Himself.[88] This was an important point which Hilary made. A certain interpretation of the Arians may agree with the logic of human reason, and nevertheless contradict the testimony of God Himself, e.g. the text in Deut. 6:4. The Arians deduced from this text that there is but one God, and it is a reasonable conclusion. But it contradicted the testimony of God which is found elsewhere.

Hilary declares the Scriptures to be the source of perfect wisdom.[89] He exhorts his readers therefore to read what has been written and to understand what they read, after which they can fulfil the duty of perfect faith.[90]

To summarize, we may state that Hilary demonstrated the value of man's faculty of reason, because it was this faculty in man which sought knowledge of God. Hilary however, was very conscious of the limitations of man's reasoning powers. That which was impossible for the reason to obtain, viz. knowledge of God, was possible through faith. Perfect wisdom is revealed in the Scriptures, and faith and reason must harmoniously combine in the interpretation thereof.

In this the Arians erred. They did not have the true faith and therefore they reasoned incorrectly. On the other hand, because of their abuse of reason, they could not attain true faith. We find this interaction between faith and reason.

The Church interprets the Scriptures correctly.[91] Hilary wrote with the full consciousness that his confession of faith was the true doctrine, being that of the Catholic Church, of the Apostles and of the Gospels. To indicate this, Hilary used the expressions "catholic faith, faith of the church, evangelic faith and apostolic faith," in all, nearly seventy times.[92]

On the other hand, the heretics also claimed that their doctrine was in accordance with the Scriptures. Alluding to this, Hilary stated in one of his works, that all heretics deceived themselves; thus Marcellus did not understand the word when reading it; Photinus did not know the man, Jesus Christ; Sabellius, Montanus, Manichaeus and Marcion all erred when they read the Scriptures. "They all talk about the Scriptures without

---

[88] *Ibid.* VII 16 (PL 10.211D–212A).
[89] *Ibid.* XII 39 (PL 10.457A).
[90] *Ibid.* VIII 14 (PL 10.247A).
[91] In addition to p. 50 n. 80 above, see *Comm. in Matt.* 13,1 (PL 9.993C). Cf. J. N. D. Kelly, *Early Christian Doctrines*, London, 1958, p. 47.
[92] Smulders, *op. cit.*, p. 107 n. 1.

understanding Scripture and they pretend faith without faith. For the Scriptures are not in the reading but in the understanding; not in prevarication, but in love."[93] Reinkens rightly remarked: "Das heisst: wer in der Gesinnung des alten Adam die h. Schrift liest, fasst nur den Buchstaben und den Wortlaut; wer aber dem Gesetze der Charitas huldigt, durch welche der zweite Adam herrschet, der dringt durch die Hülle zu dem geheimnisvollen Inhalt."[94]

Hilary did not use the phrase "regula fidei" but that is more or less what he implied when he mentioned the "fides evangelica" or "fides apostolica" or "fides ecclesiastica." The heretics did not understand the Scriptures and built up a doctrine which suited their own needs rather than being "secundam evangelicam fidem."[95] Hilary thought that Sabellius was ignorant of the "evangelical and apostolic sacraments" when he preached his false doctrine.[96]

As previously stated, Hilary did not specifically speak of a "regula fidei" as criterion to distinguish between heresy and the Church. He maintains that the heretics err in their reasoning by not having the true faith and vice versa. The true faith is based on the Scriptures and only the Church interprets these correctly. As a scholar pointed out: with the holy Scriptures the true interpretation was given in the Church; and our modern problem—where is the objective criterion to know and test this interpretation?—which became acute in the Reformation, did not exist in the early Church. The faith was congruent with the Church.[97]

On the one hand, Hilary did mention some criteria according to which the Scriptures should be interpreted, viz. the reader must not have preconceived ideas but accept the Scripture as it is written; the context in which a text is read should be carefully studied; the meaning of the words must be taken into consideration and all the relevant texts must be considered and compared before a conclusion is reached. These constitute objective criteria. However, the whole case again becomes subjective, because the Scriptures are only interpreted with preconceived ideas, when a doctrine disagrees with that of the Church. Finally it is the Church alone

[93] *Ad Const.* (II) 9 (CV 65.204,9-11; PL 10.570A): omnes scripturas sine scripturae sensu loquuntur et fidem sine fide praetendunt. scripturae enim non in legendo sunt, sed in intellegendo neque in praeuaricatione sunt, sed in caritate.
[94] Reinkens, *op. cit.*, pp. 64-5.
[95] *De Trin.* X 2 (PL 10.345C).
[96] *De Trin.* VI 11 (PL 10.165A).
[97] J. N. Bakhuizen van den Brink, "Traditie," *Pro Regno Pro Sanctuario*, Nijkerk, 1950, p. 13. In connection with this problem, see from the same author: "Traditio," *Nederlands Theologisch Tijdschrift*, Vol. 2 (1947-8), pp. 321-340 and "Traditio im theologische Sinne," *Vigiliae Christianae*, Vol 13 (1959), pp. 65-86.

who decides whether a person is a heretic, for it is only the Church who interprets the Scriptures correctly.

3. HIS REFUTATION OF THE HERETICS

a. Introduction

As indicated above, Hilary first instructed his readers in the orthodox faith and in the fourth book began to expound his actual refutation of the heretics. He never referred by name to living opponents, seldom even using the names of Arius, Sabellius or any of the other heretics. Watson thought the reason for this was that "Hilary certainly intended his work to be regarded as a whole; as a treatise *Concerning the Faith*, for it had grown into something more than a refutation of Arianism. ... it is, though cast inevitably in a controversial form, a statement of permanent truths."[1] It may also be that Hilary was faithful to the precepts of classical rhetoric and to avoid that the theological disputes be troubled by personal suscep- tibility, he refrained from calling his living opponents by name.[2]

Another problem confronting Hilary when he wrote his work was how to begin his refutation, as different nuances of opinion had arisen among the Arians. Watson, in keeping with his view mentioned above, thought that Hilary had deliberately chosen to refute the Epistle of Arius to Alexander, which had been written almost forty years earlier and was, by then, purely of historical interest. "It was no recent creed, no confes- sion to which any existing body of partisans was pledged. ... And it was no extreme statement of the Arian position."[3] Galtier thought that because of the different groups among the Arians, Hilary chose this letter of Arius as a starting point as it was generally accepted by the Arians, and had been composed by the true father of Arianism.[4] This document did afford him an advantageous point from whence to launch his attack upon the heretics, and he not only refuted the arguments contained in this letter of Arius, but in the course of his work, he mentioned and disproved many other current heretical views. It was of course only possible to refute the main arguments of the heretics in this work which was of a general character.

Hilary addressed the Arians as "heretics, fools, Ariomanites, serpents, adders who conceal their deadly poison"[5] etc. Förster reproaches Hilary

---

[1] Watson, *op. cit.*, p. xxxiv.
[2] Smulders, *op. cit.*, p. 92.
[3] Watson, *loc. cit.*
[4] Galtier, *op. cit.*, p. 89.
[5] Cf. for example *de Trin.* VIII 28; V 25; VII 7; VIII 40; VI 7. Athanasius used similar names in his *Or. c. Ar.*, e.g. Ariomanites, I 4 (PG 26.20A), III 58 (PG 26.444C); and in I 3 (PG 26.17C) he said that they are not Christians.

for committing the same fault as his orthodox-minded contemporaries who were unable to appreciate in any way the viewpoint and arguments of their adversaries.[6] It must however, be borne in mind that Hilary, just as Athanasius,[7] saw in the denial of Christ as true God and Son of God, a matter of life and death and he explicitly states that there is no other way to eternal life than that of confessing Jesus Christ as the Son of God.[8] As already pointed out,[9] Hilary thought the Arians incapable of correct reasoning as they did not have the true faith, and not attaining to the true faith, because they reasoned wrongly. They were therefore, in the true sense of the word "foolish."

Hilary began his refutation by enumerating some of the general views held by the Arians. They denied that Christ was born of God and held that He was God's Son by adoption in the sense in which many are sons of God; and likewise that He was God in the sense in which many are gods. He was however greater than the other adopted sons since His adoption preceded that of the others. Confessing God's omnipotence, they maintained that Christ was created into God's likeness out of nothing.[10] The Arians objected to the *homoousion* because the meaning they attached to it was that the Father was also the Son and that the Father had taken a body from the virgin and gave to Himself, in this body which He had assumed, the name of Son. Secondly they believed that it implied a substance anterior to the Father and the Son in which both participated. Each of the Two is of a nature pre-existent to Himself and Each identical in matter with the Other. The term *homoousios* does not distinguish between the Father and the Son and makes the Father subsequent in time to that matter which He has in common with the Son. Their third objection to this word was that it implied that the Son originated from a division of the Father's substance. The part cut off from the whole, continues to share the nature of that from which it has been severed. The Arians maintained that God is unchangeable and therefore cannot be divided as this term implied.[11] Another assertion of the heretics was that with the confession that the Son was born, His eternity was rejected, because according to them the Son was born within time and time therefore, was anterior to Him.[12]

The Church however, according to Hilary, confesses one God from

[6] Förster, *art. cit.*, p. 649.
[7] A. van Haarlem, *Incarnatie en verlossing bij Athanasius*, Wageningen, 1961, pp. 97–8.
[8] *De Trin.* VI 24 (PL 10.175B).
[9] Cf. pp. 45–48 above.
[10] *De Trin.* IV 3.
[11] *Ibid.* IV 4.
[12] *Ibid.* IV 5.

Whom are all things and one Lord Jesus Christ through Whom are all things. In the One from Whom all things are, she recognizes the majesty of the Unborn and in the One through Whom all things are, she venerates the Power which does not differ from His Source. The Church believes in one Unborn God and one Only-begotten Son of God. She confesses an eternal Father and believes that the Son's beginning is from eternity; He is not from a beginning within time but from Him Who has no beginning. He was born from eternity, receiving the birth from the eternity of the Father.[13]

Hilary then quotes many texts from which the Arians maintained that unmistakably God (the Father) alone is true, righteous, wise, invisible, good, mighty, immortal etc. This, however, was upheld with the object of denying the Son any of these attributes and eventually depriving Him of His divinity.[14] Hilary corrects the view that the conceding of any of these attributes to the Son would entail subtracting some dignity from the Father. On the contrary, he maintains that the honour of the Son contributes to the majesty of the Father, for the Source, from which comes that which merits glory, must be even more glorious.[15]

The exact terms in which the Arians express their beliefs concerning the Son, is given by quoting the letter of Arius to Alexander.[16] Hilary proceeds by analysing this document and refuting the views expressed in it.

b. Distinction within the Godhead

Hilary declares that the main tenet of the Arians is that they "believe in one, only God" and as Scriptural proof they refer to Deut. 6:4. To this he replies that the truth expressed in this text had never been doubted. But belief in One God from Whom are all things, does not however mean the denial of the Divinity of the Son of God. Hilary proceeded to search the books of Moses to ascertain whether he, who proclaimed that God is One, made a distinction within the Godhead.[17]

After stating that the words: "One God the Father, from Whom are

---

[13] *Ibid.* IV 6.
[14] *Ibid.* IV 8–9.
[15] *Ibid.* IV 10.
[16] *Ibid.* IV 12–13 (PL 10.104B–107A). It is repeated in VI 5–6 (PL 10.160A–161B). There are a few minor differences between these two texts. The Greek text is found in Athanasius, *de Synodis* 16 (PG 26.708C–712A; Hahn, § 186 p. 255).
[17] *Ibid.* IV 15. Tertullian, *adv. Praxean* 18 (ed. Evans p. 111), had stated that the confession of one God, the Father, does not deny the Son, but denies another God; but the Son is not another God.

all things and one Jesus Christ, our Lord through Whom are all things"[18] constitute a perfect confession concerning God, Hilary investigates the origin of the world according to Moses. In Gen. 1:6,7 we read: "And God said, Let there be a firmament .... And it was so, and God made the firmament, and God divided the water ... ." Here mention is made of the God from Whom and the God through Whom are all things. In 2 Macc. 7:28 we learn that all things were made out of nothing, but through Whom this was done, is found in John 1:3: "All things were made through Him." The evangelist also instructs us as to Who this is, viz.: "In the beginning was the Word, and the Word was with God, and the Word was God ..." (John 1:1-3). It cannot be denied that the Father said: "Let there be a firmament," for in Ps. 148:5(LXX) it is confirmed that "He spoke and they were made; He commanded and they were created." The words: "Let there be a firmament" were thus uttered by the Father; and the words: "And it was so" refers to the Person through Whom it was done. It is not stated that He willed it and then did it; neither do we read that they came into existence because it so pleased Him, as that would make the office of Mediator between Himself and the things that were to be created, unnecessary. God from Whom are all things, commanded, and God through Whom are all things, executed; and one and the same name is confessed for Him Who commanded and Him Who fulfilled the command. This Agent is the Son, as is evident from John 1:3 and 1 Cor. 8:6. It is illogical to contend that the words: "He commanded and they were made," indicate one solitary and same Person.[19] If God had been alone it would have been unnecessary for Him to command Himself as to what had to be done, for it would only have been necessary for Him to will it, and it would have been done.[20]

When God created man, He said: "Let Us make man after Our image and likeness" (Gen. 1:26). With this profession of fellowship, He dispelled any idea of being alone. An isolated being cannot be in fellowship with himself. The words: "Let *Us* make" are inconsistent with solitude and "*Our* image" also proves that He was not alone. Furthermore, "Our image" could not have been used if the words had been addressed to One who had nothing in common with the Speaker. The words "Let Us

---

[18] 1 Cor. 8:6. Hilary's text read: ... et unus Dominus noster Jesus Christus per quem ... .

[19] *Ibid.* IV 16.

[20] *Ibid.* IV 17 (PL 10.110B–C). Athanasius, *Or. c. Ar.* III 29 (PG 26.385A–388A), used a similar argument. He cites John 1:1–3, Phil. 2:6–8 and states that if one reads the Scriptures with these words in mind, it will be clear that God the Father spoke to the Son in the beginning when the world was created and man was made (Gen. 1:3,6, 26).

make" and "Our image" reveal that there is neither one solitary God, nor one who differs. And the fact that He said "Our image" and not "Our images" proves that there was but one nature. If Genesis had testified of a solitary God, we would have read: "And He made him after His own image."[21]

The Arians cannot interpret these words of God as though they were equivalent to "I made man after My own image," because in the above-mentioned letter of Arius he confessed that all things are from the Father but all are made through the Son. According to Hilary the words "let Us make" indicate that the Source of all things is from Him Who spoke these words, while "God made him after the image of God" points to Him through Whom the work was done.[22] Furthermore the Arians, who confess the Wisdom to be Christ, are confronted by the words of Wisdom that He was with God when He was establishing the fountains and the foundations of the earth etc. (Prov. 8:28–31 LXX). Wisdom was with God, and not only was she with God, but she set the things in order. Here again it is the Father Who through His commands is the Cause, and the Son Who executes, setting in order that which has been commanded.[23] In a subsequent book, Hilary discusses at length this question of the Wisdom.

Various texts do illustrate that God was not represented as Solitary in His dealings with the Patriarchs. Hilary refers to Hagar in the desert (Gen. 16). In verse 9 the Angel bids her to return to her mistress but in the following verse the Angel says: "I will multiply your seed." The multiplying of nations is not within the power and ministry of an angel; and in verse 13 Hagar called this Angel God. Hilary draws attention to the fact that the Son of God is elsewhere called "Angel of great counsel" (Isaiah 9:5 LXX). It is also written that God said to Abraham that He will make Ishmael fruitful and multiply him (Gen. 17:20). That there may be no doubt that He Who spoke to Hagar was the same Speaker as He Who addressed Abraham, there is written: "And I have blessd him and will multiply him" (Gen. 17:20). The Angel of the Lord spoke to Hagar but to Abraham He spoke as God; for the Angel of God is God, the Son of God.[24]

---

[21] *Ibid.* IV 17–18. Cf. Tertullian, *adv. Prax.* 12 (ed. Evans p. 101), for a similar argument. Novatian, *de Trin.* XXVI 146 (ed. Weyer p. 166), cited the account of the creation to prove that Christ was not the Father but the second Person in the Trinity, for in Gen. 1 the Father spoke to the Son.
[22] *Ibid.* IV 20.
[23] *Ibid.* IV 21-22.
[24] *Ibid.* IV 23–24. Novatian, *de Trin.* XVIII 103 (ed. Weyer p. 124), drew attention to the fact that the Angel was called Lord and God.

Three men visited Abraham but through faith Abraham knew that
One of them was the Lord. The Lord promised that Sarah would have
a son (Gen. 18:10) and the Lord later revealed to Abraham that Sodom
and Gomorrah were to be punished for their sins (Gen. 18:17ff.).[25] It is
the Angel of God Who executes the ministry of announcing the counsels
of God; but He himself is in name and nature God.[26] Of the destruction
of Sodom and Gomorrah is written: "The Lord rained brimstone and
fire from the Lord" (Gen. 19:24).[27] In the "Lord from the Lord" Hilary
sees a difference of Divine Persons, but as a modern scholar pointed out,
"from the Lord" does not necessarily denote a second Person, but may
mean "from heaven."[28] In Gen. 35:1 God commands Jacob to erect an
altar at Bethel for God Who appeared to him in his dream. In these words
Hilary distinguishes between God Who speaks, and God of Whom He
speaks.[29] The Angel of the Lord also appeared to Moses (Ex. 3). It is said
that the Angel of the Lord appeared in the burning bush (vs. 2), but "the
Lord called" (vs. 4 LXX) and He announces Himself as "the God of
Abraham, Isaac and Jacob" (vs. 6).[30] Hilary therefore concludes that in
the books of Moses it is clear that the Arians cannot use the assertion of
Moses that God is one, to disprove the Divinity of the Son of God.[31]
Moses therefore, does not serve as witness for the assertion that God is a
solitary God.

Hilary then examines the evidence in the other books of the Scriptures.
He quotes Ps. 44:8 (45:7): "Unxit te, Deus, Deus tuus." There is a clear
distinction between the Anointer and the Anointed. "Tuus" refers to
the Author and "te" to the Author's Offspring. The Father is His
God, because He (Son) was born from Him as God. The Father
and the Son are mentioned here and Both of them by the same name

[25] *Ibid.* IV 25, 27. Novatian, *de Trin.* XVIII 105 (ed. Weyer p. 126f.), refuted those
who thought that God was visible here, by stating that it was the Son Who was seen.
Novatian saw in this receiving of the Son as a guest by Abraham, a foreshadowing
of the Incarnation. Cf. Hilary, *de Trin.* IV 27 (PL 10.117B): sacramentum scilicet
futurae corporationis agnoscens.
[26] *Ibid.* IV 26.
[27] *Ibid.* IV 29. Irenaeus, *adv. Haer.* III 6,1 (ed. Harvey II p. 21), said that the Son
received power from the Father to judge Sodom. Cf. IV 58,4 (ed. Harvey II p. 280).
Novatian, *de Trin.* XVIII 106 (ed. Weyer p. 128), also thought it was the Son of God
Who caused the rain of fire. Athanasius, *Or. c. Ar.* II 13 (PG 26.173A), cited the same
text to illustrate that Christ was Lord and King.
[28] Antweiler, *op. cit.*, Vol. I p. 201 n. 2.
[29] *De Trin.* IV 30.
[30] *Ibid.* IV 32. Contrary to this view, Athanasius, *Or. c. Ar.* III 14 (PG 26.352A),
declared that the angel was not the God of Abraham, but that God spoke through
the angel just as He spoke in a cloud to Moses in the tabernacle.
[31] *Ibid.* IV 34.

(God) which denotes that They have the same nature and majesty.[32]

The text in Isaiah 43:10: "For I am, and before Me there is no other God, nor shall be after Me," is also no confirmation of the Arian view, for in this same verse God states that His chosen Servant witnesses with Him. Matt. 12:18 teaches that this Chosen Servant is Christ. Thus Hilary concludes that God and His Servant witness that there shall be no God after Him, but They do not deny that God, the Son had previously been born from Him.[33] In Hosea 1:7 God says: "I will save them (Judah) in the Lord their God." The Father here calls His Son "God."[34] Hilary cites Isaiah 45:11-16 and contends that the worship of the Sabaeans and the labour of Egypt and merchandise of the Ethiopians which would be offered to *Him*, must be understood as offered to *Christ*.[35] The last part of verse 14: "God is in Thee and there is no God beside Thee(LXX)" clearly suggests that the solitary God did not say it to Himself and thus points to a distinction of Persons in the Godhead, and the words "God is in Thee" shows a distinction of Person only, not of nature.[36]

Hilary concludes that it must be understood that when Israel hears that her God is one, God the Father and God the Son are one, not by a union of persons but by a unity of substance.[37]

c. The Other Person (Son) is true God

Hilary, having illustrated that although God is One (Deut. 6:4), a distinction nevertheless had to be made between God and another Person in the Godhead, then considers another article in the Arian confession, viz.: "We confess One true God." Hilary remarks that the heretics confess "One God" and "One true God" in order to deny the Son of God the nature and reality of God. Although Moses preached One God, he never-

---

[32] *Ibid.* IV 35. Irenaeus, *adv. Haer.* III 6,1 (ed. Harvey II p. 21), said that it was the Father Who anointed and the Son Who was anointed. Tertullian, *adv. Prax.* 13 (ed. Evans p. 102), said that Two are called "God" in this text. Athanasius, *Or. c. Ar.* I 46 (PG 26.108A), used this text to refute the Arian view that Christ was anointed to become God. Athanasius contended that He was already God and King and therefore He was anointed for our sake.

[33] *Ibid.* IV 36.

[34] *Ibid.* IV 37.

[35] *Ibid.* IV 38. Cf. Tertullian, *adv. Prax.* 13 (ed. Evans p. 102). Athanasius, *Or. c. Ar.* II 23 (PG 26.196C), used this text to illustrate how the Son will be worshipped by all nations.

[36] *Ibid.* IV 40.

[37] *Ibid.* IV 42 (PL 10.128B): pater Deus et filius Deus unum sunt, non unione personae, sed substantiae unitate. *Unio* was a technical expression used to indicate the doctrine of Sabellius and corresponds to the Greek μονάς. It differs from *unitas* in that unitas refers to the nature and unio to the persons. Cf. PL 10.128 n. f and Smulders, *op. cit.*, p. 122 n. 27.

theless indicated that the other Person in the Godhead, the Son of God, was God. Hilary therefore set himself the task of establishing that Moses did believe that the Son of God is true God; for Hilary emphatically states that the genuineness of anything arises from its nature and its power.[38]

Hilary contends that the creation of the world did not disprove the assertion that the Son is true God, for the apostle wrote: "All things are through Him, and in Him" (Col. 1:16). Because all things are through Him, no element of true Divinity is wanting in Him Who possesses the nature and the power of God.[39]

When the world was created, God spoke and God created. If He Who spoke is truly God, then He Who performed the creation is also truly God. The power to execute what has been said, proves that He Who performed the creation is equal in nature to Him Who spoke. The Son of God is equal to God in name, truly God, and equal to true God in power. As the mighty God is revealed when God spoke, so also is the mighty God manifested in the deed of creation.[40]

Hilary then directs his attention to the creation of man: "Let Us make man after Our image and likeness" (Gen. 1:26). It is impossible to distinguish between a true and a false God in these words. In saying "Let Us make" God clearly indicates One Who does not disagree with Himself, or is alien to Him or powerless, but One able to execute what had been said. "Our" shows that there is no question of only one Person, or of a diversity of Persons. Man is created after Their common image and both are therefore true God for there can be nothing in common between the true and the false. God the Speaker is speaking to God and man is therefore made after the image of the Father and the Son, but They do not differ in name or in nature. There is only one image after which man was created. Hilary defies the heretics to attempt to separate the true God from any false God in this image common to Both.[41]

God made man after the image of God. All things however are through the Son. If man is created through God the Son after the image of God the Father, he is also created after the image of the Son, because it cannot be denied that the words "after Our image and likeness" were spoken by God to the Son. While God the Son is recognized in the creative action, He is also true God because of the joint possession of the image of God.

---

[38] *Ibid.* V 3: Nulli autem dubium est, veritatem ex natura et ex virtute esse (PL 10.131C). Cf. Itaque quia naturae virtus praestat veritatem (PL 10.132A).
[39] *Ibid.* V 4.
[40] *Ibid.* V 5.
[41] *Ibid.* V 7–8.

Hilary concludes therefore that since the created man is created after the image of Both, then Both are true God.[42]

Concerning the appearance of the Angel who spoke to Hagar, Hilary contends that the title of "Angel" is an indication of function and not of nature, and if He indeed is true God, then His words and acts must be those of God. It is not within the power of an angel but only of God to increase Ishmael into a great people; and thus having the true power for this act, the true nature of God cannot be denied Him.[43]

Hilary points out the absurdity of the distinction which the Arians made between "true God" and "not true God."[44] One cannot speak of "fire" and "not true fire," "water" and "not true water." A true specimen of any object differs in no way from another true specimen of the same kind. If it be fire, it must be true fire and while it retains its nature it cannot be anything else but true. When water is deprived of its nature as water, it will no longer be water, but as long as it remains water, it is true water. The only way in which anything can lose its nature is by losing its existence, but if it continues to exist, it must be truly itself. The Son of God is God only if He is true God; if He is not true God, then He cannot be God at all. If He does not possess the nature, then He has no right to the name of that nature; thus, if He justly has the name of the nature, then He must have the true nature.[45]

Hilary rejects the argument that when the Angel of God was named God, this was granted as a name of adoption and that He thus did not have the true Godhead. If His nature as God was inadequately revealed when He was called the Angel of God, He did however manifest His true Godhead when, in an even more inferior nature, as a Man He spoke to Abraham who worshipped Him as God.[46]

In the destruction of Sodom and Gomorrah, "the Lord rained ... from the Lord" (Gen. 19:24). Hilary reminds the Arians that God Who they confessed as "alone true," they also confessed to be "alone the righteous Judge."[47] The Lord Who rained from the Lord is the righteous Judge,

[42] *Ibid.* V 9–10.
[43] *Ibid.* V 11,13. Novatian, *de Trin.* XVIII 103 (ed. Weyer p. 124), also remarks that the Angel could not have promised a blessing of offspring if He had not been God. The context however in which Novatian used this text, was to prove that not God the Father was seen as an Angel but the Son of God.
[44] Cf. Arius in his *Thalia* (Athanasius, *Or. c. Ar.* I 6 PG 26.21C–24A).
[45] *De Trin.* V 14.
[46] *Ibid.* V 15.
[47] It is not quite clear to which confession Hilary refers. In the above-mentioned letter of Arius (*de Trin.* IV 12), Hilary has "omnium creatorem" instead of "omnium judicem" which is the reading of the Greek text. It may however be a reference to Ps. 7:12 which is cited in *de Trin.* IV 8 (PL 10.101B), where Hilary quotes a number of texts which the Arians adduced as proof that God the Father was One.

for Abraham called Him thus in Gen. 18:25. The Righteous Judge is also true God, as the Arians confessed; thus they will have to deprive the Son of His judgeship, before depriving Him of His true Divinity.[48] Hilary therefore quotes Gen. 19:24 as an indication of the distinction within the Godhead: for according to him the Lord Who caused the fire to rain was Christ, Who was described by Abraham as the Judge. But the Judge was true God, according to the Arians although they of course thought the Father to be the Judge.

The Patriarch Jacob was also adduced as a witness by Hilary, for Jacob struggled with a Man (Gen. 32:44f.) and while being the stronger, he yet entreated His blessing, because through the eyes of faith, he saw in the Man, true God.[49]

In his dream Jacob saw God (Gen. 28:13). Later God commanded him to erect an altar to the God Who had appeared unto him (Gen. 35:1). Hilary maintains that according to the Gospel (John 14:6 and Matt. 11:27 God can only be known through God. It is by God that we are initiated into the worship of God. The one God teaches us the Godhead of the other. Since there is one name (God) for the one nature of Father and Son, God the Son can be no other than true God.[50]

It is the Angel of God Who appeared to Moses in the burning bush and it is God Who spoke from the bush. The heretics cannot insinuate that the name God is only one by adoption, because it is God Who is, Who spoke to Moses. "And God said to Moses: I am that I am" (Gen. 3:14). He spoke thus so that He may be known by the name which is His by nature; and God Who is, sent Moses to Israel so that He may be known as true God.[51]

The Arians added a word to the text in Isaiah 65:16(LXX) in order to change the meaning. Hilary rebukes them for their dishonesty and stupidity in presuming that their own reading of a text would be indubitably accepted by others without they themselves referring to the Scriptures. They read: "Benedicent te Deum verum" instead of "Benedicent Deum verum" to prove that the name God is not used in the true sense and to argue that the Son of God is God only in name and not in

---

[48] *Ibid.* V 16. Cf. 17 fin.
[49] *Ibid.* V 19. Tertullian, *adv. Prax.* 14 (ed. Evans pp. 104–106), maintained that God had said that no one could see His face and live. Yet Jacob said that he had seen God (Gen. 32:30) and therefore it was the Son Whom he had seen. Novatian, *de Trin.* XIX 112–113 (ed. Weyer p. 134), said that Jacob had struggled with a Man and yet entreated His blessing because he knew that it was God. Cf. Athanasius, *Or. c. Ar.* III 12 (PG 26.348A).
[50] *Ibid.* V 20.
[51] *Ibid.* V 22.

nature. The added pronoun implies that another person is addressed, but according to the correct reading the name God refers to the Speaker of the words, which according to Hilary, is Christ,[52] and He did not say: "They will bless Thee, the true God" but "They will bless the true God."

Having thoroughly examined the passage in Isaiah 65:13–16, Hilary concludes that Paul[53] had ascribed the words of Isaiah 65:1,2, that He appeared to them who did not seek Him, that He was found by those who did not ask for Him and that He stretched out His hands to a people who did not listen, as referring to the Lord Jesus Christ. The heretics were not more honest and reliable in their interpreting of the words of the prophets, than Paul.[54] In many other prophecies concerning God, the name *God* alone sufficed to indicate the Divine majesty and nature, but in this passage in Isaiah it is said that the *true* God was to be blessed. Hilary's explanation is that this was a prophecy of future events and because of the mystery of His Incarnation, the true Divinity in Him would not have been recognized by all people and the prophet therefore testified that it is the true God Who will be blessed.[55] The people who will bless the true God are those who had received a new name, viz. the new Israel, i.e. the Christians.[56]

Hilary realized that it could be argued that the apostle was not inspired by the Spirit of prophecy when he used these words of the prophet. He therefore stresses that in the beginning of this passage in which it is said that they will bless the true God, viz. in Isaiah 64:3(LXX), Isaiah declared that he had seen no God but Him. But the God Whom the prophet saw was according to John 12:41, the Only-begotten.[57] Isaiah thus saw God, but this God was the Only-begotten Son of God.

The heretics thus did confess one true God but they astutely used the pious teaching of the Scriptures to support their own godless assertions. They confessed that God is one and true, in order to deny that the Son also was truly God. They do not deny that the Son of God is God, but they insist that He is not true God, for He is not confessed to be God by nature but only in name.[58] In the above however, Hilary has successfully refuted these assertions.

[52] *Ibid.* V 26 and 25 (PL 10.146A).
[53] Rom. 10:13ff. Especially vss. 20,21.
[54] *De Trin.* V 32. In 31 Hilary pointed out that the context shows that in vss. 1 and 2 the Speaker was the same as in 13–16.
[55] *Ibid.* V 27.
[56] *Ibid.* V 28–30.
[57] *Ibid.* V 33.
[58] *Ibid.* V 25. Cf. 34.

d. Christ, true Son of God

Hilary has pointed out that Moses, who spoke of the God of Israel as one, also taught that there is a second Person within the Godhead. Hilary then indicated that this God, the Son of God, is indeed true God; and proceeds to prove that this Son of God is the *true* Son of God and not merely a Son by adoption.

The Arians used many phrases which seemed orthodox but this was done to infuse the poison of their heresy. The Son of God was mentioned by the name of "Son," but they were silent about His nature. They maintained that the Son was not born of God but created by an act of His will. He is called Son not because He was born of God but because He was created by God. They maintained that the Son was called "Son" in the sense in which others were called "sons of God" as in Ps 81:6(82:6). He is thus Son by adoption, God in name only, Only-begotten by favour, First-born in order, in every sense a creature and in no sense God.[59]

Hilary once rebuked the heretics for not according words their true and only meaning, but for interpreting them in their own arbitrary way. When the name "father" is heard, the nature of a son is contained in that name.[60]

The very words of God the Father indicate that the Son was not an adopted Son, but His own Son. When Jesus Christ was baptized, the Father spoke from heaven: "This is My beloved Son, in Whom I am well pleased" (Matt. 3:17). The pronouns used here indicate the true meaning of the names and therefore special attention must be paid to them. Elsewhere God said: "I have begotten sons, and have raised them up" (Isaiah 1:2). God did not however, say "My sons." Christ might have shared this common name of "Son" with others, if one instance could be cited where God said of another: "This is My Son." These words of God therefore indicate that although many others have received the name of "son" by adoption, Jesus Christ is God's own Son. God did not want us to be ignorant as to the identity of Who was being baptized.[61]

God the Father once again indicated Christ as His Son, when Christ was speaking to Moses and Elias upon the mountain: "This is My beloved Son in Whom I am well pleased; hear Him" (Matt. 17:5). Even the glory which was seen was not sufficient attestation of His majesty, but God also proclaimed Him as His Son. In addition to the words "This" and "My"

---

[59] *Ibid.* VI 7 and 18. Cf. IV 3.
[60] *Ibid.* II 3 (PL 10.52A); VIII 40 (PL 10.267A). Cf. Athanasius, *Or. c. Ar.* III 6 (PG 26.333A).
[61] *Ibid.* VI 23.

we are bidden "hear Him." Since God commanded us to hear the Son, Hilary proceeds to examine what the Son said of Himself.[62]

When the Father speaks of "My Son" and when the Son refers to "My Father's house" and "My Father," we must believe in these names and understand the nature which is indicated by them. The noun which follows the pronoun "My" belongs to the speaker. Hilary accuses the Arians of depriving the Father of all credibility, taking away the assertion of the Son and causing the words to be meaningless. They distort the words of God into a sense which the words cannot bear.[63] To the Son is also attributed that: "All things are delivered unto Me of My Father and no one knows the Son but the Father, neither does anyone know the Father but the Son and he to whom the Son will reveal Him" (Matt. 11:27). The Son can only be known by a mutual attestation through the Father, and the Father through the Son. Furthermore, all things are delivered to Him and from this "all" nothing is excepted. They have an equal power, the secret of their knowledge is equal and Hilary therefore concludes that They are in truth what Their names indicate, i.e. Father and Son.[64]

Not only by an appeal to the name, but to the power does the Only-begotten teach His Sonship, for He said: "For the works which the Father has given Me to finish, the same works which I do, bear witness of Me, that the Father has sent Me. And the Father Himself which has sent Me, has borne witness of Me" (John 5:36,37). His works prove that the Father had sent Him, but for the unbelievers the works are not sufficient witness that God had sent Him; and thus the Father also witnesses of Him. We have the Father's witness to His Sonship and through His works the Son equalled the witness of the Father. Christ did not therefore receive the name of Son through adoption.[65] Elsewhere Hilary states that the miracles performed by the Lord confuse the human reason and it is beyond its comprehension, but the power of God is manifest in the things which the Lord did.[66]

Hilary proceeds with another argument. Jesus said: "You neither know Me, nor do you know whence I am;[67] and I am not come of Myself, but He that sent Me is true, Whom you know not, but I know Him for

---

[62] *Ibid.* VI 24.
[63] *Ibid.* VI 25.
[64] *Ibid.* VI 26. Irenaeus, *adv. Haer.* IV 11,5 (ed. Harvey II p. 161), said that only the Son can reveal knowledge of the Father to mankind.
[65] *Ibid.* VI 27.
[66] *Ibid.* III 5–7.
[67] Hilary changed the text by making it negative. His version might be a combination of John 7:28 and 8:19.

I am from Him and He has sent Me" (John 7:28–29). The Son often assures us that no man knows the Father. The reason that only the Son knows the Father is that He is from the Father; and He is from the Father either as the result of an act of creation or of a genuine birth. If it is an act of creation, then all created things are from God; but then all should know the Father. If the Son was created and not born of the Father, then He should have been just as ignorant of the Father[68] as all other created beings. If it is peculiar to the Son to know the Father because He is from Him, then it is also peculiar to the Son to be from the Father, i.e. that He is true Son born from the nature of God. For He alone knows God, because He alone is from God. The peculiarity of alone knowing God is a peculiarity of generation. Therefore because He is from the Father, it does not signify an act of creation but a true birth from the Father, as a result of which He alone knows the Father, while all other things which are created by the Father, do not know Him.[69]

The Arians maintained that all things, without exception, are from nothing; even the Only-begotten God.[70] Christ however said: "You neither know Me, nor do you know whence I am." Hilary argues, "Why then do the Arians not know Christ or from whence He is?" If something comes into existence out of nothing, then there can be no ignorance of its origin. The fact therefore that it is not known whence Christ is, is an indication of the nature from which He came.[71]

When the Jews spoke of God as their Father, Jesus Christ replied: "If God were your Father, you would surely love Me, for I went forth from God and came; neither came I of Myself, but He sent Me" (John 8:42). Christ did not blame those who confessed Him as the Son of God, for assuming the name of "sons of God" and calling God their Father; but according to Hilary, He did reprove the Jews for claiming God as their Father, while they did not love Him (Christ). All who believe in God as Father, confess Him as Father by the same faith which confesses Jesus Christ to be the Son of God. There is no pre-eminence in the faith which confesses Jesus Christ to be the Son of God only in the sense in which many are sons of God, i.e. that Christ therefore is Son of God not in nature but only in name. In the text: "He that hates Me, hates My Father also" (John 15:23), the possessive pronoun is an indication of a

---

[68] Arius in his *Thalia* (Athanasius, *Or. c. Ar.* I 6 PG 26.24A), had asserted that the Father was invisible to the Son and that the Logos was unable to see or know His Father.
[69] *De Trin.* VI 28.
[70] Cf. Arius in his *Thalia* (Athanasius, *Or. c. Ar.* I 5 PG 26.21A).
[71] *De Trin.* VI 29.

relation between Christ and the Father which is shared by none other. In the text "... and believe that I went forth from God and came from the Father into this world" (John 16:27-28), the words "went forth from God" indicate that there is no other way of origin or being, than by birth, and none other but God could go forth from God, i.e. come into existence through birth. The words "came from the Father into this world" refer to the incarnation, while the preceding words indicate His nature. Hilary thus distinguishes between "coming from the Father" and "going forth from God," i.e. His incarnation and birth.[72]

The apostles too did not consider Christ as Son of God by adoption but by virtue of His birth. Their reaction to the Lord's words in John 16:27-28 mentioned above, was: "Now Thou speakest plainly and speakest no proverb. Now we are sure that Thou knowest all things and needest not that any man should ask Thee: by this we believe that Thou went forth from God" (John 16:29-30). Before this the disciples had known Him as the Christ, foretold by Moses and the Prophets; Nathanael had confessed that He is the Son of God and the King of Israel (John 1:49); He had reproached Philip for not perceiving the Father in the Son (John 14:9-12); they had witnessed all the healings and miracles wrought by the Lord; and yet only after He had told them that He "went forth from God" did they grasp the full truth, which opened their eyes to perceive from His works His divine nature. Not His coming from the Father, but His coming forth from God proved that He had the nature of God. Previously they had known that He, like God, could do all things, but they had been ignorant of His birth from God. They knew that He had been sent from God, but they did not know that He had gone forth from God. Now they understood the ineffable and perfect birth of the Son and thus confessed that He had spoken to them not as through a proverb.[73]

If the Son of God had only received this name by adoption and was not indeed by nature Son of God, Hilary rightly asks why Simon confessed: "Thou art the Christ, the Son of the living God" (Matt. 16:16)? If Christ was only son of God as all believers through regeneration are born as sons of God, what could the revelation be which had been made to Peter, "not by flesh and blood, but by the Father in heaven"? There would be no merit in a confession which declared that He is a son of God as all believers are sons of God. Peter had not been ignorant of the names "Father" and "Son" for he had heard them often, e.g. Christ's words in

[72] *Ibid.* VI 30-31. Novatian, *de Trin.* XV 83 (ed. Weyer p. 104), said that had Christ merely been a man, He could not have said that He had gone forth from God (John 8:42), for man was created by God and did not go forth from God.
[73] *Ibid.* VI 33-34.

Matt. 11:27. But Peter's confession revealed that he was the first person
to recognize the Divine nature in Christ. Peter had not only confessed
Christ as Son of God, for he had repeatedly heard Christ proclaimed as
Son of God, but he now realized that Christ was Son of God by virtue
of His nature.[74] He who would deny this truth and confess Christ a creature must first deny the apostleship of Peter, his faith, his blessedness, his
episcopate, his martyrdom; having denied all this, such a person will
realize that he is far from Christ, for Peter obtained all this by confessing
Him as true Son of God.[75]

The witness of John concurred with that of Peter, for he wrote: "No
man has seen God at any time, except the Only-begotten Son, which is in
the bosom of the Father" (John 1:18). The nature of the Son was apparently not set forth clearly enough by the mere name of Son and further support had to be added in order that the difference between His Sonship and
that of all others would be clearly indicated. Therefore, in addition to
"Son" he called Him "Only-begotten" and thus wholly removed any
suspicion of adoption; that He is Only-begotten proves the truth of His
name.[76]

Hilary thereupon probes the correct meaning of the word "Only-
begotten." The Arians asserted that it meant "a perfect creature of God";
"Only-begotten" being equivalent to perfect, and "Son" a synonym for
creature.[77] John however, had described the Only-begotten Son as God,
not as a perfect creature, for he had heard his Lord say: "For God so loved
the world that He gave His Only-begotten Son ..." (John 3:16). God gave
His Only-begotten Son as a token of His love for the world. Hilary then
advances a strong argument to prove his point, viz.: If the faith in His
love relied upon the fact that He offered a creature to creatures, and on
behalf of the world He gave a worldly being; and to redeem creatures
raised up from nothing He gave one also raised up from nothing, then
this cheap and petty sacrifice does not effect a faith of great merit. God
Who loved the world gave not an adopted Son, but His own, His Only-
begotten, and thus His love is proved.[78]

John's reason for writing his book was: "But these things are written
that ye may believe that Jesus is the Christ, the Son of God" (John 20:31).
Hilary insists that to believe that He is the Christ, is not sufficient for

[74] *Ibid.* VI 36.
[75] *Ibid.* VI 37. Cf. 38 fin.
[76] *Ibid.* VI 39.
[77] Hilary probably alluded to the cited letter of Arius (*de Trin.* IV 12) which read:
genuisse filium unigenitum ante omnia saecula ... creaturam Dei perfectam.
[78] *Ibid.* VI 40.

salvation, but that "Son of God" must be added. True faith is not only to believe in Christ, but in Christ the Son of God; and the name of Son, which is essential for salvation, is therefore not merely a name of adoption. Salvation consists in confessing the name and the name must therefore express the truth; but if the name expresses the truth, then He cannot be a creature.[79]

There are other examples found in the writings of John to prove that Christ is true Son of God: "Everyone that loves the Father, loves Him that is born from Him" (1 John 5:1). Hilary contends that to be born from Him cannot mean to be created by Him. The evangelist certainly did not lie in asserting the birth of the Son; on the contrary, he maintained that "He who denies the Father and the Son is antichrist" (1 John 2:22). The heretic must not try to deceive himself by thinking that he can describe the Father and the Son as Creator and Creature, and then through an ambiguity of language escape being recognized as antichrist. He who denies the Son, is without the Father, for it is written: "He who denies the Son does not have the Father: he who confesses the Son, has both the Son and the Father" (1 John 2:23). These are no adoptive names but they express the true Divine nature.[80]

John taught the true Divinity of Christ as is evident from the following words: "For we know that the Son of God came and was incarnate for us, and suffered, and because He rose again from the dead He took us for Himself,[81] and gave us a good understanding that we may know Him, that is true, and we may be in His true Son Jesus Christ: He is true and is life eternal and our resurrection" (1 John 5:20). Hilary stresses that the apostle, who lay upon the bosom of the Lord, who followed Him to the cross, who ran to the sepulchre, and who saw many signs of heaven, did not receive the doctrine that the Father is no Father and the Son no Son. There is neither life eternal, nor resurrection for them who deny that He is truly Son of God.[82]

Paul delivers the same message as John, for in texts such as Rom. 5:10, 8:3 and 1 Cor. 1:9, Christ is referred to as "His Son, Son of God," but no mention is made of "His adoption" or of "God's creature." The name expresses the nature, the attribute expresses the true relation; the Divine nature of the Son could not have been more completely described. Paul also distinguished between those who were children only by adoption,

---

[79] *Ibid.* VI 41.
[80] *Ibid.* VI 42.
[81] The words following "and was incarnate ..." are a creedlike interpolation, as well as "our resurrection" at the end.
[82] *Ibid.* VI 43.

who, by merit of their faith were called thus: "For as many as are led by the Spirit of God, they are the sons of God. For you have not received the spirit of bondage again to fear, but you have received the Spirit of adoption, whereby we cry, Abba Father" (Rom. 8:14,15). This is the name which is granted to those who believe through regeneration. The cry which the believers raise is "Abba, Father," but this does not express an essential nature. There is a difference between addressing God as Father, and God being the Father of His Son.[83]

Hilary clearly distinguishes between the sonship of man and the Son being the Son of God. We are sons of God but sons because we have been made such, for we were once sons of wrath (Eph. 2:3), but through the Spirit of adoption we have been made sons of God and we are called thus, rather than being born thus. Before this we were not sons of God, but now we are, not born thus but made sons of God; not generated but acquired. God acquired a people for Himself and thus He begot them. God however never begot sons in the strict sense of the term. He does not say: "I begot My sons" but "I begot sons."[84] We have been named adopted sons of God through His goodness, but Christ is the one, true Son of God.[85]

The objection may be raised that Israel was also called "My firstborn" in Exod. 4:22: "Filius primogenitus meus Israel," so as to deprive the Son of the characteristic property of birth. The epithet "My" used in Matt. 17:5: "Hic est filius meus dilectus" would therefore not be solely applicable to the birth of God, for it is also used in the case of those who were clearly not born as sons. In one of the Psalms both the birth and creation of the people of God are mentioned: "A people which shall be born, whom the Lord has made" (Ps 21:32 LXX).[86] Hilary however, upholds the Sonship of the Son, by pointing to the order of the words in Scripture. Of Christ it is said: "Filius meus dilectus" and of God's people: "Filius primogenitus meus." In the case of the Son, God's ownership comes first and then His love. In the case of Israel, the people have the

[83] *Ibid.* VI 44.
[84] *Ibid.* XII 13.
[85] *Ibid.* XII 2. Smulders, *op. cit.*, p. 152 n. 59, pointed out that here Hilary, who merely teaches an external sonship – the sonship of man being more of a new designation than a new being – differs from Athanasius, who saw an intimate relationship to God in our sonship. The believers, although by nature creatures, later become sons of God and thus have God the Creator as their Father. The Father, seeing His Son in us, therefore also calls us sons (Athanasius, *Or. c. Ar.* II 59 PG 26.272B–273C). P. T. Wild, *The Divinization of Man according to Saint Hilary of Poitiers*, Mundelein, 1950, p. 50 n. 9, corrected Smulders' view to some extent, because in Hilary's *Commentary on the Psalms* he does consider the adoption of man as something more intimate than a mere granting of the name of son. Cf. Wild, *op. cit.*, pp. 55–6 n. 42.
[86] *Ibid.* XII 14.

character of a firstborn, having been elected from among the nations, and then comes the ownership of God. The birth of this chosen people must be seen in the sense of having been chosen from among the nations. Before this it was a people among the nations and after having been chosen, it was born a son, but being born within time, it is not son in the true sense of the word as is the case with Christ, Who has always been Son and Who has not existed as anything but Son.[87]

Hilary continues Paul's witness to the Sonship of the Lord Jesus Christ by quoting the text: "What then? If God be for us, who can be against us? He that spared not His own Son, but delivered Him up for us" (Rom. 8:31–32). The apostle wished to manifest God's love towards us by using this comparison so that we may know how great that love is. God did not give an adopted son on behalf of those who were to be adopted, nor a creature for creatures, but His Son; His own for those who were to share in the name of son. Hilary draws attention to the fact that in the above-mentioned text the apostle used the words "(His) own," while He had previously often spoken of "His Son" or "Son of God."[88] Hilary points out that some manuscripts read "suo filio" instead of "proprio filio," but the original Greek is more accurately rendered by "proprium"; for "suum filium" is the translation of "τὸν ἑαυτοῦ υἱόν" while in this text, the passage reads: "ὅς γε τοῦ ἰδίου υἱοῦ οὐκ ἐφείσατο," and the correct Latin rendering would be: "qui proprio filio non pepercit," which expressly indicates His true Divine nature. Paul has pointed out that there were many sons through the Spirit of adoption, but he indicates the peculiarity of God the Only-begotten Son.[89]

Other examples of confessions that Christ is the Son of God, are also found in the Scriptures, e.g. Martha (John 11:27); the blind man who was healed by Christ (John 9:35ff.)—where the Lord said: "Do you believe in the Son of God?" to indicate His Divine Sonship for He could have said: "Do you believe in Christ?"—and even the devils had to confess, against their will, that He was "Son of God most High" (Luke 8:28).[90]

Hilary considers that the guilt of the Jews in denying the Divinity of Christ was less than that of the Arians, for the Jews sinned in ignorance. The Jews knew that the true Christ would be Son of God. When the priest asked Him: "Art thou the Christ, the Son of the Blessed?" (Mark

[87] *Ibid.* XII 15. Cf. J. P. Baltzer, *Die Theologie des h. Hilarius von Poitiers*, Rottweil, 1879, p. 12; Wild, *op. cit.*, p. 51 n. 16.
[88] The Latin words are respectively "proprium," "suum" and "eius."
[89] *Ibid.* VI 45.
[90] *Ibid.* VI 47–49.

14:61), the question was not whether Christ was the Son of God, but whether He was Christ. They were therefore wrong as to the Person of Christ, not as to His Sonship. The charge they brought against Christ was that He called Himself the Son of God (John 19:7). The Arians too denied that He is the Son of God and their offence is thus the same as that of the Jews; but the Jews sinned in ignorance, for they did not believe that the son, born of Mary, was the Christ, but they never doubted that the Christ would be Son of God. The Arians however, did know that Christ was born of Mary and yet they refused Him the name of Son of God. The Jews, because of their ignorance, could perchance accept the faith; but the gates to salvation were closed to the Arians because they denied that of which they could not have been ignorant. The Arians knew that He is Son of God, but they only granted this title as a name of adoption. They denied Him the Divine nature and would have denied Him His divine name, if they could, but not succeeding in this they stripped the name of its nature so that He Who is called Son, will not be the true Son of God.[91]

Hilary quoted further examples: after the Lord had calmed the storm, the apostles declared: "Of a truth, this is the Son of God" (Matt. 14:33); and the centurion, having witnessed the mighty deeds that were done, confessed: "Truly this was the Son of God" (Matt. 27:54).[92]

Hilary also cites the text: "That all men may honour the Son, even as they honour the Father. He that honoureth not the Son, honoureth not the Father who sent Him" (John 5:23). He argues that if the Son, Who is seen by the Arians as created rather than born, is treated with equal reverence as the Father, then no special honour is paid to the Father, since He is then shown the same reverence as that accorded a creature. The Son however, is equal to God the Father inasmuch as He is born as God from Him, and He is equal in honour, for He is a Son and not a creature.[93] There is also the clear utterance of the Lord: "From the womb, before the morning star I begat Thee" (Ps. 109:3 LXX). These words do not have to be interpreted as though they contradict the Spirituality of God. In order to reveal a spiritual truth, He uses expressions taken from human life so that the comprehending of Divine things may be more easily adapted to human understanding. In a similar way is spoken of the hands of God, His eyes, His heart; and the phrase "He begat from the womb" is therefore an assertion of the reality of the birth. He did not

[91] *Ibid.* VI 50.
[92] *Ibid.* VI 51–52.
[93] *Ibid.* XII 7.

beget the Son from His womb, just as He does not act by means of a hand nor sees by means of eyes, but these terms are used to indicate that He really acts, sees and wills, and the word "womb" is used to clarify that He really begat from Himself, Him Whom He begat.[94]

Finally, Hilary reminds us that a disciple is not above his master, nor a slave above his lord. We therefore, dare not be so presumptuous as to think or indicate that God is a creature or that the Son has been created, for our Master and Lord never spoke thus to His slaves and disciples, neither did He teach that His birth was a creation. The Father never testified that Christ was other than a Son and the Son did not profess that God was other than His own Father. He was born, not made or created, for He said: "Everyone that loveth the Father, loveth also the Son, Who is born of Him" (1 John 5:1). His works of creation, on the other hand, are acts of making, not a birth through generation. For the heaven is not a son, neither is the earth a son, nor the world a birth, for of these it is said: "All things were made through Him" (John 1:3).[95]

Hilary thought that he had thus shown that the Son of God is truly Son of God, not by adoption or through creation, but born of the Father.

e. The Son is God by nature

In this section the evidence adduced by Hilary to prove that the Son is God by virtue of His nature, will be treated. Quoting John 1:1 he states that there can be no doubt regarding the name in this text. He argues that there is no reason to suspect that He is not what His name indicates, and the name clearly describes His nature. This name "God" was neither imputed to or assumed by Him and therefore is His by nature.[96]

There are instances in which this name had been imputed to someone or had been assumed. God said to Moses: "I have made thee a god to Pharaoh" (Ex. 7:1). The addition "to Pharaoh" accounts for the title. God did not impart to Moses the Divine nature, but made him a god in the sight of Pharaoh when he performed a number of miracles. Moses was thus appointed as god, but this was not really being God. Hilary cites another text: "I have said, ye are gods" (Ps. 81(82):6). It is however obvious, that this name was only granted them, for the "I have said" proves that it is merely a description given by the Speaker; for the name of an object provides us with knowledge of that object, but on the other

---

[94] *Ibid.* XII 8–10. Cf. Smulders, *op. cit.*, pp. 138–9.
[95] *Ibid.* XII 11–12.
[96] *Ibid.* VII 9.

hand, the will of the speaker determines the description. When a title is conferred on an object, it is not an expression of its nature.[97]

In the case of Christ however, the name "God" is no mere title but is indeed an expression of His essence. John 1:1 reads: "Deus erat Verbum." The verb "was" does not indicate an accidental title, but an existing reality and an inherent character of His nature. John therefore indicated that the Word was no other than God, not only in name, but in essence.[98]

The Apostle Thomas, who was familiar with the words of the Lord in Deut. 6:4, confessed Christ to be: "My Lord and my God" (John 20:28). After the resurrection of the Lord, the whole mystery of the faith had become clear to the apostle and he could regard the Son of God as God without imperilling the faith in the one God; for the perfect birth of the Godhead had not brought a second God into being. The confession of Thomas was not a title of honour but a confession of the nature of the Son. The Lord confirmed that this was no mere profession of honour but of faith, when He said: "Because you have seen, you have believed: blessed are they that have not seen and have believed" (John 20:29). Thomas believed that Christ was Lord and God because no nature but God could have risen from the dead to life. Hilary also argues that the Son did not seek His own glory but that of Him Who had sent Him; and He would have rejected the adoration of Thomas involved in this name as being destructive of that unity of God which He had preached. But He confirmed the apostle's faith and acknowledged the name of the Father's nature as His own.[99]

Hilary maintains that the name which indicates every object also indicates an object of the same kind. The Son of God is God, because that is what the name indicates. The one name does not embrace two Gods, for "God" is the one name of a nature that is one and identical. Since the

---

[97] *Ibid.* VII 10. Irenaeus, *adv. Haer.* III 6,4 (ed. Harvey II p. 25), distinguished between people who were called "god" and the true God, and he mentioned the example of Moses (Ex. 7:1) who was only called "god." Tertullian, *adv. Prax.* 13 (ed. Evans p. 103), cited Ps. 81(82):6 to prove the Divinity of Christ by arguing that if those were called gods who by faith had been made sons of God, then the true and only Son of God has much more right to the name of God and Lord. This argument is found in John 10:34ff. Novatian, *de Trin.* XX 120 (ed. Weyer p. 140), used a similar argument in citing Ex. 7:1 and stating that if Moses received the name "god," although only with restrictions, then the title could not be denied Christ, Who without restriction, is Lord and God of the whole creation.

[98] *Ibid.* VII 11. Nam cum audio, *Et Deus erat Verbum*; non dictum solum audio Verbum Deum, sed demonstratum intelligo esse quod Deus est: quia sicut superius in Moyse deo et in cognominatis diis per appellationem nomen adjectum sit; hic autem res significata substantiae est, cum dicitur, *Deus erat*. Esse enim non est accidens nomen, sed subsistens veritas, et manens causa, et naturalis generis proprietas (PL 10.208B).

[99] *Ibid.* VII 12.

Father is God and the Son is God and Both have the name peculiar to the
divine nature, the two of them are one; and although the Son subsists
through a birth from the divine nature, the unity is preserved in the name.
The birth of the Son does not compel believers to acknowledge two Gods
since the confession of faith declares that the Father and the Son have one
nature just as They have one name. The Son of God has the Divine name
as the result of His birth.[100]

Smulders stated that since the beginning of the Arian controversy, the
question concerning the true generation of the Son was one of the main
points of dispute.[101] Arius had confessed that the Son was born: "natum
autem non putative, sed vere."[102] He considered Him to be a creature:
"creaturam Dei perfectam, sed non sicuti unum creaturarum; facturam,
sed non sicuti caeterae facturae ... sed, sicut diximus, voluntate Dei ante
tempora et saecula creatum."[103] Arius denied that the Son was born from
God. The Arians affirmed the fact, true in itself, that God is immutable
and incorporeal in order to deny the fact that the Son was born from
God, because an incorporeal nature cannot be conceived as generating
another.[104]

The Arians denied that Christ was born from God, by condemning
certain heresies and thereby casting suspicion upon the Church of com-
plicity in such errors. In the letter of Arius to Alexander it was said that
"the Son is not as Valentinus asserted, an emanation of the Father."[105]
Hilary maintains that the faith of the Church knows that the Son was
born as God from God and that His birth did not withdraw anything
from the Divinity of His Author, nor was He born other than God. Hilary
states that according to our human understanding, a birth seems to be an
emanation and because the idea of an emanation does not differ much
from an earthly birth, the Arians attempted to do away with the term
"emanation" by joining it to the Valentinian heresy, in order to cast
suspicion upon the faith in the true birth of the Son. Hilary emphasizes
that the birth of God cannot be judged according to the emanations of
human births. The birth of God from God bears no comparison to a
human birth which presupposes intercourse, conception and delivery; in

---

[100] *Ibid.* VII 13.
[101] Smulders, *op. cit.*, pp. 146–7.
[102] *De Trin.* IV 12 (PL 10.105A). Cf. VI 5 (PL 10.160B). The Greek text reads:
γεννήσαντα δὲ οὐ δοκήσει, ἀλλὰ ἀληθείᾳ (Athanasius, *de Syn.* 16 PG 26.709A; Hahn
§ 186).
[103] *Ibid.* IV 12 (PL 10.105A–B); VI 5 (PL 10.160B–C).
[104] *Ibid.* VII 2 (PL 10.200A).
[105] Cf. IV 12 and VI 5: nec ut Valentinus prolationem Natum Patris commentatus
est.

the birth of God the only important thing is that He was born.[106]

In his letter Arius wrote: "Nor is the Son, as Manichaeus taught, a portion of the one substance of the Father."[107] Manichaeus taught that a portion of the one divine substance was in the virgin and in the birth of the Son there was a division of the one substance and by the Son a portion of the substance of God appeared in the flesh. By rejecting this teaching of Manichaeus, the Arians cast suspicion upon the doctrine of the birth of the Son as well as the term "one substance." Furthermore Christ would not be truly God if He was composed of only a portion of the divine substance for the true God would possess the entire divine substance. Hilary contends that the pious faith of the Church also condemns Manichaeus, for the Son is no portion but whole God from whole God; and He was not cut off from God but born. The birth of God involves neither a diminution of the Begetter nor a weakness of the Begotten. The Church was taught this by the Lord Who should know about His own birth. It was the teaching of the Only-begotten God, that the Father and the Son are one and that the fullness of the Godhead is in the Son.[108]

In his letter Arius stated: "Nor as Sabellius who divides the union and calls Him the Son Whom he also called Father."[109] The Arians did not want to admit that the Father and the Son are one. The teaching of Sabellius did not acknowledge a birth. Hilary states that the orthodox faith rejects a union in the Godhead but acknowledges the unity of the Godhead, namely that as God from God They are one in nature, while that which by a true birth from God was formed into God received its being from no other source than from God.[110] The Arians, however, condemned the teaching of Sabellius of a union in the Godhead in order to destroy the Church's faith in a unity in the Godhead.[111]

Arius finally referred to Hieracas: "Nor as Hieracas declares, is He a

---

[106] *Ibid.* VI 9. Athanasius, *Or. c. Ar.* II 36 (PG 26.224A), argued that it is not right to seek how the Word is from God, or how God begets and what the manner of His begetting is.

[107] *Ibid.* IV 12, VI 5: nec sicut Manichaeus partem unius substantiae Patris Natum exposuit. The Greek reads: οὐδ' ὡς ὁ Μανιχαῖος μέρος ὁμοούσιον τοῦ Πατρὸς τὸ γέννημα εἰσηγήσατο (Athanasius, *de Syn.* 16 PG 26.709A; Hahn § 186).

[108] *Ibid.* VI 10.

[109] *Ibid.* IV 12, VI 5: nec sicuti Sabellius, qui unionem dividit, ipsum dixit Filium quem et Patrem. The Greek reads: οὐδ' ὡς Σαβέλλιος τὴν μονάδα διαιρῶν, υἱοπάτορα εἶπεν (Athanasius, *de Syn.* 16 PG 26.709A; Hahn § 186).

[110] *Ibid.* VI 11 (PL 10.165B): Nobis autem in confessione nativitas est: et unionem detestantes, unitatem divinitatis tenemus; scilicet ut Deus ex Deo unum sint in genere naturae, dum quod per nativitatis veritatem ex Deo in Deum exstitit, non aliunde quam ex Deo esse substiterit.

[111] *Ibid.* VI 11.

light from a light or a lamp divided into two parts."[112] Hieracas spoke of two lights from one lamp and taught that the two lights drawing oil of one vessel resembled the substance of the Father and the Son as if there was an external substance of oil in a lamp which contained the essence of two kinds of lights, or as if it was a candle which had the same wick throughout and which was burning at both ends, while the material between these ends supplied them and connected them together. Hilary states that the true faith confesses that God is born from God in the manner of a light from a light, which sends forth its substance without suffering any loss, and that that which is, is born, for nothing else is born except that which is; and the birth has received that which was and has not taken away which it has received. Both are one while He is born from Him Who is, and He Who is born does not come from anywhere else, nor is He anything else, for He is light from light. The Arians cast suspicion upon this confession by connecting it with the heresy of Hieracas but Hilary proved that these words can also be used in an orthodox sense. That which is God is wholly God and in Him there is nothing but power, life, light, blessedness and Spirit. God, because He is God, always remains what He is; and this eternal God has begotten God. They are not held together as two lamps or flames by some external nature. The birth of the Only-begotten God from God is not a lineage but a begetting, it is not an extension but Light from Light.[113] Unity is characteristic of light, not a diffusion of something which has been joined together.[114]

Hilary thus refuted the attempts made by the Arians to discredit certain phrases for he maintained that some of them could be used in an orthodox sense. The true confession of faith is that God is from God and God is in God not in a corporeal manner but by Divine powers; and God is not from God by a division or extension or emanation but by the power of His nature He was born into the same nature.[115] God Who was born from God, was certainly not born from nothing, nor from non-existing things, but He had a living nature as a source of His birth. He is not identical with the pre-existent God but He was born as God from the God Who was, and through His birth He has the nature of His Source.[116] Hilary insists that the phrase "from the womb I begat Thee" (Ps. 109:3

---

[112] *Ibid.* IV 12, VI 5.
[113] *Ibid.* VI 12 (PL 10.167A): Unigeniti ex Deo Dei nativitas non series est, sed progenies, non tractus est, sed ex lumine lumen.
[114] *Ibid.* VI 12.
[115] *Ibid.* V 37 (PL 10.154C–155A): Non enim per desectionem aut protensionem aut derivationem ex Deo Deus est, sed ex virtute naturae in naturam eamdem nativitate subsistit.
[116] *Ibid.* VI 13 (PL 10.167A). Cf. VII 2 (PL 10.200B); VI 35 (PL 10.185C).

LXX) teaches us, in a language which is understood by man, that the Only-begotten was born and is not a creation from nothing.[117]

The fact that God is immutable and incorporeal is used by the Arians as an argument against the birth of the Son from Him.[118] They argued that if the Son is from God, then God is changeable and corporeal since an emanation from Himself or an extension of Himself was made into His Son. Hilary replies that those who have been taught by God confess His birth and proclaim the Only-begotten. He could also point to examples in our world of births which are not necessarily an extension, and to beings which can come into existence without any loss to its begetter; and there are instances of living beings begetting living beings without intercourse. It would however, be impious to deal in such evidence for God's testimony about Himself must be accepted.[119]

Hilary declares that the birth of the Son of God remains a mystery to man and only the Father and the Son share the secret of His birth.[120] God is not born from God after the manner of a human birth, nor does He develop through the elements of our origin as a man from a man. His birth is pure, perfect and immaculate and is rather a proceeding forth from God than a birth.[121] It is One from One. It is not a part or withdrawal or diminution, or emanation or extension or suffering, but the birth of a living nature from a living nature. It is God going forth from God, not a creature elected to bear the name of God; He does not begin to be from nothing but went forth from Him Who always remains and to have come forth signifies the birth, not the beginning. For to go forth as God from God is something entirely different from a substance coming into existence.[122]

The nature with which God is born is necessarily the same as that of His Source. He cannot subsist as other than God, for His Source is none other than God. It is not that the Begetter was also Begotten, but the Son possesses the same nature in such a way that the Begotten subsists in all those elements, which the Begetter possesses in entirety, for the Begotten has no other origin.[123] He Who is born from the living God could not be

---

[117] *Ibid.* VI 16 (PL 10.169C–170A).
[118] *Ibid.* VII 2 (PL 10.200A).
[119] *Ibid.* VI 17.
[120] *Ibid.* II 9. Cf. II 12. Athanasius, *Or. c. Ar.* II 36 (PG 26.224A), said that this was known to God alone and to His Son and that to ask questions about the way in which the Son was generated, was irreligious.
[121] *Ibid.* VI 35 (PL 10.185C): a Deo exitio potius quam partus est. This is probably because of the words in John 16:28,30, where the Lord said that He "went forth from God."
[122] *Ibid.* VI 35.
[123] *Ibid.* V 37. Cf. VI 13 (PL 10.167B–C).

other than living and when the Living is begotten by the Living it can be called a birth, but nothing new comes into existence.[124]

The question of the origin of the Son of God played an important part in the doctrinal controversies of the fourth century because the origin of a person determined his nature.[125] Hilary has established that the Son of God has God as His only Source of origin and that He was not created out of nothing.

The birth did not introduce any new element into the nature of the Son so that He is not God. Human reason rejects the idea that anything can, through birth, be different from the nature of its origin, unless it has been conceived by natures which are different and therefore something new comes into the world, an offspring sharing the nature of both, yet diverse from either. This is customary among animals and wild beasts but even in this case, there is no real novelty for the different qualities already existed in the parental natures and the birth is not the cause of the difference of the offspring from its parents but it only accepted the diversity. Hilary declares that it is madness to conceive that through the birth of the Only-begotten God a nature was produced which differs from that of God,[126] for if the properties of the nature are not perpetuated through the birth, then it is no birth. The reason for all the furor was to prove that the Son of God was not born but created, and that the Divine nature is not His origin but that He draws from the non-existent matter a nature different from that of God. The birth of God the Son constitutes Him perfect God. Hilary indicates the difference between "He began to exist" and "He was born." A thing which has a beginning either comes into existence out of nothing or develops from one thing into something else and ceases to be what it was before, for instance gold from the earth and liquids from solids. The Son of God however, does not begin to be God from nothing, but was born, nor was He anything else before He was God. Through His birth He retained the nature out of which He came into being and since God is Spirit, the Son is also Spirit (John 3:6).[127]

With these explanations Hilary established an important point in his argument with the Arians. He proved that in a birth the one who is born

---

[124] *Ibid.* VII 27 (PL 10.223B–C).

[125] Cf. Löffler, *art. cit.*, p. 27.

[126] *De Trin.* VII 14 (PL 10.210C): Quis rogo furor est, nativitatem unigeniti Dei ad degenerem ex Deo referre naturam. "Degener" is rendered as "a nature inferior" by Watson, "herabgemindert" by Antweiler and "a spurious nature" by McKenna, but it should be taken in its original sense of "something that departs from its race or kind."

[127] *Ibid.* VII 14. In his *Or. c. Ar.* II 56–57 (PG 26.268A–C), Athanasius explained the difference between a creature who has a beginning and is created, and the Son Who was begotten and is eternal, for "in the beginning was the Word" (John 1:1).

has the same nature as he from whom he is born. If it was conceded that Christ was born from God, it would follow that He has the same nature as God and thus is God. If He was not born from God, He would be a creature. In the confession of Arius which Hilary refutes, it is said that the Son is born, but a little further on it is stated that the Son was created by the will of God before times and worlds.[128] The Arians had to confess thus for they denied that the Son was equal to God in nature.

The true birth of Christ is also taught by the Gospel: "This is why the Jews were seeking the more to put Him to death, because He was not only breaking the Sabbath but was also calling God His own Father, making Himself equal to God" (John 5:18). By calling God His own Father the equality of Their nature is manifested and birth is the only possible origin of true equality. Where equality exists there is neither a union nor a distinction, for the equality of likeness does not admit either of solitude or of diversity.[129] Hilary emphasizes that only birth can bestow an equality of nature.[130] When the Son therefore declares Himself equal with God the Father, it follows that He was born from God.

Hilary having proved that it is in accordance with human reason to state that birth brings about an equality of nature and that where there is equality there can be no diversity nor can it be alone, thereupon cites the words of the Lord as confirmation of this. He discusses John 5:19-23. The Lord said: "The Son can do nothing of Himself but what He sees the Father doing" (vs. 19). He thus reveals the nature of His birth; a nature which derives its power to work not from successive gifts of strength to do particular deeds but by a knowledge which He possesses beforehand. This knowledge is not imparted in such a way that the Son imitates what the Father has previously done, but having been born from the Father and aware of the Father's power that was with Him, He asserted that He could do nothing by Himself except what He saw the Father doing. Since the Son performs His works in the power of the Father, He claims that He could do as much as He was conscious of doing by His nature which is inseparable from that of God the Father and which He had received by virtue of His birth.[131]

---

[128] *Ibid.* IV 12. Cf. p. 75 n. 102 and 103.

[129] *Ibid.* VII 15.

[130] Cf. Förster, *art. cit.*, p. 653.

[131] *De Trin.* VII 17. Tertullian, *adv. Prax.* 15 (ed. Evans p. 108), proved to his adversaries, that it was the Son Who was always seen, and not the Father, and that the Son conversed and the Son always wrought, by the authority and will of the Father, because "The Son can do nothing of Himself ...,"—the Father doing it, of course, in His consciousness. For the Father acts by consciousness, whereas the Son sees and accomplishes that which is in the Father's consciousness (in sensu scilicet facientem. pater enim sensu agit, filius vero quod in patris sensu est videns perficit).

The last part of the verse reads: "For all things that the Father does, the Son does the same in like manner" (John 5:19). The words "all things whatever" and "the same" make it impossible that there should be any actions of His that are different from or outside the actions of the Father. He whose nature has the power to do all the same things, possesses the same nature, and where the Son does all things "likewise," the similarity of the works excludes the solitude of the One Who does the work so that all things that the Father does, the Son does in like manner. This is proof of the truth of the one and identical Godhead in the Father and the Son, that the Son, while He is doing the same things, does them in a like manner and that, while He is doing them in a like manner, He is doing the same things.[132] The Son has the same power as the Father namely to give life to whom He wills (John 5:21), through the unity of an indistinguishable nature.[133]

The Lord also said: "The Father does not judge any man but He has given all judgement to the Son" (John 5:22). This statement indicates His nature and birth, for only identical natures can possess all things and the Son cannot have anything unless it is given by the Father. The fact that all judgement has been given to the Son does not mean that all judgement has been taken away from the Father, because the judgement of the Son comes from the judgement of the Father, for from Him all judgement has been given. The reason why the judgement has been given to Him is: "that all men may honour the Son even as they honour the Father. He who does not honour the Son does not honour the Father Who sent Him" (John 5:23). The Son being equal to the Father in work, power, honour and also in insult to honour, therefore has the same nature by His birth as that of the Father. The Son can only be distinguished from the Father by the fact that He was born.[134]

The Father thus works until now and the Son works, but lest it be thought that the work of two unlike natures is to be understood, Hilary recalls what was said about the blind man: "But that the works of God may be made manifest in him: I must do the works of Him Who sent Me" (John 9:3,4). The work wrought by the Son, is the Father's work and the

Novatian, *de Trin.* XIV 76 (ed. Weyer p. 100), cited John 5:19 to prove the Divinity of Christ, for if Christ was only man, He could not have said that He could do what the Father could do. Cf. *de Trin.* XXI 122; XXII 127 (ed. Weyer pp. 142; 148).

[132] *Ibid.* VII 18.

[133] *Ibid.* VII 19.

[134] *Ibid.* VII 20. The Arians used ἀγέννητος with regard to the Father to express the essence of divinity which they denied to the Son. In the orthodox view, ἀγέννητος denoted not the essence of divinity, but the relation of the first to the second Person of the Trinity. Cf. *A Patristic Greek Lexicon*, ed. by G. W. H. Lampe, Oxford, 1961, s.v. ἀγέννητος, pp. 15–16.

Son's work is God's work. Hilary summarizes his argument as follows: He is the Son because He can do nothing of Himself; He is God because whatever the Father does, He Himself does the same things; They are one because He is equal in honour to the Father and does the very same things; He Himself is not the Father, because He was sent.[135] In the birth is thus contained the mystery embracing His name, nature, power and self-revelation.[136]

Hilary cites John 10:28–30 and says that this bears witness to the power of the Son's nature for He says: "No man shall snatch them out of My hand" (John 10:28). That it may be realized that this nature is His by birth, He said: "What the Father has given Me is greater than all" (John 10:29). He Who received it, received it at His birth, not later on and it came from Another, for He received it. But in order that it could not be supposed that He is different from that Other and that He does not exist in the nature of Him from Whom He has received, He said: "No one will be able to snatch them out of the hand of My Father" (John 10:29). The latter statement is not in contradiction with an earlier one that no man will snatch them out of the hand of the Son, for "I and the Father are one." The hand of the Son, is the hand of the Father. He has the same nature as His Father because a birth does not admit an element alien to itself. The nature and the power of the Father is in the Son.[137]

Hilary maintains that the godlessness of the Arians is much greater than that of the Jews for the Arians would again crucify the Lord if they had the opportunity. The Jews wanted to stone Christ for blasphemy because He made Himself God (John 10:31–33) when He said: "I and the Father are one." The Arians cannot stone Him but they are doing no lesser thing by their denial of His Divinity. The will is the same but the fact that He is on His heavenly throne renders their will ineffective. The Jew raised his stones against a body, the Arian against the Spirit; the Jew against One he thought to be a man, but the Arian against God; the Jew against One living on earth, the Arian against Him seated upon the throne of power; the Jew against Him that was about to die, but the Arian against the Judge of the ages.[138]

---

[135] *Ibid.* VII 21 (PL 10.217A): Filius est, quia ab se nihil potest: Deus est, quia quaecumque Pater facit, et ipse eadem facit: unum sunt, quia exaequatur in honore, eademque facit, non alia: non est pater ipse, quia missus est.

[136] *Ibid.* VII 21.

[137] *Ibid.* VII 22.

[138] *Ibid.* VII 23. Athanasius, *Or. c. Ar.* III 27 (PG 26.381A–B), thought that the Jews and Arians arrived at the same unbelief and that the daring of their irreligion was equal and the dispute with the orthodox believers a common one. While the Jews sought to kill the Lord because He had said that God was His own Father, thereby

Hilary feels that the Lord's reply to the Jews is even better suited to the Arian impiety: "Is it not written in the Law, 'I said, you are gods?'[139] If He called them gods to whom the Word of God was addressed, and the Scripture cannot be broken, do you say of Me Whom the Father has sanctified and sent into this world that I have blasphemed because I said 'I am the Son of God?' If I do not perform the works of God, do not believe Me. But if I do perform them and if you are not willing to believe Me, believe the works, that you may know and be sure that the Father is in Me and I in Him" (John 10:34–38). Christ was accused of making Himself God while only being a man and He exposes the absurdity of this charge by reminding His accusers that the Law had conferred this title upon holy men and furthermore, He Who had been sanctified by the Father and sent into this world could not be a blasphemer for asserting that He was the Son of God, for He excels the others who may call themselves gods in a reverential manner.[140]

With the words: "Ego et Pater unum sumus" (John 10:30) the Lord indicated Himself as Son of God in name, in nature and in birth. For "Ego et Pater" are the names of substantive beings; "unum" is a declaration of Their nature because Both of Them do not differ in that which They are; "sumus" does not allow any thought of a union ("unio"). And where there is no union, because "They are one," it is the birth which caused Them to be one. All this proceeds from the fact that He Who was sanctified by the Father confesses that He is the Son of God and this profession is confirmed by the words: "I and the Father are one," for birth cannot bring any other nature with it except that from which it subsists.[141]

The Lord confirmed His assertion that He and the Father are one, by

making Himself equal to God, the Arians not only deny that He is equal to God and that God is His own Father, but they seek to kill those who hold this view.

[139] A reference to Ps. 81(82):6.

[140] Ibid. VII 24.

[141] Ibid. VII 25. Tertullian, adv. Prax. 22 (ed. Evans p. 117), said that the text is an indication of two Persons; the "We are" cannot refer to one Person only; and the expression is "We are one thing" and not "We are one Person." The fact that two of the masculine gender are one in the neuter, indicates that it is not connected with singularity but with unity. In adv. Prax. 25 (ed. Evans p. 121), it is again said that the words are used with respect to unity of substance, not as regards the singular number. Novatian, de Trin. XIII 69 (ed. Weyer p. 96), said that no man could utter the words in this text but only Christ, conscious of His Divinity. Cf. XV 87 (ed. Weyer p. 108). In XXVII 148 (ed. Weyer p. 168f.), Novatian argued that if Christ was the Father, He would have said: "ego pater unus sum." But the Son separated and distinguished Himself from the Father. Athanasius cited this text frequently and said that the identity of the Godhead and the unity of essence was indicated and that They are two; for the Father is Father only and not the Son, but Their nature is one, Or. c. Ar. III 3–4 (PG 26.328B–C).

the words: "If I do not perform the works of the Father do not believe Me" (John 10:37). It must be believed that He is the Son from the fact that He carries out the works of His Father. It cannot be maintained that He was adopted or that the name of God was only bestowed on Him and that He therefore was not the Son of God by nature. A creature is not made equal or similar to God and no nature alien to God is compared to Him; only the Son born from Him is similar or equal to Him. If any being not born from God, can be found which is similar to Him and equal in power, then He has lost the privilege of God by the partnership of one who is co-equal to Him; and there will no longer be one God for there is another God who is His equal. Hilary declares that, on the other hand, there is no insult in making His own true Son His equal, because that which is similar to Him is His own, and that which is compared to Him is from Himself, and He that can do God's works, is not outside of Him. It is an exaltation of His dignity to have begotten the power without having changed the nature. The Son performs the Father's works and for that reason demands that it be believed that He is the Son of God. The Lord added: "But if I do perform them and you are not willing to believe Me, believe the works" (John 10:38). If He performs the works but seems unworthy of what He professes because of the humility of His body, He asks that His works be believed. If therefore it is not believed that the man is Son of God because of the works, then it must be believed that the works are indicative of the Son of God, for it cannot be denied that they are characteristic of God. For by His birth the Son of God possesses everything in Himself that is God's and therefore the work of the Son is the work of the Father.[142]

The relationship between the Father and the Son is seen by Hilary as follows: The Son is in the Father and the Father in the Son not by a mutual transfusion and flowing, but by the perfect birth of a living nature. God the Father and God the Son are not counted together as two Gods, for Both are one; nor is a single God proclaimed for the Two are not One Person. In confessing the Father, the apostolic faith confesses the Son; when it believes in the Son, it also believes in the Father for the name of Father contains in itself the name of Son. There is no father except through a son and the designation of son reveals a father. The nature of the Son, however, is not changed by the birth.[143] A nature can only con-

---

[142] *Ibid.* VII 26. Cf. VII 36. Athanasius, *Or. c. Ar.* II 12 (PG 26.172B), used this text to prove that Christ was manifested to be not merely man but God in a body and also Lord.

[143] *Ibid.* VII 31. In *Or. c. Ar.* I 15 (PG 26.44C), Athanasius also taught the strict unity of the Divine Essence. The Son partakes from the essence of the Father.

tain properties peculiar to itself. The truth that God is from God does not result in two Gods, nor does the birth of God admit any supposition of a unique God, yet They Who are mutual, are one. They are mutual since the one is from the one; for the One, in begetting the One, gave Him nothing that was not His own and the One has obtained from the One by His birth, only what belongs to the One.[144] The same and identical nature of God is in Both and the nature of Both has the same name "God." God in God or God from God does not result in two Gods nor in a single God.[145]

Referring to the words of the Lord to Philip: "He who has seen Me, has also seen the Father" (John 14:9), Hilary states that the Son is the Image of God not in a corporeal way. God is recognized in Christ by those who recognized Him as the Son on the evidence of the powers of His divine nature, and a recognition of God the Son produces a recognition of the Father. The Son is in such a manner the Image that He does not differ in nature but manifests His Author. Paintings and sculptures are lifeless images but Christ is the living Image of the Living, and because the Son born from Him does not have a different nature, He possesses the power of that nature which is the same as His own.[146] The Father Who is seen in the Son cannot be unique or unlike Him and the Father was made visible through the Son because They are One and are alike in nature.[147]

The nature in the Father and the Son is also clearly expressed in the words in John 14:10: "Do you not believe Me that I am in the Father and the Father in Me? The words that I speak to you I speak not of Myself; but the Father dwelling in Me, it is He Who does His works." While He Himself is speaking (this is indicated by the pronoun "I"), He speaks as abiding in the Divine substance; but while He does not speak of Himself, He bears testimony to the birth of God in Him from God the Father. He Himself is inseparable from Him and indistinguishable from Him by the unity of nature, because although He speaks by His authority, it is He Himself Who speaks. He Who does not speak by His own authority and yet speaks, does not cease to exist while speaking, and while He does not

---

[144] *Ibid.* VII 32 (PL 10.227A): Invicem autem sunt, cum unus ex uno est: quia neque unus uni aliud per generationem quam quod suum est dedit, neque unus ab uno aliud per nativitatem obtinet quam unius. Smulders, *op. cit.*, p. 227 n. 34, thought that "invicem sunt" should be translated by "l'un l'autre" and not "personne correlative."

[145] *Ibid.* VII 32.

[146] *Ibid.* VII 37. Tertullian, *adv. Prax.* 24 (ed. Evans p. 120), said that the Father becomes visible in the Son by deeds of power, not by the visible manifestation of His Person.

[147] *Ibid.* VII 38 (PL 10.231C).

speak of Himself He reveals that it is not He alone Who speaks. The fact that the Father dwells in the Son, proves that the Father is not alone and unique, and the fact that the Father works through the Son proves that His nature is not different from or outside of that of the Father. The Father thus works in the Son, but the Son also performs the work of the Father.[148]

Lest it be thought that the Father works and speaks in the Son through His own power and not through the property of the nature which is the Son's by birth, Christ said: "Believe Me that I am in the Father and the Father in Me" (John 14:11). This does not indicate a transfusion of the One into the Other but a unity of the same nature in Both of Them through the generation and the birth. The Lord wanted people to believe Him but if His assumed body, His flesh and His passion should give rise to any doubts, then at least on the evidence of His works, it should be believed that God is in God and God is from God; and that by the power of Their nature Each one is in Himself and Neither is without the Other; while the Father loses nothing of Himself in the Son and the Son receives His whole Sonship from the Father. Material natures are not so constituted that they are mutually in one another. This is proper only to the Only-begotten God, and in the mystery of the true birth is this faith and this is the work of the power of the Spirit that there is no distinction between to be and to be in God; but being in God is not as one thing in another as a body in a body, but to be and to subsist in such a manner that He is in the subsisting God, and He is within Him in such a manner that He Himself subsists. For Each One, while subsisting, is not without the Other and by the generation and birth the nature is the same.[149] Of this attempt to describe the unity of Father and Son it has been said with good reason: "Son exposé est un perpétuel combat contre l'insuffisance de notre langue humaine qui n'a pas de terme pour exprimer cette unité."[150]

Hilary thus proved that the Father and the Son have the same Divine nature. This is only possible by a birth, for in birth the one who is born receives the nature of him from whom he was born. If it is conceded that the Son was born, then He must have the nature of His Begetter and thus be God by nature. Many facts about the birth of the Son remain a mystery to the human mind and in this respect some of Hilary's arguments are not

---

[148] *Ibid.* VII 40. Athanasius, *Or. c. Ar.* II 33 (PG 26.217B), said that the true God-head of the Son is revealed in this text. The Son is not begotten from without, but from the Father.

[149] *Ibid.* VII 41. Tertullian had to refute the view that the Father and the Son were two names for the one Person and he used this text among others, to refute this view, *adv. Prax.* 24 (ed. Evans p. 120).

[150] Smulders, *op. cit.*, p. 225.

very clear, but that is due to the fact that a Divine mystery cannot be explained in human language.

f. The eternity of the Son

A point closely connected with the birth of the Son is the question of the eternity of the Son. The Arians denied that the Son was eternal and in the above-mentioned letter of Arius it was said: "Hunc Deum[151] genuisse filium unigenitum ante omnia saecula, per quem et saeculum et omnia fecit: natum autem non putative, sed vere, ... nec qui fuit ante, postmodum natum vel supercreatum in filium, ... sed voluntate Dei ante tempora et saecula creatum, et vivere et esse accipiens a Patre .... Et quidem Deus causa est omnium, omnino sine initio solitarius: Filius autem sine tempore editus a Patre, et ante saecula creatus et fundatus, non erat antequam nasceretur: sed sinc tempore ante omnia natus, solus a solo Patre substitit. Nec enim est aeternus, aut coaeternus, aut simul non factus cum Patre, nec simul cum Patre habet esse.[152]

The Arians taught that the Son was born within time. There was a time when He was not and time is anterior to Him. According to Hilary the heretics intended to support their blasphemy and justify their false accusation with the confession: "The Son did not exist before He was born." With this confession they denied that the nature of an eternal origin was in the Son. He therefore had a beginning out of nothing. If this statement was regarded as blasphemous they could justify it by saying that He Who did exist could not be born. Birth brings about the beginning of existence and He Who already existed could not be born.[153] On this point the Arians, reasoning according to ordinary human concepts and ideas, had a strong argument against the confession of the Church[154] which maintained that the Son was born and equally that He was eternal.

Hilary states that all human births involve a previous non-existence. All human beings have a beginning in time and this beginning has a cause; in respect to time it is clear that a thing which at a certain point of time had a beginning, formerly did not exist; with regard to the cause it is certain that things do not come into existence through a cause in itself

[151] The punctuation in the Greek text is different: τουτὸν θεόν is connected with the preceding and the new line begins with γεννήσαντα υἱὸν μονογενῆ κτλ. (Athanasius, *de Syn.* 16 PG 26.709A; Hahn § 186). In the text by Opitz there is no comma between θεὸν γεννήσαντα, Opitz II 1 p. 243,31.
[152] *De Trin.* IV 12–13 (PL 10.105A–106B). Cf. VI 5–6.
[153] *Ibid.* IV 5; VI 14.
[154] Reinkens, *op. cit.*, p. 148.

but all things are created by the power of God. All human beings are born from parents who did not exist before their birth and Adam, the first parent of the human race was formed from the earth, which is made from nothing.[155]

The Arians contended that if it was taught that the Son had always existed, then He could not have been born, for the purpose of birth is to bring that which does not exist, into being. It may further be argued that if He was born, then He had a beginning and at the time when He began to be, He was not and thus He did not exist before He was born.[156] Hilary warns his readers that the sophistry of the syllogistic questioning easily robs a weak understanding of the protection of its faith. The Apostle Paul had foreseen this and warned the Christians to be vigilant so that they may not be robbed by philosophy and vain deceit, according to human traditions and the elements of the world (Col. 2:8). Hilary encourages the Christians to refute the doctrines of men and not to flee from them; to instruct the simple-minded lest they be robbed by these heretics. Those who proclaim Christ to the world must face the irreverent and faulty doctrines of the world with the knowledge imparted by the wise Omnipotence. Their faith must be supported by learning so that they can strongly resist the heresies.[157]

Hilary emphatically states that it is not possible to maintain that the Only-begotten God Who is preceded by no antecedent time, at some time did not exist. He Who is born from Him Who *is*, cannot be understood to have been born from that which had not been, because in His case He Who really *is*, is the cause of the Son's existence and His birth cannot have its origin in that which is not. Therefore it cannot be said either that He has been born from nothing or that He did not exist before He was born.[158] The Son was born, for where a father is the source of being, there is also a birth; but where the Source of being is eternal, the birth is also eternal.[159] Everything which always exists, is eternal but not

---

[155] *De Trin.* XII 16.
[156] *Ibid.* XII 18.
[157] *Ibid.* XII 19–20.
[158] *Ibid.* XII 17.
[159] *Ibid.* XII 21 (PL 10.446A). Novatian, *de Trin.* XXXI 184 (ed. Weyer p. 196), said that the Son is always in the Father because the Father is always Father. Tertullian, *adv. Hermogenem* 3 (CV 47 p. 129), taught that there was a time when the Father did not have the Son. In *adv. Prax.* 7 (ed. Evans pp. 94–5), it is said that the Word was first established under the name of Wisdom, then begotten for activity and thereafter He became Son. It must however be borne in mind that for Tertullian Wisdom, Word and Son are identical. Cf. Evans, p. 225. In his *Comm. in Matt.* 16,4 (PL 9.1008C–1009A), Hilary clearly taught the eternity of the Son, e.g. that He received His eternity from the eternity of the Father and that if the Son is not always Son then the Father is not always Father. Hilary did not however, in this early work teach the eternity

everything eternal is also unborn. What is born from the eternal has the
attribute that what has been born is eternal. If that which has been born
from the Eternal is not born eternal, then the Father is not an eternal
Source of being. If any measure of eternity is lacking in Him Who has
been born from the eternal Father, then it is evident that the same thing
is lacking in His Author, as what is infinite for the Begetter is also infinite
for the Begotten. Neither our reason nor our understanding allows any
interval between the birth of the Son of God and the generation by God
the Father, since the birth consists in the generation and the generation
in the birth.[160]

All human beings that have been born, at one time did not exist. Hilary
says that there is a difference between being born of someone who once
was not and to be born from Him Who always was. Everyone is born
from a father who was also born and grew up and only later became a
father. Yet man is not always a father and furthermore did not always
beget, but where the Father is eternal, the Son is also eternal. If it is
always proper for the Father to be always the Father,[161] it must always be
proper for the Son to be always the Son. And it cannot be in harmony
with our language and understanding to maintain that He to Whom it is
proper that He always is what He was born, did not exist before He was
born.[162] To be always from Him Who always is, is eternity; but this
eternity is not derived from Himself but from the Eternal. And from the
Eternal nothing can come but what is eternal, for if the Offspring is not
eternal, then neither is the Father, Who is the Source of generation.[163]

Hilary declares that since the Only-begotten God contains in Himself
the form and the image of the invisible God, He is made equal to Him in
all the attributes that are proper to God the Father, through the fullness
of the Godhead in Himself. He Who is as mighty and as worthy of honour
as the Father, possesses the property to exist always, because the Father
is always. The meaning of the words spoken to Moses: "He Who is, has
sent me to you" (Ex. 3:14), is that it is proper for God to be what He is

of the Son's generation, but only that the Son, in His birth, received the Divine nature
which is eternal. In his *de Trin.* he teaches the eternal generation of the Son, probably
as a result of his contact with the Greek theology. Cf. Loofs, "Hilarius," p. 61.

[160] *Ibid.* XII 21. Athanasius dealt at length with the problem of the eternity of the
Son, *Or. c. Ar.* I 11–14, and said, inter alia, that the Son is the eternal offspring of the
Father, I 14 (PG 26.41B), and that the Son is eternal for He said: "I am the Truth" etc.
and not "I became the Truth," I 12 (PG 26.37B).

[161] Arius denied that God was always a Father (Athanasius, *Or. c. Ar.* I 5 PG
26.21A).

[162] *De Trin.* XII 23. Athanasius, *Or. c. Ar.* III 66 (PG 26.464B), said that as the
Father is always good by nature, so He is always generative by nature.

[163] *Ibid.* XII 25 (PL 10.448B).

and that what is, cannot be thought of as not being. To be and not to be
are contradictory to each other and these two irreconcilable meanings
cannot become united in one and the same object. We can go back in our
thoughts as far as possible but we never reach a point beyond the truth:
that He is. This attribute of God has been pointed out by Moses and
recognized by the universal understanding of men. It has also been
attributed by the Gospels to the Only-begotten God, since in the beginning
was the Word and it was with God; He was the true light; the Only-
begotten is in the bosom of the Father (John 1:1,9,18); and Jesus Christ
is the God over all (Rom. 9:5).[164]

Hilary states that time can be comprehended either by human speculation or knowledge. Since all time is within the sphere of human knowledge or speculation, man judges it according to the understanding of
human reason. It is thought reasonable to say about anything: "It was
not before it was born." But in the things of God, that is, in the birth of
God, everything is before the eternal time and it cannot be said of Him:
"Before He was born," nor can it be said that He to Whom the eternal
promise was made before the eternal time, is merely in hope of eternal
life, according to the statement of the apostle in Tit. 1:2, nor can it be
said that at one time He was not; for reason rejects the idea that He Who
existed before eternal time, began to exist after anything.[165]

It is contrary to human nature and understanding that something was
born before the eternal ages and yet in this matter God's testimony about
Himself must be believed. The apostolic faith has declared that He was
always born. What has been born before time has always been born,
because that which exists before time eternal, always exists. That which
has always been born cannot at any time have had no existence, since
non-existence at a given time is contrary to eternity of existence. The fact
that He has always been born excludes the idea that He has not always
existed and thus it cannot be conceived that He did not exist before He
was born. He Who has been born before times eternal, is before any
thought and it can never be thought that He once did not exist, since it
must be confessed that He always exists.[166] If He is within the range of
human thought, in the sense that He was not before He was born, then
both human comprehension and time are prior to His birth; because
everything which once was not, is within the power of human comprehension and the very meaning of the words "has not been," makes Him

[164] *Ibid.* XII 24.
[165] *Ibid.* XII 27.
[166] *Ibid.* XII 28.

subject to time, for what has not been, is a part of time. He Who is from the Eternal and has always been, is neither without birth nor has He not "been," since that which has always been transcends time and to have been born is birth.[167]

Hilary clearly indicates the limitations of the human mind with regard to this question of the eternal birth of the Lord. The human mind cannot grasp the idea of a timeless birth since it is inconsistent with worldly natures to be born before time. The Only-begotten God is, however, confessed to be born before the eternal ages because the apostles and prophets preached thus. If the birth before the eternal ages is no conclusion of human reasoning but a confession of faith, because a birth before time is beyond the human comprehension, then the human mind is exalted irreverently by asserting, according to human intelligence, that He was not before He was born, because an eternal birth surpasses human comprehension and worldly knowledge. Whatever transcends time, is eternal.[168]

The Arians made a very subtle objection: If it is inconceivable that He did not exist before He was born, then it must be conceivable that He Who already existed, was born. To this Hilary replies that he has not called the Son anything else than born; and to exist before eternal ages is the same as that He Who existed, was born; for the birth of One already existing is not really birth but a self-wrought change through this birth. To be always born means that through His birth He is prior to any conception of time and it is impossible for the mind to suppose that at any time He was unborn. Hence, an eternal birth before the eternal ages is not the same as to exist before being born. But to have been born always before times eternal excludes the possibility that He did not exist before birth.[169]

On the other hand, Hilary states that it cannot be assumed that He existed before He was born, for He Who transcends comprehension, transcends it in every respect. To confess His eternal birth is to confess nothing else than His birth, for the question whether He did or did not exist before His birth, is not within the grasp of human thought. He does not allow the human thought to pass judgement on Himself whether He was or was not before He was born, for existence before birth is not characteristic of birth and previous non-existence involves the idea of time. If it would have been possible for the human perception to deter-

[167] *Ibid.* XII 25 (PL 10.449A).
[168] *Ibid.* XII 26.
[169] *Ibid.* XII 29–30.

mine whether He existed or not, then the birth itself would have been after time, for someone who does not always exist, must have had a beginning after some point of time.[170]

Therefore the conclusion reached by faith, argument and thought, is that the Lord Jesus was born and always existed. As it is a property of God the Father to exist without birth, so it is also a property of the Son to exist always through birth. The fact of His birth presupposes the Father, and the name Father presupposes His birth. For if God is always Father, there is always a Son and whatever period of time is denied to the Son, making His Sonship non-eternal, it follows that an equal period of time the Father must be denied His Fatherhood. This implies that while He is always God, He is not always the Father in that infinitude in which He is God.[171] It is incompatible either with reason or logic to teach that from a Father Who is eternal, anyone else but an eternal Son can proceed.[172]

Hilary declares that if the Arians confess that He is always God but not always the Father, they condemn the statement of Paul that the Son is "before the eternal ages" (Tit. 1:2); and they find fault with the testimony of Wisdom about Itself, that It was established before the ages and It was present when the Father prepared the heavens. In order to attribute to God a beginning of His being a Father, the Arians would, according to Hilary, first of all have to establish the starting point at which Time must have begun, and if Time had a beginning, then the apostle who declared that it was eternal, is a liar. It is customary to reckon time from the creation of the sun and moon, for it is written: "And let them be for signs and times and years" (Gen. 1:14). But He Who is before the heaven, which even in the view of the Arians is before time, is before the ages and even before the generations of generations which precede the ages. Wisdom does not say that It is after anything but before all things. David said that Christ is before the sun (Ps. 71:17 LXX) and before the moon are the generations of generations (Ps. 71:5 LXX). Men who were deemed worthy of prophetic inspiration, looked down upon time, and the human mind has not been afforded any opportunity for reaching into the ages before the birth which transcends times eternal.[173]

The Arians objected that Wisdom Itself taught that It was created: "The Lord created Me for the beginning of His ways" (Prov. 8:22

[170] *Ibid.* XII 31.
[171] *Ibid.* XII 32.
[172] *Ibid.* XII 41.
[173] *Ibid.* XII 34.

LXX).[174] According to Hilary this was said lest it be thought that Wisdom did not exist before Mary; and It did not wish Its birth to be understood as a creation. Wisdom also stated that It was established before the ages so that no one may suppose that this creation for the beginning of the ways, which is indeed the beginning of human knowledge about divine things, meant that His birth is subordinate to time. Hilary distinguishes between being created for the beginning of the ways and for the works, and being established before the ages. For the latter is prior to the creation and before time, while creation for the beginning of the ways and for the works is after the commencement of time. The terms "creation" and "establishing" are no obstacle to the faith in the divine birth, for it is written: "Before He made the earth, before He established the mountains, before all the hills He begot Me" (Prov. 8:24, 25 LXX). In the following verses (26–30 LXX) it is said that when God prepared the heavens, Wisdom was with Him and when He placed fountains under the heavens and made firm the foundations of the earth, Wisdom was with Him forming all things. From these words it is clear that time plays no part. It is not sufficient to say that He was born before the mountains and hills for, although He is prior to these things, it would make Him subject to time to say that He was prior to them. For that which is antecedent to temporal things, stands in the same relation to time as they do.[175]

The Word of God however, teaches that He is prior not to temporal but to infinite things. When the heavens were prepared, He was present with God. The preparation of the heaven is not an act of God within time as though He suddenly thought of doing it and then sought material and instruments for building the world. The prophet said: "By the word of the Lord the heavens were established; and all their power by the breath of His mouth" (Ps. 32:6 LXX). The heavens were in need of a command of God to be established. Although all things have a beginning in so far as their creation is concerned, they do not have a beginning in so far as the knowledge or power of God is concerned. The prophet is witness to this: "O God, Who has made all things which shall be" (Isaiah 45:11 LXX). Things that still have to be created, have already been made in so far as God is concerned because to Him there is nothing new and unexpected in the things that are to be created. It belongs to the dispensa-

---

[174] *Ibid.* XII 35. Hilary's text read: Dominus creavit me in initium viarum suarum. According to the Benedictines the *in* would have to be omitted to agree with the LXX, but that would not be in accordance with the mss. and Hilary's exposition of this text, see PL 10.454 n. f.
[175] *Ibid.* XII 36–38.

tion of time for them to be created but in the prescient working of the
divine power, they have already been created. When Wisdom teaches
that It was born before the ages, It teaches that It is prior not only to
the things that are created but also that It is co-eternal with things
eternal, that is, in the preparation of the heavens. Wisdom reveals Its
eternity in being present with Him as He prepares, and Its function in
forming with Him Who forms. Therefore It declared that It was begotten
before the earth, mountains and hills, because It wished to teach that It
was present at the preparation of the heavens in order to prove that at the
time when the heaven was prepared, these things had already been made
in the counsel of God, because there is nothing new to God.[176]

The preparation of the things to be created is perpetual and eternal.
God did not think of the things one after the other so that He first
thought of the heavens and then the earth and then thought it better to
have mountains etc. The entire preparation for these things is co-eternal
with God. Although, as Moses taught, each act of creation had its proper
order, there is not an element of time discernable in the creation of the
heavens, earth and other elements, because the concept of their creation
is co-eternal with God.[177]

The fact that the term creation was used could have been disturbing if
it had not been that a birth before the ages and a creation for the beginning of the ways of God was preached. Birth cannot be understood to
denote creation since this birth preceded a cause while creation is the
result of a cause. He Who was created for the beginning of the ways of
God and for His works, existed before the preparation of the heaven
and was established before time.[178]

Hilary rejects the idea that the phrase "He was created for the works"
be interpreted as though He was created because of the works, for this
would mean that Christ had been created for the sake of the works which
He had to perform. But He was born as the Lord of glory and not as a
slave and builder of the world. God the Father is the Maker and Creator
of the world but Wisdom was present with Him, and with Him prepared
all things and formed all things. Hence Wisdom was not created because

---

[176] *Ibid.* XII 39. Hilary distinguishes between on the one hand, "parare" and
"componere" which indicate the creative work of God within time, and on the other
hand, "praeparare" which is used for the eternal activity. Cf. Baltzer, *op. cit.*, p. 15 n. 1.
[177] *Ibid.* XII 40.
[178] *Ibid.* XII 42. Athanasius, *Or. c. Ar.* II 51 (PG 26.256A), explained that when it
was said that He was created "for the works," He thereby did not want to signify
His essence but the economy which came after His being. He was created for a specific
purpose while in the case of creatures they are created to exist and only later are they
given a certain task to perform.

of the works, for It was present at their eternal preparation.[179]

The interpretation in accordance with the Catholic doctrine which should be given to Prov. 8:22: "The Lord created Me for the beginning of His ways and for His works," is made clear by the previous verse: "If I shall make known to you the things that are done each day, I shall remember to recount those things that are in time" (Prov. 8:21 LXX). Prov. 8:22 thus refers to the deeds which were performed from the beginning of time and in no way indicates the generation before time.[180]

Hilary enquires into the meaning of the saying that God, born before the ages, was again created for the beginning of the ways of God and His works. Where there is a birth before time it signifies an eternal generation, while He was created in time for the ways and works of God. Since Christ is Wisdom, He is Himself the beginning of the way of the works of God, for He said: "I am the way. No one goes to the Father but through Me" (John 14:6). He is created for the beginning of the ways for the works of God, because He is the way and leads to the Father. He was also created within time for the ways of God when He subjected Himself to the visible form of a creature and assumed the form of a created being.[181] This refers to the manifestations of the Son (according to Hilary) in the Old Testament. Adam heard One walking in paradise and His approach could have been heard only if He had assumed the form of a creature. In some guise He spoke to Cain, Abel and Noah and was present to bless Henoch. An Angel spoke to Hagar, but it was this same God (Christ). A man came to Abraham but was adored as God. He also came to Jacob in a human form and even wrestled with him. Later He was revealed to Moses as a fire so that it might be comprehended that this created nature was related to His outward appearance rather than to the substance of His nature. Christ appeared in different guises to Joshua, Isaiah, Ezechiel and Daniel and in all these manifestations He could lay aside the created

---

[179] *Ibid.* XII 43.

[180] *Ibid.* XII 44. Athanasius, *Or. c. Ar.* II 44 (PG 26.240C–241A), said that concerning this passage in Proverbs, it should be remembered that proverbs are of a figurative nature and should be interpreted; their sense must be unfolded. It is understood that this is done with the help of the regula fidei.

[181] *Ibid.* XII 45. Tertullian, *adv. Prax.* 6–7 (ed. Evans pp. 94–5), saw in Prov. 8:22ff the establishment of Wisdom Herself, or rather the establishment in Her of the world as proposed for creation in the mind of God, and then after Wisdom had received expression as the Word, the creation of the world through the Word as God's Agent. Cf. the notes by Evans, pp. 220–225. Athanasius, *Or. c. Ar.* II 45 and 51 (PG 26.241C, 256A), also emphasized that the phrase: "The Lord created Me for the beginning of His ways," is an indication of His manhood and the economy which took place. Smulders, *op. cit.*, p. 193 n. 61, rightly asserted that although Athanasius and Hilary are in accord on this point, they differ on the details in their interpretation of this text.

form by the same power through which He had assumed it.[182]

Hilary admits that the Apostle Paul referred to the true birth of the flesh, which was conceived within the virgin Mary, as something created and made, because a being of our own created nature was born.[183] Hilary contends that there is a difference between the creation within time for the beginning of the ways of God and the birth before the ages. The term "creation" cannot be applied to that which had been established and born before all the ages, but only to what had been created since the beginning of time for the ways and works of God.[184] The apostle was justified in saying that He was "made of a woman," because the word "made" excluded the idea of a conception from human intercourse, while on the other hand, the apostle knew that He was born from the virgin. There is a great difference between the apostle's assertion that He had been "made," in order that there may be no doubt that He had been born from One, and the interpretation of the heretics that He had received His being from nothing, just as a creature does.[185]

Hilary asserts that the apostolic faith knows that Christ was created in the dispensation of time and born in the eternity of time. He was born as God from God, born before all things, and His birth testifies to the Author and implies that there is no incongruity between Him and His Author.[186] The Son's birth is before the eternal ages. Being from the Father, He is second to Him in the sense that He derives His eternal origin from the Father and being His Son, He is not to be separated from the Father, for the Father has never been without His Son.[187] Hilary does not concede that the word "creation" be used of the Holy Spirit, for He proceeds from the Father, sent through the Son.[188]

The fact that man cannot comprehend the eternal birth does not permit him to deny and reject it. Hilary confesses that there are many things in this world which he does not understand; the stars, the ebb and flow of the sea, the hidden power which restores decayed seeds to life and multiplies it, but this causes him to admire God all the more. He cannot grasp

---

[182] *Ibid.* XII 46–47.
[183] *Ibid.* XII 48.
[184] *Ibid.* XII 49. Athanasius, *Or. c. Ar.* II 60 (PG 26.276A), stressed the difference between a creature and an offspring. If the Word was a creature and there was no difference between creature and offspring, it would not have been necessary to add the sentence "But before all the hills He begat Me" to the preceding "The Lord created Me for a beginning of His ways."
[185] *Ibid.* XII 50.
[186] *Ibid.* XII 51.
[187] *Ibid.* XII 54.
[188] *Ibid.* XII 55.

the origin of the Only-begotten, but that does not lessen his belief in the omnipotence of God.[189]

g. Unity of Father and Son

Hilary also gave his attention to the question of the unity of the Father and the Son. His adversaries had reasoned that Christ was not God, for there would no longer be one God if Christ was also to be acknowledged as God. If God is one, whoever else there may be, will not be God. The orthodox faith however, preached the true birth of the Only-begotten God from God the Father. By this it is maintained that He is true God and not alien to the nature of the one true God. Thus it could not be denied that He is God, nor could He be called another God, because the birth made Him God and the nature within Him of one God from God did not separate Him into another God. Human reason led to the conclusion that different natures do not meet together in the same nature, and this was also manifested from statements of the Lord Himself, e.g. "I and the Father are one" (John 10:30) and "If you know Me, you also know My Father" etc. (John 14:7–11).[190]

The heretics could not deny these words which are clearly stated and understood, according to Hilary, but they distorted the meaning. They refer to the words in John 10:30 as an agreement of unanimity, so that there is a unity of will and not of nature in these words. To confirm this view, the Arians cited the text in Acts 4:32: "And the multitude of believers were of one heart and soul," to prove that a diversity of souls and hearts leads to a unity of one heart and soul, through a mere conformity of will. They also quoted the words in 1 Cor. 3:8: "Now he who plants and he who waters are one," to show that there is a unity of will in both, since there is no difference in the ministry for our salvation, and the effecting of it. The prayer of the Lord, John 17:20,21: "Not for these only do I pray but for them who shall believe in Me through their word, that all may be one, as Thou, Father, in Me and I in Thee, that they also may be one in us," proves, according to the heretics, that, since men cannot be fused back into God and cannot themselves be united into one indistinguishable mass, this oneness proceeds from a unity of will, since all of them do things that are pleasing to God; the sentiments of their minds are in harmony and thus it is not the nature which makes them one, but the will.[191]

[189] *Ibid.* XII 53. Cf. Baltzer, *op. cit.*, p. 18.
[190] *Ibid.* VII 3–4.
[191] *Ibid.* VIII 5. Cf. VIII 10. Novatian, *de Trin.* XXVII 151 (ed. Weyer p. 172), in

Hilary replied to this view by declaring that he could refute the heretics with the very words which they adduced as proof of their interpretation.[192] The believers who were one in soul and heart were one through their faith in God; and there is but one faith, as there is one Lord, one baptism etc. (Eph. 4:4,5). The believers are therefore one, through the nature of the one faith, and there is therefore a natural unity among those who are one by the nature of the one faith. They are all reborn to innocence, immortality, to the knowledge of God and to hope, and thus cannot differ within themselves as there is one hope, one God, one Lord and one baptism. If these are one by assent rather than by nature, then a unity of will may be ascribed to those who have been reborn to these things. If they have been reborn into the nature of one life and one eternity whereby they are one soul and heart, then the unity of assent ceases to apply in the case of those who are one in the generation of the same nature.[193]

Hilary points out that this unity of the faithful arises from the nature of the sacraments. In Gal. 3:27,28 we read: "For as many of you as have been baptized into Christ have put on Christ. There is neither Jew nor Greek, nor slave nor freeman, there is neither male nor female; for you are all one in Christ Jesus." The fact that they are one amid so great a diversity of race, condition and sex does not arise from the agreement of will, but from the unity of the sacrament, since they all have one baptism and have put on the one Christ.[194] Likewise the text concerning "he who plants and he who waters" being one, means that they are one because they themselves have been reborn in the one baptism and form the one ministry of one regenerating baptism. They have been made the same thing, having all put on Christ, and are ministers of the same thing and the same power.[195]

Hilary rebukes the Arians for maintaining that the unity between the Father and the Son was no more than an agreement of the will. There was no lack of suitable words which the Lord could have used in His

explaining the text John 10:30: "I and the Father are one," quoted 1 Cor. 3:6–8 to illustrate that Paul, while accepting a unity of concord distinguished between the persons.

[192] *Ibid.* VIII 6.

[193] *Ibid.* VIII 7. Si ergo per fidem, id est, per unius fidei naturam unum omnes erant; quomodo non naturalem in his intelligis unitatem, qui per naturam unius fidei unum sunt? Omnes enim renati erant ad innocentiam, ad immortalitatem, ad cognitionem Dei, ad spei fidem ... Si vero regenerati in unius vitae atque aeternitatis naturam sunt, per quod anima eorum et cor unum est; cessat in his assensus unitas, qui unum sunt in ejusdem regeneratione naturae (PL 10.241B–C).

[194] *Ibid.* VIII 8.

[195] *Ibid.* VIII 9.

prayer, had He wished thus to express this. He could have prayed: "Father, as We are one in will, so let them also be one in will, etc." In a very striking and apt passage, Hilary then asks: "Or was He, Who is the Word, perchance unacquainted with the meaning of words; and did He, Who is the Truth, not know how to utter the truth; and did He, Who is Wisdom, go astray in foolish talk; and was He Who is Power, so weak that He could not speak what He wished to be understood?" The prayer of the Lord is for those of whom it is said: "That all may be one," and the progress of unity is seen by an example of unity, when He says: "As Thou, Father, in Me and I in Thee, that they also may be in us."[196]

Hilary also teaches the unity of Christians with Christ through the glory bestowed on them. The Son said: "And the glory which Thou hast given Me, I have given to them, that they may be one, even as We are one" (John 17:22). The Son has given the glory that He has received from the Father, to all who believe in Him. The glory of the Son is not different from that of the Father, for the glory of the Son elevates all the believers to the unity of the glory of the Father. Hilary's teaching on the unity of Christians in honour has been termed unusual[197] because he frankly admits at the end of the paragraph, that he cannot explain how the glory that has been given, causes all to be one.[198]

Hilary also dwells on the unity with Christ in the eucharist. The Lord has indeed become flesh and the believers receive the Word as flesh in the food from the Lord and He dwells in them naturally. The believers are thus one because the Father is in Christ and Christ in them. He calls the union of Christians with Christ and fellow-Christians through the eucharist the "image" ("sacramentum") of the perfect unity of the Father and Son.[199] In the eucharist the believers receive the true body of Christ: "My flesh is meat indeed and My blood is drink indeed. He who eats My flesh and drinks My blood, abides in Me and I in him" (John 6:55–56). Christ is thus in those who receive these things, and the believers are in Christ.[200] Another text is quoted by Hilary illustrating that a unity of will is not indicated: "Since I am in My Father, and you in Me and I in you" (John 14:20). The sequence of the unity that was to be brought about, excludes a mere volitional unity and indicates that He was in the Father through the nature of the Deity and the believers are in Him through His

[196] *Ibid.* VIII 11.
[197] Wild, *op. cit.,* p. 104.
[198] *De Trin.* VIII 12.
[199] *Ibid.* VIII 13. For the different meanings of "sacramentum" in Hilary's works, cf. J. P. Brisson, ed. *Traité des mystères,* Paris, 1947, p. 24 n. 1.
[200] *Ibid.* VIII 14.

corporeal birth, while He is in them through the mystery of the sacraments, and thus there is a perfect unity by means of the Mediator.[201] The
effect of the union with Christ and His Father is life. Quoting John 6:57:
"... as I live through the Father, so he who shall eat My flesh shall live
through Me," Hilary concludes that the believers live naturally through
Christ because they have the nature of His flesh, while Christ lives
naturally through the Father, because He has the Father's nature. He
lives in the Father because His birth did not bring Him a foreign and
different nature, inasmuch as His being is from the Father.[202]

It must be pointed out that Hilary thought the unity of the believers
with God to be a real and natural one. Nevertheless he never avers that
the natural unity that binds the Christian to God is the same as that which
binds the Father and Son together. He merely insists that both are natural.
By natural unity he means one founded on the nature either of the two
things joined together or of the bond joining them. By opposing this
natural unity to a unity of wills, he must mean a physical unity, or at least
one that more closely approaches physical unity than a clearly moral
union does.[203] In the above argumentation it must be remembered that
for Hilary, faith, glory and the eucharist are natures and a nature has
objective reality and here means a reality over and above a product of
the mind and will; and when he speaks of a natural unity based on faith
etc. it is a reality over and above mere unity of wills.[204]

According to Hilary, the Father and Son are one, not through the
mystery of the dispensation, but through a birth of nature. They are one
because those things that are not snatched from His hands are not snatched from the hands of the Father (John 10:28); when He is known, the
Father is known; when He is seen, the Father is seen; what He speaks,
the Father Who remains in Him, speaks; in His works the Father works;
for He is in the Father and the Father in Him (John 14:7,9,10,11). This
is not granted by creation but by birth; it is not brought about by will
but by power. There is a difference between willing the same thing and
being able to do the same thing.[205]

By denying that harmony alone is the basis of unity between the Father
and the Son, the orthodox doctrine does not necessarily deny unanimity
between God and Christ. Hilary clearly teaches that the Father and the

[201] *Ibid.* VIII 15.
[202] *Ibid.* VIII 16.
[203] Wild, *op. cit.*, pp. 108–9.
[204] Wild, *op. cit.*, pp. 88, 113.
[205] *De Trin.* VIII 18. Athanasius, *Or. c. Ar.* III 5 (PG 26.329B–C), said that the
attributes of the Father are ascribed to the Son because the Son is the Offspring from
the Father and only because He is the Offspring.

Son are one in nature, glory and power, and the same nature cannot will things that are contrary.[206]

Hilary also dwells at length on some of the texts in which Christ told the disciples about the coming of the Holy Spirit, especially the following texts: "When the Advocate has come, Whom I will send you from the Father, the Spirit of truth, Who proceeds from the Father, He will bear witness concerning Me" (John 15:26). "He (Spirit) will glorify Me; for He will receive of Mine and will declare it to you. All things that the Father has are Mine. That is why I have said that He will receive of what is Mine and will declare it to you" (John 16:14,15). The Spirit of truth proceeds from the Father but He is sent by the Son from the Father. All the things that belong to the Father, belong to the Son. Whatever He, Who is to be sent will receive, He will receive from the Son, because everything that the Son has, the Father has. There is no difference in this unity of Father and Son nor does it make any difference from Whom it is received, for what is given by the Father is also represented as given by the Son.[207]

The words of Paul (Rom. 8:9–11) also bear witness of this unity of Father and Son, for the Spirit of God which is in us, is also the Spirit of Christ. Though the Spirit of Christ is in us, yet the Spirit of Him Who raised Christ from the dead, is also in us, and thus the Spirit of God is in us. Hilary challenges the heretics to separate the Spirit of Christ from the Spirit of God; and to part the Spirit of Christ that was raised from the dead from the Spirit of God which raised Christ from the dead.[208] From the following texts (Luke 4:18; Matt. 12:18,28; Acts 2:16,17) Hilary points out that the expression, the "Spirit of God," may serve to designate the Father or the Son and is also used in the strict sense of the Paraclete.[209] Hilary further contends that the Father and the Son are called "Spirit," lest it be thought that the Son is in the Father or the Father in the Son in a corporeal manner.[210] But while the Spirit of Christ dwells in us, it is also no other than the Spirit of God in us. The Holy Spirit is as much the Spirit of God as the Spirit of Christ, and the nature of the Son is identical

---

[206] *Ibid.* VIII 19 (PL 10.250A).
[207] *Ibid.* VIII 19–20. Novatian, *de Trin.* XVI 90 (ed. Weyer p. 112), said that John 16:14 affirmed that Christ could not have been merely a man, for the Spirit does not receive anything from man but grants knowledge to man. Athanasius, *Or. c. Ar.* II 24 (PG 26.197B), referring to John 16:15 said that it is a property of the Son to have the things of the Father.
[208] *Ibid.* VIII 21.
[209] *Ibid.* VIII 25 and 23. Tertullian, *adv. Prax.* 11 (ed. Evans pp. 100–101), cited Luke 4:18 with other texts to indicate that there is a distinction within the Trinity, viz. Father, Son and Spirit.
[210] *Ibid.* VIII 24.

with that of the Father, since the Holy Spirit Who is the Spirit of Christ and of God, is the property (being) of one nature. The Spirit of Truth proceeds from the Father, He is sent by the Son, and receives from the Son. The Spirit is a Being of the nature of the Son, but the same Being is of the nature of the Father.[211] Hilary also quotes the words of the Lord in John 14:23: "... and My Father will love him, and We will come to him and make Our abode with him." There are not two Spirits in the believer, but one, the Spirit of Christ Who is also the Spirit of God, and He dwells in the believer in a unity of nature.[212] The unity of Father and Son is therefore more than one of will, but is one of nature.

Hilary also deals at length with the diversity of spiritual gifts of which Paul wrote in 1 Cor. 12, and contends that this chapter teaches that it is the same Spirit in the varieties of gifts and the same Lord in the varieties of ministries and the same God in the varieties of works; yet it is the one Spirit Who works and distributes as He wills. It also teaches that the one body has many members; and that the various gifts are from the one Lord Jesus Christ, Who is the body of all. In 1 Cor. 12:28 Paul says that God ordained the ministrations and operations, while in Eph. 4:11 it is said of Christ. The Son as Giver must be one with the Father Who is also Giver and one with the Spirit.[213]

Hilary rejects the charge which could be made with reference to the words in 1 Cor. 12:5,6 namely "The same Lord and the same God." These words cannot be used to attest that They are not in unity of nature. Even the text where Paul mentions "one God, the Father ... and one Lord Jesus Christ" (1 Cor. 8:6) is wrongly interpreted by the Arians. Hilary reasons that if the fact that the Father alone is God has not left the possibility for Christ to be God, then it must also follow that the one Lord Christ does not leave God the possibility of being Lord, because the heretics contended that to be One is characteristic and peculiar to Him Who is one. But if God is not Lord, what will His power amount to and what will the strength of the Lord be if He is not God; for being God is perfected by being Lord and being Lord is constituted by being God.[214]

---

[211] *Ibid.* VIII 26.

[212] *Ibid.* VIII 27. Novatian, *de Trin.* XXVIII 158 (ed. Weyer p. 178), quoted this text to prove that Christ was not the Father. Athanasius, *Or. c. Ar.* III 11 (PG 26.344 A–C), maintained that the likeness and oneness must be referred to the Essence of the Son and Father and as such They dwell in the believer.

[213] *Ibid.* VIII 29–33.

[214] *Ibid.* VIII 34–35. Cf. 41. Athanasius, *Or. c. Ar.* III 4 (PG 26.329A–B), said that since the Father and the Son are one, and the Godhead Itself one, the same things which are said of the Father are said of the Son, and in this sense he quoted 1 Cor. 8:6.

[215] *Ibid.* VIII 40.

Thus unless through the unity of Spirit there is one Lord, the Father cannot be Lord.[215]

The words "I and the Father are one" (John 10:30) do not therefore teach us the solitude of a single Person but the unity of the Spirit, because the one God the Father and the one Christ the Lord, although each is Lord and God, do not admit two Gods and two Lords in our faith.[216] Paul spoke of Christ not only as Lord, but also as God (Rom. 9:5: "... Christ, Who is over all things God").[217] Hilary summarizes this argument which he derived from the writings of the Apostle Paul thus: "Since he (Paul) has specially ascribed to God that all things are from Him and has assigned as a peculiar property to Christ that all things are through Him; and it is now the glory of God because all things are from Him and through Him and in Him[218]; and since the Spirit of God is the same as the Spirit of Christ; and in the ministry of the Lord and in the working of God the one Spirit works and distributes, They cannot but be one Whose properties are those of one; since in the same Lord the Son, and in the same God the Father, one and the same Spirit distributing in the same Holy Spirit accomplishes all things."[219]

Hilary also uses another example, viz. that God the Father has set His seal upon the Son of Man (John 6:27).[220] Hilary explains this by referring to the words of Jesus that He does everything that the Father does, that He has received all judgement from the Father and that He must be honoured like the Father (John 5:19–23) and that as the Father has life in Himself, so He has given to the Son to have life in Himself (John 5:26). This, according to Hilary, indicates the unity of the same nature through the mystery of His birth; for when He says that He has what the Father has, He means that He has the Father Himself, for God is not as a human, fashioned of composite things so that there is a difference between possessor and possessed. The total that He has is life, and this life He gave as He possessed it.[221] While it is true that seals do manifest the entire form that has been impressed on them, Hilary warns that this comparison

[216] *Ibid.* VIII 36.
[217] *Ibid.* VIII 37. Irenaeus, *adv. Haer.* III 17,2 (ed. Harvey II p. 84), cited this text to prove that Jesus Christ was one Person and the Son of God. Tertullian, *adv. Prax.* 13 (ed. Evans p. 104), used the same argument as Hilary. Cf. Novatian, *de Trin.* XIII 69 (ed. Weyer p. 96). Athanasius cited this text a few times but not always to emphasize the Divinity of Christ. In *Or. c. Ar.* I 11 (PG 26.33C), the eternity of Christ was being stressed.
[218] Rom. 11:36.
[219] *De Trin.* VIII 39.
[220] *Ibid.* VIII 42.
[221] *Ibid.* VIII 43. Novatian, *de Trin.* XIV 76 (ed. Weyer p. 100), cited John 5:19 and 26 to prove the Divinity of Christ, for had He only been man He could not have uttered these words. Cf. XXI 122 (ed. Weyer p. 142).

does not adequately exemplify the Divine birth, because with sealing there is matter, difference of nature and an act of impression whereby the likeness of the stronger nature is impressed upon that of a more yielding one. But the Only-begotten God desiring to point out to us the likeness of His Father's proper nature in Himself, made known that God had set His seal upon Him. What God had set His seal upon could produce from itself nothing less than the form of Him Who had set His seal upon it.[222]

Hilary continues that God did not form anything else from Himself into God but God, and He Who is in the form of God is then in His entire being nothing else but God.[223] This however must not lead to the conclusion that the apostolic faith leads to the confession of two Gods, and the confession that God the Son is inseparable from the Father does not afford the opportunity to teach that God is single and solitary. He Who is in the form of God (Phil. 2:6) does not develop into another God, nor can He not be God; just as He Who is in the glory of God (Phil. 2:11)[224] cannot be other than God and since He is God in the glory of God, He possesses the nature of God in Himself from Him in whose glory He is.[225]

Hilary then explains the sense in which Christ is the image of God (Col. 1:15). An image must express the form of that of which it is an image. Christ is the image of the Father through the power of His works, quoted in Col. 1:15–20. He is the image of the nature and not of the form, because by the power of His nature and not by invisible attributes does He have the nature of God. From the above-mentioned text in Col. 1:15ff. declaring that He is the head of His body, the Church, and the first-born of every creature, it is seen that in all things He has the pre-eminence and in Him all things are reconciled to God. He is the image of God, for all things are created in Him through (or unto) Him. Since all things are created in Him, it must be understood that He Whose image He is, also creates all things in Him. Since all things which are created in Him are also created through Him, then in Him, Who is the image, there is also the nature of Him in Whose image He is. Since all things are reconciled through Him, He reconciles all things to the Father in Himself, which He reconciled through Himself.[226] Creation and reconciliation is the joint work of the Father and the Son.

[222] *Ibid.* VIII 44.
[223] *Ibid.* VIII 46.
[224] The Latin text reads: et omnis lingua confiteatur quia Dominus Iesus Christus in gloria est Dei Patris.
[225] *De Trin.* VIII 47. Novatian, *de Trin.* XXII 126–131 (ed. Weyer pp. 146–152), fully treated this passage and concluded that it clearly taught that the Lord Jesus Christ was also God. Cf. Athanasius, *Or. c. Ar.* I 40 (PG 26.93B–C).
[226] *Ibid.* VIII 48–51. Tertullian, *adv. Prax.* 7 (ed. Evans p. 95), said that Christ was

The meaning of the words: "I and the Father are one" (John 10:30) are thus unambiguous. Whatever the Son did and said, the Father did and said in the Son. This is not characteristic of a nature alien to God Himself, or of one made into God by creation, or formed into God from a portion of God, but of the Divinity that has been begotten into the perfect God by the perfect birth. Nothing of the Godhead is lacking in Him in Whose working, speaking and manifestation, God works, speaks and is seen. Once again Hilary emphasizes that there are not two Gods distinct in nature, work, speech and manifestation but One. Neither is He a solitary God Who worked, spoke and was seen as God.[227]

The text "For in Him dwells the fullness of the Godhead bodily" (Col. 2:9), is adduced by Hilary as further proof of the unity of nature between the Father and the Son. If it is maintained that the Father is in the Son in a corporeal manner, then the Father, while dwelling in the Son, will not exist in Himself. It is therefore more likely that the God Who dwells in Him bodily signifies the true nature of God in Him, and God is thus in Him not by will but by generation and He was born by His divine birth to be God.[228] Where a unity of nature is proclaimed an agreement of will cannot be denied, but the latter must not lead to a profession of merely a mutual agreement. Thus the bodily dwelling of the incorporeal God in Christ brings about a unity of nature.[229]

h. Christ is true God and man

In this section other objections to the orthodox faith raised by the Arians will be discussed. Hilary quotes a number of texts which the Arians used to substantiate their denial of the divinity of Christ, e.g. Mark 10:18; John 17:3, 5:19, 14:28; Mark 13:32.[230] Before giving the correct interpretation of these texts and the refutation of the heretics, he proceeds to expound the true faith. He asserts that Jesus Christ is true God and true

"first-begotten" because He had been begotten before everything. Novatian, *de Trin.* XXI 123 (ed. Weyer pp. 142f.), also thought that "firstborn of all creation" proved the Divinity of Christ and referred to the generation of the Son before the creation. Hilary follows this interpretation and referred it to the eternal generation. Cf. *De Trin.* VIII 50. Athanasius, *Or. c. Ar.* II 62–63, thought these words referred to Christ's incarnation, the coming of the Logos to the creatures through which He became the "brother of many" (Rom. 8:29) and the first-born of the new creation.

[227] *Ibid.* VIII 52.
[228] *Ibid.* VIII 54.
[229] *Ibid.* IX 1. Athanasius, *Or. c. Ar.* III 5 (PG 26.329B–332A), said that the attributes of the Father were ascribed to the Son, and the Son is the proper Offspring of the Father's essence. The Son is in the Father and the Father in the Son.
[230] *De Trin.* IX 2.

man. He was constituted as Mediator for the salvation of the Church and through the mystery of the Mediatorship between God and man, He alone is both. The two natures are united in Him in such a way that He is not wanting in either of the two, so that He does not cease to be God by His birth as man, nor does He fail to be man because He remains God.[231]

It is contrary to all human experience that Christ should be born as man and yet remain God. In nature we are used to development and growth. It is God alone Who could become something else than what He was, and still be what He had been, Who could shrink within the limits of the womb, cradle and infancy, and yet remain in the power of God.[232]

Christ was Son of God and Son of man. Hilary insists however, that as man He could speak and perform all deeds which are characteristic of God, and, as God, could speak and perform all deeds characteristic of man; and when He spoke He indicated that He was man as well as God. He revealed the one God the Father, but declared that He Himself possessed the nature of the one God by His true birth. He is subject to the Father in His dignity as Son and as man, because all flesh must be considered weak when compared to God. Hilary asserts that the heretics misrepresented the Son's statements which were made as man, as having been made through the weakness of His divine nature.[233] Hilary stresses that in order to understand the words of Christ correctly, the period in His life to which He refers, must be borne in mind, i.e. before the Incarnation, during the Incarnation and after His resurrection.[234]

Continuing his discussion on Christ's two natures, Hilary states that His birth, passion and death was all for the sake of man. In Christ the believers receive from the fullness of the Godhead which dwells in Christ. Christians are buried with Him in His baptism but they rise again in Him through faith in God.[235] He Who died and He Who raised the dead to life are not two, but one Person; for Christ laid down His life but also took it up again,[236] and He hereby proved that He is God and that the resurrection is His own work, and yet He referred all these things to the authority of His Father's command (John 10:18).[237] Paul had pointed out the Lord's human infirmity and His divine power and nature (2 Cor. 13:4).

---

[231] *Ibid.* IX 3.
[232] *Ibid.* IX 4.
[233] *Ibid.* IX 5.
[234] *Ibid.* IX 6.
[235] *Ibid.* IX 7–9.
[236] John 10:17,18. Cf. John 2:19 where Jesus said that He would raise the temple in three days.
[237] *De Trin.* IX 10–12. Novatian, *de Trin.* XXI 121–122 (ed. Weyer p. 142), said that only the Word, Christ, Who proved to be God and man, could say these words.

Christ is a Person of two natures; in the form of God and in the form of a slave. It was one and the same Christ Who changed His outward appearance and assumed that of a human being.[238]

Hilary then examines the arguments of the Arians. They denied that our Lord Jesus Christ is God, because He said: "Why do you call Me good? No one is good but one, God" (Mark 10:18). Hilary emphasizes that Christ did not rebuke the youth for calling Him "good," but His criticism was levelled against the use of the phrase "good master" if the youth saw Christ only as a teacher of the common precepts of the law. Christ did not repudiate the use of "good" for Himself if given to Him as God. He illustrated this in Mark 10:21 in which He promises heavenly treasures (which only God can do), and He did not reject being regarded as "master" because He offered to lead the youth. Jesus Christ accepted the fact that His apostles called Him Master (John 13:13, Matt. 23:10), for this title was from the faithful, but He rejected it when He was not acknowledged as Lord and Christ. Hilary also stresses the point that when Christ called the one God alone "good," He did not separate Himself from God, for He asserted that He Himself is Lord and Christ and a guide to the treasures of heaven.[239]

The text: "but this is life eternal, that they may know Thee, the only true God, and Him Whom Thou hast sent, Jesus Christ" (John 17:3), was adduced by the Arians as evidence that Christ is not true God. When He used the words "Thee, the only true God" they thought that He separated Himself from the true nature of God by restricting it to a solitary God, for "the only true God" can only be understood as a solitary God. Hilary agrees that the apostolic faith forbids us to believe in two true Gods. There cannot be one true God, if, outside the nature of the one true God, there exists a true God of a different nature which is not His by birth.[240]

Hilary states that in this text (John 17:3) there is nothing to suggest that Christ is not God, for other titles e.g. "Son of man" or "Son of God," which are given to Him, are not used, but only "Him, Whom Thou hast sent, Jesus Christ."[241] Many texts in the Lord's last discourse (John 14–16)

[238] *Ibid.* IX 13–14.
[239] *Ibid.* IX 15–18.
[240] *Ibid.* IX 28. Athanasius, *Or. c. Ar.* III 15 (PG 26.352C–353A), emphasized that the orthodox faith does not confess many gods. The Word has no other Godhead than that of the Only God, because He is born from Him.
[241] *Ibid.* IX 33. Novatian, *de Trin.* XVI 91 (ed. Weyer p. 112), said that this text proved the Godhead of Christ. He wanted to be acknowledged as God. Athanasius, *Or. c. Ar.* III 9 (PG 26.337C–340A), stated that if the Father be called the only true God, this was said not to deny Christ when He said: "I am the Truth," but to deny those who by nature are not true as the Father and His Word are true. The Lord at

mention the true Godhead of Christ. In the beginning of this discourse Christ said that he who has seen Him, has also seen the Father (John 14:9) etc., and the disciples confessed: "Now we know that Thou knowest all things and dost not need that anyone should question Thee; by this we believe that Thou comest forth from God" (John 16:30). They perceived in Him the nature of God by the divine powers which He exercised. The Lord also said that He "came out from God" and with these words He signified His birth, because He added "I came out from the Father" (John 16:27,28).[242]

From John 17:3 Hilary deduces that if the confession of the only true God, and of Jesus Christ gives us eternal life, then the name Jesus Christ has here the full sense of that of God. It is futile to believe in the only true God unless we also believe in Him Whom God had sent.[243] Because there is one God, the Father, this does not deprive Christ of being the one Lord,[244] and because there is the only true God, this does not in any way deprive Christ from being the true God. The fact that God the Father is the only true God confirms that Christ is also true God, for the one God could not produce from Himself a God of another nature. The Begotten God possesses the same nature as that of the Father. The divinity in the Son is not changed or degenerated but the Son possesses the natural power of the Father Whose nature He retains in Himself by the natural birth.[245] In John 13:31,32 it is clear that the glory of the Father is that of the Son. The Son of man is glorified and God is glorified in Him and God glorifies in Himself Him, Who is glorified in the man.[246] "If the Father glorifies Him (Christ) in Himself and the Father alone is true God, Christ is not outside the only true God: because the Father Who is the only true God glorifies in Himself Christ, Who has been glorified into God."[247]

The third text which the Arians quoted to deny that Christ was God, was John 5:19: "Verily, verily, I say unto you, the Son can do nothing of Himself, but only what He sees the Father doing." Hilary reacts to this objection to Christ's Godhead by the Arians, by citing the evidence

once added: "And Jesus Christ Whom Thou hast sent." Had He been a creature, He would not have added this.
[242] *Ibid.* IX 29–30.
[243] *Ibid.* IX 33 and 35.
[244] Cf. 1 Cor. 8:6.
[245] *De Trin.* IX 34 and 36.
[246] *Ibid.* IX 39–42. Tertullian, *adv. Prax.* 23 (ed. Evans p. 119), cited this text to prove that the Son was not the Father.
[247] *Ibid.* IX 42 (PL 10.315C): Si enim in sese eum glorificat Pater, et solus Pater Deus verus est, non extra solum verum Deum Christus est: quia glorificatum in Deum Christum, glorificet Pater verus Deus solus in sese.

of other texts. He quotes John 5:17: "My Father works until now, and I work." It might be asked what the work of the Father is, for all things visible and invisible, are through the Son and in the Son.[248] He quotes another text wherein the Lord said that the words He has spoken, He spoke not of Himself, "but the Father, Who dwells in Me, it is He Who does His works" (John 14:10). If the Father works in Christ when He works, then Christ works when the Father works.[249] When the Lord said that He could do nothing of Himself, it does not imply a lack of strength, but indicates the source of His authority. In John 5:19 the Lord also said: "For whatever the Father does, the Son also does the same in like manner." The "whatever" includes all things, without exception, and there is no weakness in the Son for there is nothing which the Father can do, which the Son cannot do likewise. Equal honour is also ascribed to the Father and the Son (John 5:23), and They therefore share the same power and are accorded equality of honour.[250]

Another statement of the Lord which refers to this matter is: "And of Myself I do nothing; but as the Father taught Me, I speak these things. And He Who sent Me is with Me and He has not let Me alone, because I do always the things that are pleasing to Him" (John 8:28,29). To the Arians this text and John 5:19 must have seemed contradictory. The Son does nothing of Himself because of the Father Who abides in Him and He does all things that are pleasing to the Father: but it is no merit not to do of Himself what He does and therefore how can the Son deserve to have the Father remain in Him? On the other hand, how are the Son's deeds pleasing to the Father if the Father Himself, abiding in the Son, be their Author?[251] The solution to the problem, according to Hilary, lies in Their unity of nature so that the Son acts through Himself in such a way that He does not act by Himself. The Son is the Subject of the works which He performs, although He does not do it by Himself, but the Father works through Him. The Father is abiding in the Son, instructs Him, and the Son in acting, does not act of Himself while on the other hand, the Son Who does not act by Himself, is Himself active, since He does the things that are pleasing to the Father. The unity of nature is preserved in Their activity; for He Himself Who works does not work by Himself and He Himself Who has not worked by Himself, works.[252]

---

[248] This is probably an allusion to Col. 1:16.
[249] *De Trin.* IX 43–44.
[250] *Ibid.* IX 45–46. Cf. the explanation of this text on pp. 80–1 n. 131–132.
[251] *Ibid.* IX 47.
[252] *Ibid.* IX 48. Ita et manendo docet Pater, et Filius agendo non ab se agit, et non

It might also have seemed that the Son had no freedom of will for He said: "All that the Father gives to Me, comes to Me and him who comes to Me I will not cast out; for I have come down from heaven not to do My own will but the will of the Father Who sent Me" (John 6:37,38). In connection with this verse, Hilary quotes another text: "Everyone who listens to the Father and learns, comes to Me; not that anyone has seen the Father except He Who is from God, He has seen the Father. Verily, verily, I say to you, he who believes in Me has life everlasting" (John 6:45-47). No one has seen the Father except the Son and no one therefore could have heard the Father. He who listens to the Father comes to the Son. When the Son is heard and teaches, the reality of the Father's nature which is heard and teaches is revealed in Him, so that when the Son teaches and is heard it must be understood that the teaching of the Father is heard. The Father teaches through the words of the Son, and He Whom no one has seen is heard when the Son is seen, because the Son by virtue of His perfect birth, possesses the properties of His Father's nature. When the Son said that He does the will of the Father, it does not mean that He does not will what He does; but He let it be known that the Father Who had sent Him, and He Who had been sent, possess an identical nature, for what He wills, does and says are the will, works and words of the Father.[253]

The Lord revealed in no uncertain language His freedom of will by the words: "For as the Father raises the dead and gives them life, even so the Son gives life to whom He will" (John 5:21). When the Father and the Son are shown as equal in power and glory, the Son's freedom of will is indicated; when Their unity is demonstrated, the love for the Father's will is emphasized, for the Son does what the Father wills. Hilary asserts that to do the Will is more than to obey the Will, because the latter implies an external necessity, but to do the will of God is an attribute of the unity, since it is an act of the will of the Son. Through Their identity of nature, the Son has a unity of will with the Father. Other texts are cited viz. that the Father wills that those who believe in the Son should have eternal life (John 6:40); the Son wills that the believers should be there where He Himself is (John 17:24), and only he to whom the Son chooses to reveal the Father, knows Him (Matt. 11:27). It is evident that the Son's will is thus free, for He imparts knowledge of Himself and the Father to whom He wishes. Thus the nature of the birth and the unity between the Father

ab se agens Filius, cum quae placita sunt facit, ipse agit. Ac sic unitas naturae retinetur in agendo: dum et ipse operans non operatur ab se, et ipse ab se non operatus operatur (PL 10.319D).
[253] *Ibid*. IX 49.

and the Son are revealed, for the Son is free in will in this sense that what He does willingly is an act of His Father's will.[254]

Hilary asserts that the Father is in the Son and the Son in the Father by unity of nature, by power, by equality in honour and by the generation of the birth. This assertion seems contradicted by the Lord's statement: "The Father is greater than I" (John 14:28). Hilary states that the Church knows nothing of two unborn Persons nor two Fathers. In the Incarnation, the Son, emptying Himself of the form of God, took the form of a slave, but the Father was not affected by this assumption of human passions by the Son and continued in the eternity of His own nature. The Only-begotten however, remained in the Divine nature but took the form of our nature and human weakness. He still had what was proper to His Divine nature, but no longer had the form of God, because by His emptying, He had taken the form of a servant.[255] The Son also bore witness to the unity of His nature with the Father's (John 14:9, 10:38, 14:11) as well as Their equality of nature, for the appearance of the Son is a guarantee that the Father has been seen.[256]

When the Only-begotten God was about to fulfil the plan of salvation in the flesh and to complete the mystery of taking the servile form, He said: "You have heard Me say to you, I go away and I come to you. If you loved Me you would rejoice that I am going to the Father, for the Father is greater than I" (John 14:28). He had already, in the earlier part of this discourse, explained all things which pertain to His Divine nature and the declaration therefore in this text does not deprive the Son of the equality of nature which His true birth has given to Him. The Son is not the source of His own origin, but existing as a living nature from a living nature He possesses the power of the nature in Himself. He acknowledges the source of His nature in order to bear witness to the honour of the

---

[254] *Ibid.* IX 50.

[255] *Ibid.* IX 51. Tertullian, *adv. Prax.* 9 (ed. Evans p. 97), in order to prove that the Father is not identical with the Son, described the Father as "the whole substance, while the Son is an outflow and assignment of the whole, as He Himself professes, *Because My Father is greater than I.*" The Father is thus other than the Son, as the Begetter is other than the Begotten. Cf. the notes by Evans, pp. 245–7, on the phrase "filius vero derivatio totius et portio." Tertullian did not suggest an inferior grade of deity with these words (Evans p. 247). Novatian had proved that the Son is God but to combat the heresy that, because there is only one God, Christ is therefore the Father, Novatian cited many texts and among them John 14:28, to prove that the Father and the Son are not one Person, *de Trin.* XXVI 146; XXVIII 159 (ed. Weyer p. 166; 178). Athanasius, *Or. c. Ar.* I 58 (PG 26.133B), quoted this text to emphasize the fact that the Son has the same nature as the Father. If He did not have the same nature as the Father, Christ would have said: "My Father is better than I." But He used the word "greater," not in greatness or in time, but because of His generation from the Father.

[256] *Ibid.* IX 52.

Father and to render Him gratitude by His obedience. This obedience does not weaken the unity of the nature and so He, Who became obedient unto death, received after His death, a name above every other name (Phil. 2:9).[257]

If He appears to be unequal to the Father because this name was given to Him, the mystery of the humiliation must be borne in mind. His birth brought about a new nature and His form was changed through the assumption of the form of a slave and the bestowal of this name above all others restored to Him equality of form. What was given to Him is a property of God and such a gift does not therefore lead to a degradation of the divine nature. To Jesus is given "that all things in heaven and those on earth and under the earth bend the knee before Him and every tongue confess that Jesus is Lord in the glory of God the Father" (Phil. 2:10). The Father, as the One Who gives, is greater by reason of His authority to give but He, to Whom it is given to be one with the Giver, is not less. The Father is greater than the Son for He allows the Son to be as great as He Himself; because He imparts the image of His unbegotten nature to the Son through the birth; because He again renews Him from the form of a slave into the form of God; and since He permits Christ, born as God, to return to the glory of God again after His death.[258]

Hilary therefore concludes that the Father is greater because He is Father, but the Son, because He is Son, is not less. The birth of the Son establishes the Father as greater, but the nature of the birth does not allow the Son to be less. The Father is greater because He is asked to restore glory to the manhood which was assumed, but the Son is not less for He resumes glory with the Father. Thus the mystery of the birth and dispensation of the Incarnation are fulfilled.[259] Consequently the birth of the Son does not lead to an inferior nature for He is in the form of God, as He is born from God. The Begotten is not outside the nature of the Unbegotten for He derived His substance from the Father and none other. Unlike the Father the Son was born and through His birth He received from the Unbegotten God the nature of Divinity.[260]

Finally Hilary treats the words in Mark 13:32: "But of that day or hour no one knows, neither the angels in heaven, nor the Son but the Father only." The heretics said that this text proved that the Only-begotten God does not possess the perfection of Divine nature because He is subject to ignorance. The heretics contended that this confession is inevitable and

257 *Ibid.* IX 53.
258 *Ibid.* IX 54.
259 *Ibid.* IX 56.
260 *Ibid.* IX 57.

had to be believed because the Lord spoke thus and because it would be the height of blasphemy to distort a statement of the Lord by giving it a different meaning of our own.[261]

Before Hilary examines the meaning and occasion of these words, he appeals to the judgement of common sense to decide whether it is credible that He Who is the Author of everything that is and that is to be, can be ignorant of anything. The Lord Jesus is aware of the thoughts of man not only at the present moment but also those which will arise from future desires, as the evangelist testified: "For Jesus knew from the beginning who they were who did not believe and who it was who would betray Him" (John 6:64). If He possesses power over things foreign to Himself, can He be impotent in things pertaining to Himself? Of Him was said: "All things have been created through Him and in Him and He is before all creatures"[262] (Col. 1:16,17) and: "For it has pleased Him (Father) that in Him (Son) all fullness should dwell and that through Him all things should be reconciled unto Him" (Col. 1:19–20). All the fullness is in Him and all things are reconciled through Him and in Him and that day (Mark 13:32) is the expectation of our reconciliation. Is He ignorant of this day when its time depends on Him and when it is connected with the mystery of the dispensation? Is Christ ignorant of the day of His own coming, for it is His day according to the same apostle: "Because the day of the Lord is to come as a thief in the night" (1 Thess. 5:2).[263]

Hilary states that the trembling conscience of man dare not presume to think that He Who was born as God is ignorant of anything nor that the Father denied something to the Son because He was motivated by ill-will and begrudged the Son the knowledge of His future achievement. Hilary uses another illustration namely that a father is father with his whole personality: one cannot be partly father and partly not. God as Father must be Father to His begotten in all that He Himself is, for the perfect birth of the Son makes Him perfect Father in all respects. If He is truly Father to the Son, the Son must possess all the properties of the Father. How can this be if the Son does not have the attribute of pre-

---

[261] *Ibid*. IX 58. In connection with the mystery of the birth of Christ, Irenaeus declared that concerning the ineffable mysteries of God, man had to acknowledge that they were only known to God, for even the Son declared that only the Father knew the day of judgment (Mark 13:32), and man therefore did not know exactly how the Son came forth from the Father, *adv. Haer*. II 42,3 (ed. Harvey I p. 355).

[262] Hilary's text read: "et ipse est ante omnes."

[263] *Ibid*. IX 59. Athanasius also dealt at length with the explanation of Mark 13:32. He used arguments which Hilary also used. Athanasius said that the Lord by Whom all things were made and the Son Who knows the Father, could not be ignorant of the day. He had spoken of the events preceding this day and therefore He must have known the day, *Or. c. Ar*. III 42 (PG 26.412A–C).

science and if, through His birth, He lost some of the attributes of the Father? Almost everything will be deficient in Him if He does not have all that which is proper to God and surely knowledge of the future is a property of God?[264]

To teach that the Only-begotten God was ignorant of anything contradicts the words of Paul: "Being instructed in love unto all riches of complete understanding, unto knowledge of the mystery of the God Christ, in Whom are hidden all the treasures of wisdom and knowledge" (Col. 2:2-3). Hilary contends that a part and the whole cannot be together in the same object and if the Son does not know the day, all the treasures of knowledge are not in Him. It must be remembered that those treasures of knowledge are hidden in Him, though not, because hidden, wanting in Him. In Him are hidden all the treasures of knowledge and His ignorance is rather the plan of salvation than lack of knowledge. This is the reason for His ignorance and from this one cannot conclude that anything is unknown to Him.[265]

Whenever God says that He does not know, He professes ignorance, but He is not subject to ignorance, so that it is not because of the infirmity of ignorance that He does not know; either it is not yet the time to speak or the dispensation causes Him to refrain from action. Hilary cites the example in Gen. 18:20-21. God knows that the sins of Sodom and Gomorrah are very great but He comes down to see whether they have been done. Hilary concludes that it can be seen that He is not ignorant because He does not know, for when the time comes for action, He knows.[266]

God's knowledge depends upon the occasion, it is a question of the right moment to divulge what is known rather than to acquire this knowledge. The example of Abraham illustrates this point (Gen. 22:12). God commands Abraham not to lay his hand upon his son because God now knows that he fears God. God knew beforehand that Abraham believed in Him (Gen. 15:6) but only chose to make this knowledge

---

[264] *Ibid*. IX 60-61.

[265] *Ibid*. IX 62. Nam cum ignoratio ejus, secundum quod omnes thesauri in eo scientiae latent, dispensatio potius quam ignoratio sit; habes causam ignorandi sine intelligentia nesciendi (PL 10.331B).

[266] *Ibid*. IX 63. In omnibus enim, quae ignorare se Deus loquitur, ignorantiam quidem profitetur, sed ignoratione tamen non detinetur: dum ad id quod nescit, non nesciendi infirmitas est, sed aut tempus est non loquendi, aut dispensatio est non agendi... Scire ergo Deum, non est ignorantiae demutatio, sed temporis plenitudo. (PL 10.331B,332A). Athanasius, *Or. c. Ar*. III 50 (PG 26.428C), used the examples of God asking Adam "where art thou" and Cain "where is your brother Abel." As God asked Adam and Cain and yet knew what He had asked, so the Son (as God) knew, and yet asked.

known when Abraham was about to sacrifice his son. Therefore, when in the Old Testament God does not know something, the cause lies not in His ignorance, but in the occasion.[267]

In the Gospels examples are to be found of the Lord not knowing many things which He knows. He declares that He does not know the works of iniquity (Matt. 7:23) and yet He knows that there are workers of iniquity. Similarly He declares that He does not know the foolish virgins (Matt. 25:12) but in both these cases they are unworthy of being known by Him to Whom nothing is unknown. From another text it is learnt that the Lord even knows the thoughts of people, for Jesus said to the Scribes: "Why do you think evil in your hearts" (Matt. 9:4). Some examples of occasions when the Lord asked about words and deeds as if He was ignorant of them are: when the woman touched the hem of His garment; when the apostles were dissenting amongst themselves and when people were weeping at the tomb of Lazarus. His lack of knowledge must be ascribed not to ignorance, but to His manner of speaking. It is the economy of salvation that He, Who knows all things, sometimes referred to the very things that He knew, as if He did not know them. Therefore it is clear why He declared that He did not know the Day. He was not really ignorant because in Him are hidden all the treasures of wisdom and knowledge. Consequently the knowledge is hidden and because it must be hidden it was expressed at times as a lack of knowledge in order that it may remain hidden. Thus if He does not know in order that the knowledge may remain hidden, His lack of knowledge does not come from His nature, because He knows all things, but He appears ignorant only to keep it hidden. He therefore declared that He does not know the day in order to deprive us of the assurance of a certain knowledge and keep us in uncertainty so that we may always be watching for the day of His coming. This ignorance was necessary, not to deceive us, but to make us persevere. That which is denied us, does not harm us as believers, but what is unknown is to our advantage because we will continue to be watchful instead of becoming careless of the faith through the assurance of knowledge.[268]

Another objection made by the heretics was that the Son could indeed know the thoughts of human hearts because a more powerful nature has

---

[267] *Ibid.* IX 64.

[268] *Ibid.* IX 65–67. Athanasius ascribed the ignorance of the Lord to His manhood; because to be ignorant is a property of man, *Or. c. Ar.* III 45 (PG 26.417C); 43 (PG 26.416A); 46 (PG 26.420C) etc. Elsewhere Athanasius said that it was to the advantage of man that Christ said that He did not know, for that would prevent carelessness and encourage people to be always prepared for His coming, *Or. c. Ar.* III 48–49 (PG 26.424C–428A).

united itself with a lower nature, but that the Son does not know the thoughts of God the Father, since the Son is weak and He could not enter into an alliance with One Who is stronger. Hilary maintains that the Lord's own statements refuted this objection, for He said: "He who has seen Me has also seen the Father" and "Believe My works that the Father is in Me and I in the Father" and "I and the Father are one." The Father and the Son do not differ in nature for the Father is seen when the Son is seen and the Son abides in the Father and the Father in Him and They Who are one, are not different.[269]

The heretics cannot deny that the Lord used these words to signify the mystery of His birth but they attempt to evade them by referring them to a harmony of will, as if the vocabulary of the divine teaching was limited and the Lord either could not say: "I and the Father will to be one" or He expressed the same idea by His words: "I and the Father are one." Furthermore, common sense rejects the idea that the Lord could not say what He wanted or that He did not say what He said. The Lord did make use of proverbs and allegories but He did this simply to confirm His words by means of illustrations. The words: "I and the Father are one" can only be interpreted to mean exactly what the words signify. If They are one because They will to be one, They cannot be separate natures for the diversity of nature will draw Them into diversities of will. They must have the same knowledge otherwise They cannot will the same thing, since diversity in knowledge is incompatible with unity of will. Therefore in this case the fact that the Son does not know, is the dispensation of the hidden knowledge rather than an ignorance proceeding from His nature. As was said above, God's knowledge is not the discovery of what He did not know, but only the revealing of His knowledge. The fact that the Father alone knows the day, cannot be considered as an argument to show that the Son does not know, for the Son said that He did not know so that others should not know. The Son therefore said that He did not know the day because it was not the right moment to reveal it.[270]

The Son clearly taught His unity of nature with the Father (John 16:15) and since everything that the Father has is His, it is the property of His nature to will and know exactly as the Father wills and knows. Accordingly, the Son is not lacking in the knowledge of anything that the Father knows and the Son is not ignorant because the Father alone knows, because the Father and the Son remain in the unity of nature. What the

[269] *Ibid.* IX 68–69.
[270] *Ibid.* IX 70–71.

Son does not know is in accordance with the divine plan of silence. After His resurrection the apostles again asked Him about the day of His coming and then His reply was not that He did not know, but: "It is not for you to know the times or moments which the Father has fixed by His own authority" (Acts 1:7). The knowledge is denied them, and not only denied but the desire to learn is forbidden.[271] Hilary thus refuted the Arian objection that Christ was not true God because He Himself confessed His ignorance in certain matters.

i. Christ's passibility

A much disputed question is whether Hilary taught that it was possible for Christ to really experience suffering during His passion. Hilary has been accused of "sailing somewhat close to the cliffs of Docetism,"[272] but it is generally agreed that "he has escaped shipwreck."[273] There are three different interpretations of Hilary's teaching on this subject.[274] Some scholars think that Hilary denied that Christ really suffered pain. This view is held by Baltzer, Watson, Rauschen, Smulders and Galtier among others.[275] Some say that Hilary taught that Christ in His true humanity could suffer pain but where it is said He did not suffer His divine nature was referred to. Finally some scholars think that Hilary admitted the possibility that Christ could suffer pain, but that it was not of necessity by nature, and that every time Christ did suffer, it was the result of an act of His will by which He subjected Himself to the afflictions. Among the scholars who more or less hold this view are Dorner, Förster, Beck and Kelly.[276]

The Arians maintained that because of His fear during the passion and His weakness in suffering, Christ could not have the nature of God. This assertion is based upon the texts: "My soul is sad, even unto death," and

---

[271] *Ibid.* IX 73–75.

[272] Förster, *art. cit.*, p. 662, His view is shared by J. P. Baltzer, *Die Christologie des hl. Hilarius von Poitiers*, Rottweil, 1889, p. 32; Bardenhewer, *op. cit.*, p. 392.

[273] Watson, *op. cit.*, p. lxxvii.

[274] Cf. Le Bachelet, *art. cit.*, col. 2444–5; G. Giamberardini, "De Incarnatione Verbi secundum S. Hilarium Pictaviensem," *Divus Thomas*, Vol. 51 (1948), pp. 5–8.

[275] Baltzer, *Christologie*, pp. 23–32; Watson, *op. cit.*, pp. lxxiii–lxxvii; G. Rauschen, "Die Lehre des hl. Hilarius von Poitiers über die Leidensfähigkeit Christi," *Theologische Quartalschrift*, Vol. 87 (1905), pp. 424–439, and in *ZkTh*, Vol. 30 (1906), pp. 295–305; Smulders, *op. cit.*, pp. 203–206; Galtier, *op. cit.*, pp. 131–141.

[276] J. A. Dorner, *Entwicklungsgeschichte der Lehre von der Person Christi*, Berlin, 1851², Vol. I, pp. 1037–1057; Förster, *art. cit.*, pp. 660–666; A. Beck, *Kirchliche Studien und Quellen*, Amberg, 1903, pp. 82–102: "Die Lehre des hl. Hilarius von Poitiers über die Leidensfähigkeit des Leibes Christi," and in *ZkTh*, Vol. 30 (1906), pp. 108–122, 305–310; Kelly, *op. cit.*, p. 335.

"Father, if it is possible, let this cup pass away from Me," "My God, My God, why hast Thou forsaken Me" (Matt. 26:38,39; 27:46) and "Father, into Thy hands I commend My Spirit" (Luke 23:46).[277] Hilary asserts that the only things which could have caused Him fear would be His passion and death. But it is not reasonable to suppose that He was afraid to die; He, Who drove away all fear of death from His apostles and exhorted them to martyrdom with the words: "He who does not take up his cross and follow Me is not worthy of Me; and he who finds his life will lose it and he who loses it for My sake, will find it" (Matt. 10:38–39).[278]

The human life is either hastened to its end by external circumstances such as fever, wounds, accidents etc. or the body is overcome by old age. The Only-begotten God, however, Who has the power to lay down His life and take it up again, died of His own will. He gave up His Spirit through His own will and He thus had no dread of death because it was within His power to give up His life or not. Neither did He, through the fearfulness of human ignorance, fear the power of death. He did not fear death with regard to His body, for it was said that the Holy One will not see corruption (Ps. 15(16):10) and He knew that within three days He was to revive the temple of His body. Neither did Christ fear death with regard to His Spirit, for would Christ have feared the abyss of hell while Lazarus rejoiced in the bosom of Abraham? The willingness to die and the power to come to life again is incompatible with fear, for death cannot be feared where there is readiness to die and the power to live.[279]

In order to ascertain whether it was the physical pain of hanging on the cross, the cords that bound Him or the wounds where the nails were driven in which caused Him to fear, Hilary examines what body the man Christ had. Bodily matter in itself is senseless but by association with the soul it acquires the sense of feeling: pain, hunger, cold etc. When this association between the soul and body is severed the feeling of pain ceases: e.g. a cut off limb is senseless and on the other hand, the power of the soul can be rendered insensible by medicine so that an operation can be performed without causing distress. The animated body experiences pain because of its union with a weak soul.[280]

If the man Jesus Christ had a body and soul of the same origin as our body and soul, He may have felt the pain of our body. But if He assumed

[277] *De Trin.* X 9.
[278] *Ibid.* X 10.
[279] *Ibid.* X 11–12. Quia et voluntas moriendi et potestas reviviscendi extra naturam timoris est, dum timeri mors non potest et in voluntate moriendi et in potestate vivendi (PL 10.352A).
[280] *Ibid.* X 13–14.

through Himself the flesh from the virgin and He Himself from Himself joined a soul to the body that was conceived through Himself, then the nature of His suffering must be in accordance with the nature of His soul and body. Although accepting the form of a slave and without losing anything from Himself and His power, God the Word formed a perfect, living man. What the virgin begot she begot only by His Holy Spirit, although for the birth of His flesh she supplied from herself as much as women do when they receive the seeds of the bodies which are to be born. Jesus Christ however, was not conceived in the same way as a human being.[281]

The Lord Himself revealed the mystery of His assumption of manhood by declaring: "No one has ascended into heaven but He Who has descended from heaven, the Son of Man Who is in heaven" (John 3:13). Mary was not the cause but only the means of His human life. "Son of Man" refers to the birth of the flesh conceived in Mary and "Who is in heaven" refers to the power of His eternal nature. He descended from heaven and is the Son of Man but the Word Which was made flesh did not cease to be the Word. The apostle expressed this mystery in the words: "The first man from the slime of the earth, the second man from heaven" (1 Cor. 15:47).[282] Calling Him "man" the apostle, according to Hilary, taught the birth from the virgin and by saying that "the second man was from heaven" He testified that His origin was from the Holy Spirit Who came upon the virgin. Therefore the Lord said: "I am the living bread Who has descended from heaven. If anyone eat of My bread he shall live forever" and "unless you eat the flesh of the Son of Man and drink His blood, you shall not have life in you" (John 6:51,53).[283]

Jesus Christ by His power was a man of flesh and soul as well as God, possessing in Himself whole and true manhood and whole and true Godhead.[284] The Arians denied that God the Word was a substantial God but they made Him the utterance of the voice of God. The Word of God was, according to them, in Jesus just as the Spirit of prophecy was in the prophets. The heretics even charged the orthodox doctrine with teaching

---

[281] *Ibid.* X 15. Quod si assumpta sibi per se ex Virgine carne, ipse sibi et ex se animam concepti per se corporis coaptavit; secundum animae corporisque naturam, necesse est et passionum fuisse naturam (PL 10.353A–B).

[282] Hilary's text reads: Primus homo de terrae limo ... (PL 10.356A). One manuscript reads: de terra terrenus.

[283] *Ibid.* X 16–18. In Hilary's text John 6:51 reads: "Si quis manducaverit de pane meo."

[284] *Ibid.* X 19 (PL 10.357B): Ut sicut per naturam constitutam nobis a Deo originis nostrae principe, corporis atque animae homo nascitur, ita Jesus Christus per virtutem suam carnis atque animae homo ac Deus esset, habens in se et totum verumque quod homo est, et totum verumque quod Deus est.

that Christ was not born as a man of our body and soul because according
to the orthodox confession the Word was made flesh and Christ, emptying
Himself of the form of God assumed the form of a slave and although
being born as man, He did not cease to be God.[285] Hilary states that two
things, in contradiction to one another, are brought together in Him:
He truly remained in the form of God and He truly accepted the form
of a slave. Thus it is confessed that He is in the form of God by virtue
of His divine nature and in the form of a slave by the conception of the
Holy Spirit, being found in the appearance of a man. It is the same
Christ Who descended from heaven, was born, died, arose again and
ascended to heaven.[286]

The man Jesus Christ, the Only-begotten God, assumed a true manhood according to the likeness of our manhood without sacrificing His
Divinity. When a blow struck Him or He was wounded, He experienced
the impulse of the passion but not the pain of the passion. A weapon which
passes through water, penetrates fire or wounds the air, inflicts pains which
are proper to its nature for it penetrates, pierces and wounds, but it is
without effect in these cases for it is contrary to nature that a hole is made
in water or that air is wounded. The Lord Jesus truly suffered when He
was struck, suspended, crucified and died. The suffering which came upon
the body of the Lord was indeed suffering but it did not have the natural
effect of suffering: His body suffered the violence of the pain but without
feeling it. The body of the Lord would have had the nature of our pain,
if our body was of such a nature that it could tread upon water without
sinking and even penetrate solid matter so that a closed door was no
obstacle to it. He possessed a body to suffer and He suffered but He did
not have a nature which could feel pain. His body had a nature peculiar
to Himself; it was transformed into heavenly glory on the mountain, it
put fevers to flight by its touch and it gave new eyesight by its spittle.[287]

It could be objected that He Who wept, was thirsty and hungry, must
have had the nature of other human sufferings. To this Hilary replies that
he who is ignorant of the mystery of the tears, thirst and hunger, should
remember that He Who wept, also brought back to life and that He Who
was thirsty, bestowed rivers of living water. He was exposed to suffering

[285] *Ibid.* X 21.
[286] *Ibid.* X 22.
[287] *Ibid.* X 23. Passus quidem est Dominus Jesus Christus, dum caeditur, dum
suspenditur, dum crucifigitur, dum moritur: sed in corpus Domini irruens passio,
nec non fuit passio, nec tamen naturam passionis exseruit: dum et poenali ministerio
desaevit, et Virtus corporis sine sensu poenae vim poenae in se desaevientis excepit
(PL 10.362A). Habens ad patiendum quidem corpus, et passus est; sed naturam non
habens ad dolendum (PL 10.363A).

but not in such a way that He was prostrated by the injuries of the sufferings. His weeping was not for Himself and His thirst needed no water to quench it. It is never said that the Lord ate or drank or wept when He was hungry or thirsty or sorrowful. He assumed the custom of our body to prove the reality of His body so that according to the custom of our nature the custom of the body was satisfied. When He accepted food and drink it is to be attributed not to the body's necessity but to its custom.[288]

Christ did indeed have a body but a unique one of His own origin. He bore our humanity through the form of a slave but He was free from the sins and defects of a human body, so that we are in Him by His birth from the virgin but our defects are not in Him by the power of His origin that proceeded from Himself. From the words of the apostle in Phil. 2:7 it may be seen that the outward appearance and the truth of the body testified to His humanity but He Who was seen as a man did not have the defects of our nature. His birth was in the likeness of our nature and not in the possession of our defects. Paul also testified of this in Rom. 8:3. His outward appearance was not as if it were that of a man but as that of a man, nor was His flesh the flesh of sin but the likeness of the flesh of sin. Jesus Christ therefore was man and as man had the birth of man and as Christ He was not subject to the sinful weakness of man.[289]

Hilary examines the actual events as they took place, because His words cannot indicate fear if His deeds displayed self-assurance. The Lord of glory was not afraid of suffering for He rebuked Peter as "satan" and "stumbling-block" when he erred through his ignorance. Neither was He afraid when He went to meet the armed band so that He could be captured and there was no weakness in Him when He offered Himself to the chains and the crowd of persecutors fell to the ground because they could not endure His majesty. He could not have feared the pain of wounds, for what horror could the nail that was driven into His hand have had for Him Who, by His mere touch, restored the ear of the servant which Peter had cut off?[290]

The heretics concluded that His nature was weak because His soul was sorrowful unto death. But how did they explain His words to Judas, as he departed to betray Him: "Now is the Son of Man glorified" (John 13:31). If the passion was to glorify Him, how did the fear of the passion

---

[288] *Ibid.* X 24. Neque enim tum, cum sitivit aut esurivit aut flevit, bibisse Dominus aut manducasse aut doluisse monstratus est: sed ad demonstrandam corporis veritatem, corporis consuetudo suscepta est, ita ut naturae nostrae consuetudine consuetudini sit corporis satisfactum. Vel cum potum et cibum accepit, non se necessitati corporis, sed consuetudini tribuit (PL 10.364A–B).

[289] *Ibid.* X 25–26.

[290] *Ibid.* X 27–28.

make Him sorrowful? It could be thought that He feared to such an extent that He prayed that the cup be taken from Him (Mark 14:36) but, according to Hilary, this view is refuted by His words: "Shall I not drink the cup which the Father has given Me?" (John 18:11). The cry of the Lord: "God, My God, why hast Thou forsaken Me?" (Mark 15:34) is no proof that because of the humiliation of the cross the Father withdrew His help from the Son, for Christ also said: "Hereafter you shall see the Son of Man sitting at the right hand of power and coming with the clouds of heaven" (Matt. 26:64).[291] Finally it can be asserted that the words: "Father, into Thy hands I commend My Spirit" (Luke 23:46), proved that He feared the descent into the lower world. But His words to the thief on the cross: "Amen I say to thee, today you shall be with Me in paradise" (Luke 23:43), proves that the power of His nature cannot be restricted not even by the region of the infernal world.[292]

The weakness of a corporeal nature was not in the nature of His body and although suffering was inflicted upon His body, He did not feel pain. Although the form of our body was in the Lord, our sinful weakness was not in the body of Him Who did not share our origin because the virgin brought Him forth by the conception of the Holy Spirit. Mary performed the function of her sex and begot a body from herself but one which was conceived by the Spirit. That body was truly a body because it was born of the virgin but it was above the weakness of our own bodies because it had its beginning from a spiritual conception.[293]

The heretics thought that the words: "My soul is sad, even unto death" (Matt. 26:38) proved the weakness of His nature. To this objection Hilary replies by pointing out the difference between being "sad even unto death" and "because of death." The latter means that death is the cause of the sadness while in the former case the sadness is removed by death. To understand the cause of the sadness of the Lord, the events preceding and following this declaration must be borne in mind. During the Passover supper the Lord declared that all His disciples would be offended because of Him. Peter protested but Christ said that Peter would deny Him thrice. Then He took Peter, James and John with Him and declared that He was sad unto death. He left them and prayed: "My Father, if it is possible, let this cup pass away from Me; yet not as I will, but as Thou

---

[291] *Ibid.* X 29–31.

[292] *Ibid.* X 34.

[293] *Ibid.* X 35. Genuit (=virgo) etenim ex se corpus, sed quod conceptum esset ex Spiritu; habens quidem in se sui corporis veritatem, sed non habens naturae infirmitatem: dum et corpus illud corporis veritas est quod generatur ex virgine; et extra corporis nostri infirmitatem est, quod spiritalis conceptionis sumpsit exordium (PL 10.371B–C).

wilt" (Matt. 26:39). He did not pray that it may not be with Him, but that it may pass away from Him. "And He came to His disciples and found them sleeping and He said to Peter: could you not watch one hour with Me? Watch and pray that you enter not into temptation. The spirit indeed is willing but the flesh is weak" (Matt. 26:40,41). Through the weakness of the flesh the disciples were offended and the Lord therefore did not pray for Himself and was not sad on His own account, but He warned the disciples to be vigilant so that the cup of passion should not overwhelm them and He prayed that it might pass from Him so that it might not remain with them.[294]

Therefore, says Hilary, the Lord was sad unto death because at His death the earthquake, the darkness, the rent veil, the opened graves and resurrection of the dead, would again strengthen the faith of the apostles which had been shaken by the arrest of the Lord, the scourging and all the events which culminated in His crucifixion. Knowing that all this would come to an end with His passion, He was sad unto death for He knew that this cup could not pass away unless He drank it.[295]

The explanation which Hilary offers to the question of why the Lord, after praying for a third time, returned and said to the disciples: "Sleep on now and take your rest" (Matt. 26:45), is to be found in Luke (22:43) where it is said that an angel stood by Him comforting Him. The angel was sent to watch over the apostles and when the Lord had been comforted by him so that He no longer was sad on their account, He, without fear of sadness, said "sleep on." Hilary did not overlook the fact that in some of the Latin and Greek manuscripts nothing was said of the coming of the angel. On the other hand, if this text was maintained, he asserted that the heretics should not conclude that this confirmed the Lord's

---

[294] *Ibid.* X 36–38. Irenaeus, *adv. Haer.* III 31,2 (ed. Harvey II p. 122), cited many texts to prove that Christ had indeed taken true flesh from Mary and in this context quoted Matt. 26:38. Tertullian, *adv. Prax.* 27 (ed. Evans pp. 124–5), stated that Jesus Christ was both God and man; He was two natures in the one Person for He manifested deeds of power, but on the other hand the flesh experienced sufferings, e.g. He wept, and was "sad unto death." Watson, *op. cit.*, p. lxxvi, called Hilary's explanation of Matt. 26:38–39 an ingenious misinterpretation. Cf. Galtier, *op. cit.*, p. 134: une exégèse aussi arbitraire qu'ingénieuse.

[295] *Ibid.* X 39. Cf. *Comm. in Matt.* XXXI 4–5 (PL 9.1067B–1068B), where Hilary gave the same explanation of Jesus' words in Gethsemane. Athanasius, *Or. c. Ar.* III 34 (PG 26.396A–B), emphasized that Christ suffered "for us in the flesh." He taught that the Word Himself is impassible by nature, and yet because of the flesh which He put on, it was said that He suffered. Cf. III 55 (PG 26.437B). In III 57 (PG 26.441B–C) Athanasius said of Matt. 26:39 that for the sake of the flesh Christ combined His own will with human weakness so that by overcoming weakness, He might make man undaunted in face of death. Cf. van Haarlem, *op. cit.*, pp. 154–8, who concluded that traces of Platonism are found in Athanasius' attempt to combine the Word and the body.

weakness so that He needed the help and comfort of an angel. The Creator of the angels did not need the support of His creatures. This comforting must also be explained in the same way as His sadness. He was sad for us, on our account and He must also have been comforted for us, on our account. Nor is the fact that He sweated blood to be attributed to His weakness, for it is contrary to nature to sweat blood. The bloody sweat does however, confirm the reality of His body.[296]

The Gospels mutually complement one another, for John wrote that He had prayed: "Holy Father, keep them in Thy name. While I was with them I kept them in Thy name: those whom Thou hast given Me I have kept" (John 17:11,12). The prayer was not for Himself but for His apostles and He was not sad on His own account because He warned them to pray that they be not tempted. The angel was not sent to Him Who if He had wished, could bring down twelve thousand legions from heaven. It was not for Himself that the Lord prayed that the suffering be taken away but He begged the Father to protect the apostles during His coming passion.[297]

There is no anxiety of human fear in that nature which is above man and a body which does not trace its origin to the elements of the earth is not subject to the ills of an earthly body. The soul which is joined to the body vivifies the body to feel the pain which afflicts it and when the soul in the body is not from an earthly origin, a body is formed which has its own sensation and life in its sufferings so that it ceases to feel the pain which it endures. But at times even earthly bodies are indifferent to pain and fear. Hilary quotes the examples of the Jewish youths who were un-afraid of the flames of the Babylonian furnace. The men who threw them into the furnace were burnt because of the great heat but the youths were unharmed. Daniel did not fear the lions' den. The apostles rejoiced in suffering for the name of Christ. Martyrs were executed while singing hymns and thus the consciousness of faith took away the weakness of nature so that they did not experience pain. Could it then be ascribed to Jesus Christ, the Lord of glory, Who had the power to heal the blind, the ill and the man with a withered hand, that His body was in that weakness of pain from which the spirit of faith in Him had rescued the martyrs?[298]

The Only-begotten God suffered all the weaknesses of our sufferings which pressed upon Him, but He suffered them in the power of His own

[296] *Ibid.* X 40–41.
[297] *Ibid.* X 42–43.
[298] *Ibid.* X 44–46.

nature just as He was born in the power of His own nature, for although He was born He did not lose His omnipotent nature through His birth. It is thus a mistake to think that He experienced pain because He suffered. He bore our sins while He assumed the body of our sins and yet He Himself did not sin. He was sent in the likeness of our sinful flesh. He endured pain for us but He did not endure pain with the feeling of our pain because He Who was found in the appearance of man, with a body which could feel pain, did not have the nature that could feel pain, for while His appearance was that of a man, His origin was not that of a man for He was born by the conception of the Holy Spirit.[299] Paul knew nothing about the fear of pain in Christ but only knew of His passion as a triumph: "Forgiving you all sins, cancelling the handwriting that was against us in the decree which was hostile to us, taking it away, nailing it to the cross, stripping Himself of the flesh, He led the principalities and powers away, triumphing over them in Himself" (Col. 2:13-15).[300]

The statement: "God, My God, why hast Thou forsaken Me" (Matt. 27:46) was considered by the heretics to be a very important proof of Christ's weakness because it was His own words. Hilary contends that this deduction of theirs is opposed by the whole tenor of all which the Lord said. He Who hastened to death, Who was to be glorified by it, with all these blessed expectations, He could not have feared death.[301]

Hilary mentions different heretical views, e.g. that: God the Word was merged into the soul and did not remain God the Word; that Christ did not exist before His birth from Mary because Jesus Christ was a man with merely an ordinary soul and body. All these views have been rejected by the Church which has been inspired by the teaching of the apostles.[302] Hilary reminds us of the limitations of human understanding and he exhorts man not to strive to know more than is possible because in the end,

---

[299] *Ibid.* X 47. Passus igitur unigenitus Deus est omnes incurrentes in se passionum nostrarum infirmitates; sed passus virtute naturae suae, ut et virtute naturae suae natus est: neque enim, cum natus sit, non tenuit omnipotentiae suae in nativitate naturam (PL 10.380B). Fallitur ergo humanae aestimationis opinio, putans hunc dolere quod patitur. Portans enim peccata nostra, peccati nostri scilicet corpus assumens, tamen ipse non peccat. Missus namque est in peccati carnis similitudine; portans quidem in carne peccata, sed nostra. Et pro nobis dolet, non et doloris nostri dolet sensu: quia et habitu ut homo repertus, habens in se doloris corpus, sed non habens naturam dolendi, dum et ut hominis habitus est, et origo non hominis est, nato eo de conceptione Spiritus sancti (PL 10.381A).

[300] *Ibid.* X 48.

[301] *Ibid.* X 49. Tertullian cited this text to prove that it was not the Father as Son Who suffered, but it was the Son Who as a different Person from the Father, cried out to His Father, *adv. Prax.* 25; 26; 30 (ed. Evans pp. 121; 123; 128).

[302] *Ibid.* X 50-52.

overstraining his faculties, he loses the power of attaining that which was possible to attain.[303]

Hilary cites two examples in which it is said that Christ wept, viz. Luke 19:41 where He wept for Jerusalem and John 11:35 when Jesus wept at the grave of Lazarus. Hilary emphasizes that there is no doubt that Jesus Christ truly wept. The problem is to know what it was that wept in Him: God the Word or His human soul? It is also difficult to ascertain what prompted Him to weep in the case of Lazarus. It was not because of his death because this was for the glory of God (John 11:4). Neither did Christ weep because He was not with Lazarus at the time of his death because He said that He rejoiced that He was absent so that the disciples might believe in Him (John 11:15). Thus there seems no necessity for His tears and yet He wept. It is not characteristic of Him Who was about to give life to Lazarus to weep nor of Him Who was to be glorified to feel pain and yet He wept and felt pain.[304]

In trying to find a solution to this problem it is evident that Hilary acknowledges the fact that in these matters we are dealing with the mystery of the incarnation of the Son of God and that it is impossible to explain precisely all the aspects of His Person and conduct. As Hilary puts it: "The Lord accomplishes and performs actions that are not known in spite of the knowledge of them, actions of which we are not ignorant but which cannot be understood, for the actions are real but the power behind them is a mystery." Hilary substantiates this statement by the Lord's words: "For this reason the Father loves Me because I lay down My life[305] that I may take it up again. No one takes it from Me, but I lay it down of Myself. I have the power to lay it down, and I have the power to take it up again. This commandment I received from the Father" (John 10:17–18).

Hilary thereupon makes contradictory statements to stress the problem with which he is dealing. The Lord said that He lays down His soul of Himself. Hilary asserts that there is no doubt about the fact that Christ is God the Word. On the other hand the Son of Man is composed of a soul and a body. But who laid down the soul? It could not be the body because without the soul it is lifeless. If it is contended that God the Word laid down His soul in order to take it up again, it must first be proved that God the Word died, that is, that He was without life and feeling

---

[303] *Ibid.* X 53.

[304] *Ibid.* X 55–56. Non est vivificaturi flere, nec glorificandi dolere: et tamen vivificat, qui et flevit, et doluit (PL 10.388B).

[305] It is evident that *anima* in this text and in Hilary's explanation which follows can be translated either as "life" or as "soul."

because He took up again His soul in order to live. On the other hand no one will assign to God a soul. It is said that God's soul hates the sabbaths and the new moons (Isaiah 1:14) but this expression is used in the same sense in which arms, eyes and a heart are ascribed to God. God is not infused with life in a corporeal manner through the activity of an interior soul but He Himself is life. God therefore could not lay down His soul to death and then take it up again to live.[306]

The solution to the problem according to Hilary, is to recognize as God He Who is recognized as man, and to recognize as man He Who is recognized as God. Jesus Christ must not be divided because the Word was made flesh. It must not be thought that He was buried, of Whom it is known that He rose from the dead; it must not be doubted that He Whose burial dare not be denied, rose from the dead. Jesus Christ died and at the moment of death cried out: "My God, why hast Thou forsaken Me." Yet He also said: "Verily I say to thee, this day thou shalt be with Me in paradise." He Who promised paradise to the thief declared in a loud voice: "Father, into Thy hands I commend My spirit."[307] Hilary clearly alluded to the two natures in one Person Jesus Christ. It cannot be said that God died and human nature cannot bring itself back to life: yet Hilary states that it is known that Jesus Christ died, was buried and rose again.

Hilary says that it is one and the same Lord Jesus Christ, the Word made flesh, Who expressed Himself in all the above-mentioned words. He is man when He says that He is abandoned to death, but while still man, reigns as God in paradise. While He reigns in paradise, He commends His spirit to the Father but as Son of Man He surrenders His spirit, which He had commended to the Father, to death. In the mystery of the Son of God and the Son of Man, He Who reigns dies and He Who dies, reigns. Christ therefore wept, not for Himself but for us, to prove the reality of His assumed manhood. He did not die for Himself, but for us so that the life of mortal men may be renewed through the death of the immortal God. It is one and the same Person Who died and reigns, Who was buried and rose again and He Who descended to earth was the same as He Who ascended to heaven.[308]

The apostolic doctrine, according to Hilary, was taught not by the knowledge of the flesh but by the gift of the Spirit since the preaching of Christ was a stumbling-block to the Jews and foolishness to the Gentiles (1 Cor. 1:23). To the believer Christ is the power and the wisdom of God,

[306] *Ibid.* X 57–59.
[307] *Ibid.* X 60.
[308] *Ibid.* X 62–63.

but a wisdom unknown to the world and not understood by the wise men of the world (1 Cor. 2:7–8).[309] The apostle expressed the mystery of this doctrine as follows: "For though He was crucified through weakness, yet He lives through the power of God" (2 Cor. 13:4). In the same Person there was both weakness in suffering and the power of God to live again and therefore He Who suffered and lived is neither another Person nor one separated from Himself.[310] Hilary thus emphasizes that it is one Person, Jesus Christ Who died and Who arose again and he thereby rejects any idea that Jesus died but that the Word, Christ, lived and ascended to heaven.

Hilary finally extols the true faith which is found in and confirmed by the Scriptures. He quotes the words of Paul: "I delivered unto you ... that Christ died for our sins according to the Scriptures, and that He was buried and rose again the third day according to the Scriptures" (1 Cor. 15:3–4).[311] Through faith man knows that the laws which govern man are no hindrance to the power of God.[312] The perception of the human mind cannot attain to knowledge of the divine but neither does a religious faith doubt the works of God.[313]

To summarize Hilary's teaching on the passibility of Christ: he said that man experiences pain because of the connection between the matter of the body with the soul (14). Christ had a heavenly origin in so far as He was not conceived in the same way as other human beings but by the Holy Spirit. Hilary emphasized that Christ, although He took His own soul,[314] received from Mary all that women give in birth (15;22). He was true man and true God (19). Christ however, was free from sin (25–26) yet He took our sins and human needs (55–56; 67). He drank and ate, not of necessity, but according to human custom (24) to prove His true humanity. He was not subject to the ills of earthly bodies because His origin was different from ours.

Hilary seems to make contradictory statements on the question of whether or not Christ suffered pain. On the one hand he said that Jesus Christ could not feel pain, but he also emphatically stated that Christ did weep and feel pain. Hilary distinguished beween *pati* and *dolere*. Christ had a body to suffer but not the nature to suffer (47). His body therefore

---

[309] *Ibid.* X 64.
[310] *Ibid.* X 66.
[311] *Ibid.* X 67 (PL 10.394C).
[312] *Ibid.* X 68 (PL 10.396A).
[313] *Ibid.* X 69 (PL 10.396B–C).
[314] Hilary has been accused of Docetism because of this statement, cf. Harnack, *op. cit.*, p. 316 n. 2; Loofs, "Hilarius," p. 61. Hilary however, held the creationist view that even the ordinary human soul is never derived from its human parents.

could undergo the *impetus passionis* without feeling the *dolor passionis*. He experienced the impulse of pain, but did not suffer the natural effect of this impulse. He had a true body, but a suffering according to His own nature (23; 35). Hilary stated that Christ truly wept (55), but that it is wrong to assume that He felt pain (47). He Who was conceived in His own way suffered in His own way, just as a weapon goes through water without the water experiencing pain, because it does not have the nature to experience pain (23).

Most scholars agree that Hilary taught that Christ's nature was not naturally subjected to the feeling of pain. A group of scholars hold the view that Christ therefore, according to Hilary, experienced no bodily suffering.[315] As Smulders said, torments were truly inflicted upon His body, but pain did not reach His soul.[316] Galtier put it as follows: "On peut et l'on doit dire que le Christ les (coups) a endurés: en ce sens, il a souffert; la passion a exercé sur lui son office d'expiation"; but like water and air, Christ did not experience pain.[317] Giamberardini thought that Hilary taught that it was not necessary that Christ suffered and felt pain but that we know and believe that Christ did suffer. Giamberardini wrote that because Christ was God: "Potuit pati, quin doluerit, quia praeter verum hominem, verus quoque Deus est."[318]

Another group of scholars say that according to Hilary, Christ could not suffer pain by nature, but by an act of His will He did suffer and experience pain.[319] Dorner even said that if Christ could not suffer at all, that would mean that Christ was restricted.[320] Beck however, asserted that by nature Christ could experience pain, but that He never did because the cause of suffering in human beings, namely sin, was absent in His case. When Christ did suffer for us, it required an act of His will.[321] Beck maintained that if Hilary taught that Christ could not suffer by nature, Hilary was not free from docetism.[322] Kelly agreed that "there was a decidedly Docetic strain in Hilary's thought."[323] On the other hand Harnack[324] overemphasized the importance of the expression which

---

[315] Baltzer, *Christologie*, p. 32; Watson, *op. cit.*, p. lxxvi; Rauschen, *Theol. Quart.*, p. 433.

[316] Smulders, *op. cit.*, pp. 204–205.

[317] Galtier, *op. cit.*, p. 135.

[318] Giamberardini, "De incarnatione Verbi," pp. 9–12.

[319] Förster, *art. cit.*, p. 665; Kelly, *op. cit.*, p. 335.

[320] Dorner, *op. cit.*, p. 1056. Cf. pp. 1052–1055 where he said that every suffering was an act of Christ's will.

[321] Beck, *Kirchliche Studien*, pp. 98–9.

[322] Beck, *ZkTh*, p. 110.

[323] Kelly, *op. cit.*, p. 335.

[324] Harnack, *op. cit.*, p. 317 n. 1.

Hilary used in *De Trin.* X 18 (corpus caeleste). In the whole context of Hilary's work (if it is borne in mind that he maintained that Christ was truly man) the corpus caeleste only indicates that Christ had a different origin than the ordinary human being. Hilary is not a docetist in the strict sense of the word, because he emphasized that Christ had a true body and even that Christ died. Some of Hilary's ideas on this subject are found in later Aphthartodocetic circles.

Thus it can be said that Hilary maintained that Christ did suffer, but in His own way, in accordance with His body which was conceived by the Holy Spirit. Christ did not sin and therefore could not experience pain in the same way as man who falls into sin and experiences pain because of his weak soul. Christ did suffer for mankind yet He Who wept at the grave of Lazarus was to be glorified by restoring Lazarus to life and yet "et flevit, et doluit" (56). How should we understand this? Hilary replies: it is a sacramentum that Christ wept (55) and that Christ Who reigns in paradise, died (62); but it must nevertheless be believed, for it is "according to the Scriptures" (67).

i. The equality of the Father and the Son

Hilary deplored the fact that because of all the heresies the one faith of which Paul had written in Eph. 4:5, was no longer accepted by all. Hilary emphasizes that whoever preaches Christ other than He is, namely, that He is not the Son or that He is not God, preaches another Christ.[325] The heretics indeed, preach another Lord Christ, as well as another God the Father. For the Father is no Begetter but a Creator and Christ is not the Begotten, but a creature. Christ is no true God and God is no Father.[326] The Arians stressed all the incomparable attributes of God so that by eliminating any comparison with Him, it could be asserted that the Only-begotten God had a weaker nature and one that was different from that of God. Hilary however, argued that if the Only-begotten God is the Image of the unborn God, then the divinity of the perfect and complete nature of God is in Him and through this He becomes the image of the true nature. The apostle declared that Christ is the Image of the invisible God (Col. 1:15).[327]

The Arians quoted some texts to prove their assertion that the Son was not equal to God the Father. The Lord said: "I ascend to My Father

[325] *De Trin.* XI 2 (PL 10.401A).
[326] *Ibid.* XI 4 (PL 10.401C–402A).
[327] *Ibid.* XI 5.

and your Father, and to My God and your God" (John 20:17). According to them the Son thus has the same weakness as a human being, for in having the same Father we are made equal as sons and in the service of the same God we are equal as servants. We however, are of created origin and slaves by our nature and because there is a common Father and God between us and the Son, He in common with our nature is a creature and a servant. The Arians also cited: "O God, Thy God hath anointed Thee" (Ps 44(45):8), to prove that Christ did not possess the Divine nature.[328]

Hilary begins his refutation by stating that he who does not know the God Who was born, is ignorant of the God Christ. But if it is confessed that God was born, it follows that He possessed the Divine nature because He had no other Author but God. Hilary quotes a number of statements made by the Lord Jesus Christ which showed that the confession that He was born did not offer any insult to His Divinity and that His reverent obedience did not infringe upon His sovereign nature: Christ as the Begotten did not withhold the homage due to His Begetter but He was also fully conscious of His participation in that nature of His Father, e.g. the Lord's words: "He who has seen Me has also seen the Father" illustrate His consciousness of possessing the Divine nature but: "The words that I speak I speak not from Myself" shows that He was indebted to His Begetter for what He said.[329]

Because of the Incarnation, He Who was already the Father of the divine birth, also was the Lord of Him Who had assumed the form of a slave, for He Who was in the form of God was also found in the form of a slave. The Father therefore is His Lord for no other reason than that He, because of the Incarnation, was a slave. When Jesus Christ uttered the words under discussion, He spoke as a servant to servants and His words may therefore not be applied to His other nature which has nothing of a slave in it. In this sense, as incarnated man, God is His Father and the Father of men, His God and the God of servants. Hilary draws attention to the words which precede those which were cited by the heretics, viz.: "But go to My brethren and say to them: I ascend to My Father and your Father... ." Hilary concludes that "His brethren" is surely not understood to refer to His form as God but to His form as a servant. Thus according to the dispensation He has brethren and in this sense Paul called Him not only the first-born from the dead (Col. 1:18) but also the first-born among many brethren (Rom. 8:29). God has brethren according to the flesh because the Word was made flesh and dwelt amongst us, but the

[328] *Ibid.* XI 10.
[329] *Ibid.* XI 11–12.

Only-begotten God, unique as the Only-begotten, has no brothers.[330] The Son thus has God as His Father by reason of His nature but also by reason of His earthly state. For God is the Father of all since all things are in Him and through Him and He is therefore Father to the Only-begotten because the Word was made flesh. His Fatherhood also extends to Him Who was with God in the beginning as God the Word.[331]

The words which were spoken by David: "God, Thy God has anointed Thee with the oil of gladness above Thy fellows" (Ps. 44(45):8), do not according to Hilary, refer to the Word Who was in the beginning God. This is clear from the fact that we are His fellows only by the assumption which made Him flesh, and God the Word Who was God in the beginning had no need to be anointed. The Only-begotten is our brother and fellow only in so far as the Word was made flesh and dwelt among us.[332] Thus the words cited by the Arians must be ascribed to the Son in the mystery of the dispensation and do not prove His inequality with God, the Father.

Another text which the Arians quoted was: "But when He saith, all things are put in subjection, He is excepted Who subjected all things unto Him. But when all things have been subjected to Him, then He Himself will be subjected to Him, Who subjected all things to Him, that God may be all in all" (1 Cor. 15:27-28). According to them this meant that Christ is included in the common subjection of all to God and by the condition of subjection loses His Divinity: surrendering His Kingdom He is no longer King: Christ loses His power at the end.[333] Hilary then examines each of the three points which are disputed: the end, the delivering and the subjection.

From different texts Hilary proves that the end is not a final destruction and dissolution but a perfection: "Christ is the end of the law" (Rom. 10:4), and it is known that He did not come to destroy the law but to fulfil it (Matt. 5:17). In the same sense the Lord exhorted us to remain faithful to the end: "Blessed is he who shall persevere to the end" (Matt.

[330] *Ibid.* XI 13-15. Tertullian twice cited John 20:17 to prove that the Father and the Son are different Persons and that the Son could not have been the Father. The Father could not go to the Father! *Adv. Prax.* 25; 28 (ed. Evans pp. 121; 126). Novatian refuted the same heretical view as Tertullian and among other texts, he quoted John 20:17 to prove that the Son is the Second Person in the Godhead, *de Trin.* XXVI 146 (ed. Weyer p. 168).

[331] *Ibid.* XI 16.

[332] *Ibid.* XI 18-20. In *de Trin.* IV 35 (see p. 59 n. 32). Hilary used this text to prove the distinction within the Godhead and concluded that the Father and the Son are Both mentioned in this text by the same name "God" and that They are one in majesty. The Son was born from God to share the Godhead.

[333] *Ibid.* XI 21 and 25. Tertullian used this text to prove that the Father and the Son are two Persons and that the monarchy is not harmed although it is with the Son Who will restore it to the Father, *adv. Prax.* 4 (ed. Evans p. 92).

10:22). Paul warned us of the end of the wicked: "Whose end is ruin ... but our expectation is in heaven" (Phil. 2:19,20). If the end is interpreted as a dissolution then the blessed and the godless, true worship and impiety would be treated equally. The end of the godless cannot be destruction for that would mean that they were not punished. The end is therefore a culmination, a perfection and a condition which is unchangeable.[334]

Hilary establishes that if the delivery of the kingdom to the Father is to be understood as a loss of ownership and that the Son by delivering the kingdom, will no longer possess it, it follows that the Father lost possession of the things which He handed over to the Son, for the Lord said: "All things have been delivered to Me by My Father" (Luke 10:22) and "All power in heaven and on earth has been given to Me" (Matt. 28:18). If the Father did not cease to possess what He had delivered to the Son, it can be assumed that the Son will retain what He will deliver to the Father. Hilary's conclusion is that only the dispensation explains why the Father still possesses what He delivered to the Son and why the Son will not forfeit what He will give to the Father.[335]

On the question of the subjection Hilary states that it is not meant in the sense of subordination of servitude to domination or weakness to strength: i.e. qualities which are mutually contrary. The Son is not subject to the Father because of a diversity arising from a different nature. The apostle said that when all things are subject to the Son, then He will be made subject to the Father and with this "then" He was referring to the temporal dispensation. No other explanation of the subjection should be given, for that would lead to the assumption that because He will be subjected at some future date, He is not subject at the moment and that would make Him a hostile, impious rebel who was subdued into subservience by the necessity of time. The Lord however, frequently declared that He did not come to do His own will but that of the Father (John 6:38, 8:29; Matt. 26:39; Phil. 2:8). The subjection of the Son is not a sign of a new obedience but one of the dispensation of the mystery, for the obedience already exists and the subjection is an event within time. The subjection is therefore a revelation of the mystery.[336]

The Lord Jesus Christ sits at the right hand of God and God has placed all things at His feet, all the authority and power and dominion; and the apostle described the future events as if they had already taken place

---

[334] *Ibid.* XI 28.
[335] *Ibid.* XI 29.
[336] *Ibid.* XI 30.

(Eph. 1:19–22) so that we may perceive the unchangeable power of Christ.[337] The Son subjects the powers to Himself in the sense that God subjects them to the Son for in all the works of the Son, we see the works of God (cf. John 6:44; 14:6).[338] The last enemy, death, is also conquered by Him (1 Cor. 15:26) through the resurrection from the dead; "when the body of our humiliation will be conformed to the body of His glory, according to the works of His power, by which He is able to subject all things to Himself" (Phil. 3:21).[339]

When we have been conformed to His body we may share the splendour with which He reigns in the body. Hilary states that the glory of the body of Christ was shown to the apostles by His Transfiguration on the mountain (Matt. 17:1–2). The Lord promised His apostles that they would share in this glory of His: "Then the righteous will shine forth like the sun in the Kingdom of their Father" (Matt. 13:43).[340] Then He will deliver the Kingdom to God the Father not in the sense that He will renounce His power by delivering it, but rather we, conformed to the glory of His body, will become the Kingdom of God. Hilary draws attention to the fact that Paul said: "He will deliver the Kingdom" (1 Cor. 15:24), and not "He will deliver His Kingdom," that is, deliver to God those who have been made the Kingdom through the glorification of His body. He will deliver us into the Kingdom, as it is said in the Gospel: "Come, blessed of My Father, take possession of the Kingdom prepared for you from the foundation of the world" (Matt. 25:34).[341]

Hilary's explanation of the phrase: "That God may be all in all" (1 Cor. 15:28) is that in accordance with the divine economy of salvation, the Son became the Mediator between God and man. As a result of this dispensation He has the nature of flesh and by the subjection He will receive everything that belongs to God and He will become God not in part but wholly and entirely. The end will be the time when no trace of His earthly body will remain in Him and He Who previously had two natures will then only be God not by casting the body aside but by transforming it through the subjection; not by losing it through dissolution but by its change through the glorification. Thus He will gain our human nature for God rather than that God lost His Divinity by His assumption of our human nature. His subjection will not end His existence but it ensures that God will be all in all.[342]

337 *Ibid.* XI 31.
338 *Ibid.* XI 33.
339 *Ibid.* XI 35.
340 *Ibid.* XI 37–38.
341 *Ibid.* XI 39.
342 *Ibid.* XI 40. Cf. 41.

Hilary criticizes the heretics for their conclusion that the subjection of the Son to God the Father would make the Father the God Who is all in all, implying that the subjection of the Son will be necessary to complete the perfection of the Father. From this deduction it could be said that God would only become perfect by the coming of the fulness of time. Hilary states that it seems as sacrilegious to answer such objections as to support them. If God was capable of progress He must always be incomplete because a nature which is capable of progress always finds that there remains room for progress. The pious mind knows that there is nothing lacking in God and that He is complete.[343] The subjection of the Son will not make God all in all nor can anything make Him perfect, of Whom the Apostle said: "For of Him and through Him and in Him are all things" (Rom. 11:36).[344]

Although the Son of God was in the form of God, He was seen in the form of a slave but He has returned to the glory of God the Father. In the end the believers gain, for they are made conformable to the glory of the body of God; they will be renewed unto the knowledge of God and created again in the image of the Creator, as the apostle said: "Having stripped off the old man with his deeds and put on the new man which is being renewed unto the knowledge of God after the image of Him Who created him" (Col. 3:9,10). Thus is man made in the perfect image of God. Through true worship of God he advances to eternity and through eternity he will remain in the image of his Creator.[345]

In this way Hilary thought that he had refuted the views of the heretics. He began his work by refuting the confession contained in the letter Arius wrote to Alexander but Hilary also attacked other statements made by the heretics at this time. Hilary always appealed to the Scriptures to prove his doctrine and he endeavoured to gather all the Scriptural evidence concerning a certain problem so that an opinion could be formed on this basis. It has been said that by the time Hilary wrote his work every text of Scripture which could be made applicable to the point in dispute had been used to the utmost and that Hilary's treatment of the Scriptural evidence is very complete.[346]

---

[343] *Ibid.* XI 43–44 (PL 10.428B–429B).
[344] *Ibid.* XI 47.
[345] *Ibid.* XI 49.
[346] Watson, *op. cit.*, p. lxiv.

k. Conclusion

In this section Hilary's refutation of the heretics was treated and his explanation of certain texts was compared with that of his predecessors Irenaeus (*Adv. Haer.*), Tertullian (*Adv. Prax.*) and Novatian (*De Trin.*) and with the *Orationes contra Arianos* of his contemporary, Athanasius. Cases are only quoted where Hilary used the same texts as the above-mentioned writers with more or less the same interpretation or where the same theological problem is concerned. Thus to some extent could be ascertained whether the texts which Hilary discussed were generally given the same interpretation. It is only possible to reach a provisional conclusion because it is necessary to study all the writings which were written during the Arian struggle before a definite conclusion can be justified.

Some of the texts quoted by the Western theologians were used in arguments connected with the specific theological problems of their own day. Irenaeus quoted a text to prove that Jesus Christ was one Person and the Son of God (n. 217). Tertullian and Novatian had to refute the view that the Father was not the same Person as the Son (For Tertullian see n. 21, 141, 149, 209, 246, 255, 301, 330, 333; for Novatian see n. 21, 212, 255, 330). Novatian cited many texts to prove that Christ could have made certain remarks only if He had been God (see n. 72, 131, 141, 207, 221, 237, 241).

In the sections in which Hilary proved that there is a distinction of Persons within the Godhead and that the Other Person is truly God, many resemblances to the above-mentioned writers are to be found. In the creation of man, Hilary used the same argument as Tertullian and Novatian (n. 21). Hilary's argument that the Angel Who spoke to Hagar was the Son of God, had been used by Novatian (n. 24). Novatian also used the argument that not God the Father (Who is invisible) was seen as Angel, but God the Son (n. 25, 43). Hilary saw the receiving of the Son by Abraham as a foreshadowing of the Incarnation—a thought already propounded by Novatian (n. 25). Hilary said that the Son of God destroyed Sodom and Gomorrah (cf. Irenaeus and Novatian, n. 27). Jacob struggled with a Man (God) (cf. Tertullian, Novatian and Athanasius, n. 49). Ps. 44:8 was interpreted by Hilary as an indication of a distinction within the Godhead (Irenaeus and Tertullian, n. 32) as was Isaiah 45:11–16 (Tertullian and Athanasius, n. 35). Thus Hilary used traditional texts to prove his point, although he also used texts which were not employed in this context by the earlier writers in the West.

A striking difference of interpretation between Hilary and Athanasius is found in n. 30, where Athanasius said that God spoke through the angel while Hilary said that this Angel was the Lord.

In the argument as to whether Christ is the true Son of God, Hilary quoted Matt. 11:27 in the same sense in which Irenaeus used it (n. 64) although the text actually speaks for itself. Both Athanasius and Hilary used the argument that the name "father" implies a son (n. 60) but these two Church Fathers differ in their interpretation of the sonship of man (n. 85). In this section therefore Hilary mainly developed his own arguments.

In proving that the Son is God by nature Hilary and Irenaeus quoted Ex. 7:1 to show the difference between Moses, who was only named god, and the true Son of God (n. 97). Tertullian and Novatian quoted Ex. 7:1 and Ps. 81:6 and stated that if human beings were on occasions called gods, the Son of God could not be denied the name of God (n. 97). Hilary explained John 10:30 in the same way as Tertullian, Novatian and Athanasius (n. 141). In n. 131 Hilary used the same argument as Tertullian that the Son is conscious of doing the work which the Father does. Tertullian and Hilary said that the Father becomes visible in the Son by the deeds of power which the Son performs (n. 146). Tertullian quoted John 14:11 to prove that the Father and the Son are two different Persons, while Hilary developed his view of the mutual indwelling of the Father and the Son (n. 149). There are many resemblances between Athanasius and Hilary in their interpretation of texts in this section. Both said that the birth of the Son is a mystery known to God alone (n. 106, 120) and they gave an explanation of the difference between a creature and the begotten Son (n. 127). Athanasius and Hilary also drew a parallel between the godlessness of the Arians and the Jews, but Hilary thought the godlessness of the Arians to be greater than that of the Jews (n. 138). Athanasius and Hilary both taught the unity of the Divine essence (n. 143).

In connection with the eternity of the Son it was seen that Tertullian thought that the Father did not always have a Son, while Novatian said that the Father was always Father. Hilary taught the eternity of the Son in his early work on the Gospel of Matthew, but in *De Trin.* taught the eternal generation of the Son (n. 159). The text in Prov. 8:22 was seen by Hilary and Athanasius as referring to the Incarnation of the Son (n. 181) while Tertullian thought that the text referred to the establishment of Wisdom and that the world was created later through Wisdom as the Word (n. 181, 159).

In proving the unity of the Father and the Son, Hilary used texts which were similarly interpreted by other Christian writers. Luke 4:18 had been used by Tertullian to indicate the Three Persons in the Godhead (n. 209). Rom. 9:5 was also quoted by Irenaeus, Tertullian and Novatian to illustrate that Christ was God and although Athanasius also used it in this sense, he also stressed the eternity of Christ by using this text (n. 217). While Novatian quoted John 5:19 and 26 to prove the Divinity of Christ, Hilary thought it indicated the unity of the same nature (n. 221). Novatian Hilary and Athanasius thought that Phil. 2:6–11 proved the Divinity of Christ (n. 225). Tertullian, Novatian and Hilary thought the term "first-born" in Col. 1:15 referred to the generation of the Son before the creation, but Athanasius thought it referred to the incarnation of Christ (n. 226). Referring to several texts Hilary and Athanasius stressed the fact that the same properties were attributed to the Father and the Son (n. 205, 207, 214) and that Their oneness is in the essence or nature (n. 212).

Novatian, Hilary and Athanasius interpreted John 17:3 as a proof of the Divinity of Christ (n. 241). John 14:28 was quoted by Tertullian and Novatian to prove that the Father is not identical to the Son, while Athanasius and Hilary thought it taught that the Father and the Son have the same nature (n. 255). Athanasius and Hilary emphasized that the orthodox faith confesses that there is only one, true God (n. 240). With reference to the text about the ignorance of the Lord (Mark 13:32), Athanasius and Hilary declared that the Son was not really ignorant (n. 263) and they quoted examples of the ignorance of God in the Old Testament (n. 266—they cited different examples), but while Athanasius ascribed the ignorance of the Lord to His manhood, Hilary said that it was because of the economy of salvation that the Son sometimes said that He did not know. Athanasius and Hilary declared that to prevent mankind from becoming careless, Christ said He did not know (n. 268).

In the section on the passibility of Christ, Irenaeus and Tertullian interpreted Matt. 26:38 as indicative of the true manhood of Christ. Hilary only quoted the text because it was used by the heretics (n. 294). On the suffering of Christ, Athanasius said that Christ suffered for mankind, while Hilary gave his well-known interpretation that Christ was sad to death for His disciples (n. 295).

Finally the texts in n. 330 and 333 were quoted by Tertullian and Novatian to refute the heresy current in their day, that the Father and the Son are not one but two different Persons.

Hilary thus followed the same interpretation of the texts as Irenaeus, Tertullian, Novatian and Athanasius in quite a number of cases. There are however a few differences of interpretation. The work of Irenaeus contains only a few texts which were also used by Hilary and this is easily explained by the distance in time and circumstances in which they lived. More parallel interpretations are to be found in the works of Tertullian and Novatian. Hilary was greatly indebted to his Western predecessors. As can be expected, more parallels of interpretation are to be found between Hilary and Athanasius, for they contended with the same heresy and in more or less the same time. In his refutation of the heretics Hilary used many texts and arguments which Athanasius did not use. To what extent Hilary used new arguments will never be precisely known because many of Hilary's arguments might have been commonly used in this doctrinal struggle.

4. HIS ATTEMPT TO RECONCILE THE EAST AND THE WEST

According to many manuscripts[1] and according to an ancient Christian writer[2] the *De Synodis* has been regarded as the thirteenth book of the *De Trinitate.* The *De Synodis* is, however, an independent work, known to Jerome as *Liber de Synodis*,[3] and to which the Benedictine editors of the text added *seu de fide Orientalium*.

Hilary received no reply to his letters which he had sent to his friends in the West. He feared that they had succumbed to the error which was sweeping through the Church.[4] At last he received a letter and realized that his friends had not written to him because they had not known his address. To his great joy he learnt that they had not only steadfastly refused to accept Saturninus in their church communion but that they had also condemned the confession of faith promulgated by the bishops who had assembled at Sirmium (357).[5] Hilary's friends had asked him for information about the professions of faith current in the East and they also wanted to know his own opinion on these confessions. Hilary stated that it was very difficult to put into words his own feelings concerning his beliefs and that an interpretation of the thoughts of others was a difficult assignment.[6] In view of the fact that synods were to be held at Ancyra and Ariminum (Rimini) he complied with this request because it offered him the opportunity to explain some of the doctrinal phrases

---

[1] Cf. *Praefatio in librum de Synodis* I (PL 10.471B).
[2] Cassiodorus, *de institutione divinarum litterarum* c. XVI (PL 70.1132C).
[3] Jerome, *de viris ill.* c. 100 (PL 23.738B); *Ep.* 5,2 (CV 54.22,9–11).
[4] *De Syn.* 1.
[5] *Ibid.* 2.
[6] *Ibid.* 5.

which were viewed with suspicion both by the bishops in the East and
the West. He wanted to prevent those bishops, who actually agreed about
the faith, from differing with each other at the forthcoming synods because of their ignorance of the meaning of some words used by the different groups.[7] He therefore proposed to explain the different confessions
of faith which were published after the council of Nicaea[8] and he requested the readers of his book to read the whole work before they formed an
opinion of the merit of his view.[9]

It is certain that the book was written after the earthquake at Nicomedia
(24 August 358) because when he wrote it, Hilary had already learnt that
a double synod was to be held, namely at Ancyra and Rimini.[10] The work
was thus written before the emperor had finally decided that the bishops
in the East were to assemble at Seleucia. Hilary is apparently the only
writer who mentions Ancyra as a likely meeting-place for the synod.[11]
After the disaster at Nicomedia many places had been suggested and it is
very likely that Ancyra had also been mentioned as Basil of Ancyra was
at the emperor's court at this time. The *De Synodis* was therefore written
by the end of 358[12] or the beginning of 359.[13] The late spring 359[14] seems
unlikely since that would have left very little time for the letter to reach
the bishops who were to attend the synod at Rimini.

The first document which Hilary discussed was the statement published
at Sirmium (357). It was not so much a council as a "cabal of Court
bishops."[15] Hilary thought that this "blasphemy" had been composed by
Ossius and Potamius.[16] He probably made a mistake[17] and it may be
assumed that the authors were Ursacius, Valens and Germinius.

---

[7] *Ibid.* 8.
[8] *Ibid.* 7.
[9] *Ibid.* 6.
[10] *Ibid.* 8 (PL 10.485B).
[11] Cf. the footnote by the Benedictines, PL 10.486 n. e.
[12] Gwatkin, *op. cit.*, p. 168; Griffe, *op. cit.*, p. 177; Galtier, *op. cit.*, p. 51.
[13] Bardenhewer, *op. cit.*, p. 380; Schanz, *op. cit.*, p. 292; Watson, *op. cit.*, p. 1.
[14] Cf. Reinkens, *op. cit.*, p. 173 n. 3. In order to be effective before the bishops
assembled for the respective councils, Reinkens had to assume that it was distributed
very quickly.
[15] Kidd, *op. cit.*, p. 154.
[16] *De Syn.* 11 (PL 10.487A); 3 (PL 10.482B). In *de Syn.* 63 (PL 10.523A) and 87
(PL 10.539B), Ossius is also mentioned, but Hilary did not say that he wrote the creed
and Hilary might have only referred to his subscription to the creed. This may also
be the case where Hilary mentioned the "deliramenta Osii," *contra Const.* 23 (PL
10.599B).
[17] Reinkens, *op. cit.*, p. 161, thought that the Arians wanted to make the most of
the fact that Ossius had subscribed to this declaration, by spreading the false rumour
that Ossius had actually been one of the authors. Cf. Goemans, *op. cit.*, p. 127; V. C. de
Clercq, *op. cit.*, pp. 513–14. There is no reason to doubt the fact, as Sulpicius Severus,
Chron. II 40,5 (CV 1.93–94) did, that Ossius did sign this document.

In the statement it was said that there is one God the Father Almighty, and His only Son Jesus Christ, begotten of Him before the ages. Because of all the trouble about substance (substantia), which in Greek is called οὐσία, no further mention was to be made of ὁμοούσιος or ὁμοιούσιος because these words are not found in the divine Scriptures. The birth of the Son is beyond the knowledge of man. The Father is greater than the Son in honour, dignity, splendour, majesty and in the very name of Father. The Father is invisible, immortal and impassible, while the Son took from Mary manhood, through which He suffered.[18]

Hilary remarked that the emphasis was placed on the oneness of God the Father, in order to deny the full Divinity of the Son. The confessed ignorance about the birth of the Son led to the belief that He was either born out of nothing or from some other substance other than God the Father. The statement about the Father's superiority implied that the Son lacked those attributes which constitute the Father's superiority. While it was affirmed that the birth of the Son is unknowable, it was commanded that people were not to know that He is from God.[19]

The publication of this creed was a turning-point in the Arian struggle, for this was the first time that the Nicene creed was publicly refuted.[20] A scholar observed that, "while every creed of the central Eastern party devised since the Dedication Council had contained anathemas of Arianism as a matter of course, such anathemas are for the first time conspicuously absent here."[21] This formula was an edict of tolerance in favour of Arianism[22] and it contained nothing which Arius could not have subscribed to.[23]

This creed provoked protests both in the West and in the East, where a small number of bishops gathered at Ancyra (358). Hilary discussed twelve of the nineteen anathemas which were issued by these bishops.[24]

The contents of the anathemas were as follows[25]:

1(6). The Son is the image of the invisible God. Hilary commented that there is thus a Father and a Son and that the relationship of the Father and the Son is not merely a matter of names because by the state-

---

[18] *De Syn.* 11 (PL 10.487A–489B).
[19] *Ibid.* 10 (PL 10.486B–C).
[20] Harnack, *op. cit.*, p. 254 n. 1.
[21] J. N. D. Kelly, *Early Christian Creeds*, London, 1950, p. 287.
[22] G. Rasneur, "L'Homoiousianisme dans ses rapports avec l'orthodoxie," *RHE*, Vol. 4 (1903), p. 199.
[23] Smulders, *op. cit.*, p. 45.
[24] He did not discuss no. 1–5, 18 and 19.
[25] For the following see *de Syn.* 12–26 (PL 10.489B–500B). The numbers in the Greek text are given in brackets. Cf. Epiphanius, *Haer.* 73,10,1–11,10 (GCS 37.280–4); Hahn § 162.

ment that two things are equated with one another, one is the image of
the other.

2(8). The Son Who received life from the Father is not the same Person
as the Father Who gave life (John 5:26; 6:57). Hilary distinguished between the Recipient and the Giver.

3(7). The Only-begotten Son Who is the image of the invisible God,
is like the invisible God and Son in essence. Hilary had given a definition
of essence before he dealt with the anathemas of Ancyra. According to
him, essence is a thing which is or the elements from which it is and which
subsists inasmuch as it is permanent. One can speak of the essence or
nature or genus or substance of anything. The word essence however,
is specially used because it always exists. This again is identical with
substance, because a thing which is, necessarily subsists in itself. When
we say that essence signifies nature or genus or substance, we mean the
essence of that thing which permanently exists in the nature, genus or
substance.[26] As Smulders put it: "L'essence signifie donc ce qu'il y a de
plus profond dans les choses, ce qui constitue la chose dans son identité;
ce par quoi elle est ce qu'elle est."[27] Hilary remarked that this anathema
meant that since Christ is the Only-begotten Son of God and the image
of the invisible God, He must necessarily in species and nature be of a
similar essence. The One is not less because He is Son and the Father is
not greater because He is Father and the similarity of the Son, begotten
of the substance of the Father does not permit any diversity of substance.

4(9). The life which the Father possesses and gives to the Son (John
5:26) signifies the divine essence ($o\dot{v}\sigma\acute{\iota}a$) and a likeness of essence to
essence is indicated. Hilary stated that in the life which is begotten of life,
i.e. in the essence which is born of essence, since it is not born unlike
(because life is from life), the Son maintains in Himself a nature wholly
similar to His original, for there is no diversity in the likeness of the
essence which is born and which begets.

5(10). The words "begat Me" and "formed Me"[28] are not the same, for
the Son of God is signified as Son under two different expressions. Not

[26] De Syn. 12 (PL 10.490A): Essentia est res quae est, vel ex quibus est, et quae in eo
quod maneat subsistit. Dici autem essentia, et natura, et genus, et substantia uniuscu-
jusque rei poterit. Proprie autem essentia idcirco est dicta, quia semper est. Quae
idcirco etiam substantia est, quia res quae est, necesse est subsistat in sese; quidquid
autem subsistit, sine dubio in genere vel natura vel substantia maneat. Cum ergo
essentiam dicimus significare naturam vel genus vel substantiam, intelligimus ejus rei
quae in his omnibus semper esse subsistat.
[27] Smulders, op. cit., p. 283.
[28] The Greek text reads: $\kappa a\grave{\iota}$ $\varepsilon\check{\iota}$ $\tau\iota\varsigma$ $\tau\grave{o}$ »$\check{\varepsilon}\kappa\tau\iota\sigma\acute{\varepsilon}$ $\mu\varepsilon$« $\kappa a\grave{\iota}$ $\tau\grave{o}$ »$\gamma\varepsilon\nu\nu\tilde{a}$ $\mu\varepsilon$« $\pi a\varrho'$ $a\dot{v}\tau o\tilde{v}$
$\dot{a}\kappa o\acute{v}\omega\nu$ $\kappa\tau\lambda$. (Epiphanius, Haer. 73,11,1 GCS 37.282). Hilary's text reads: Si quis
condidit vel creavit me, et genuit me ab eodem audiens (De Syn. 16 PL 10.493A).

only formation but also Sonship is implied by these words. Hilary gave
the following explanation of this statement: Wisdom also said that she
was begotten. Her creation therefore illustrates the changeless nature of
God, Who has no need of passion, intercourse or parturition. Without
any diminution or change in Himself, He created from Himself what He
begat. Wisdom said that she was created, thereby excluding in her manner
of birth every kind of corporeal process, but she added that she was
begotten in order to explain her birth. Speaking of creation, it is implied
that the nature of the Father is changeless, but speaking of her birth the
reality of her own nature is indicated, for the substance of her nature,
begotten of God the Father is genuine and real. The Son, born of God
without any change in God, is so born as to be created and the Father,
Who is changeless and the Son's Father by nature, so forms the Son as
to beget Him.[29] In his *De Trinitate* Hilary said that the birth referred to
the eternal generation, and the creation of Wisdom was the creation in
time for the ways of God.[30] The different interpretations in his two works
are to be explained by the different purposes he had in mind when he
wrote the two works. His *De Synodis* was written to restore the unity of
the Church and he did not want to offend the Homoeousians unnecessarily in matters which were not of profound importance. In *De Trinitate*
he freely expounded his own view.[31]

6(11). Anyone who grants the Son only a likeness in activity but denies
Him a likeness in essence (which is the corner-stone of our faith) notwith-
standing the fact that the Son Himself revealed His essential likeness to
the Father (John 5:26) as well as His likeness in activity (John 5:19), such
a man robs himself of the knowledge of eternal life. Hilary said that a
similar might can only be the result of a similar nature, for a lower nature
can never attain to the might of a higher and more powerful nature. "As
the Father has life in Himself, so He has also given to the Son to have life
in Himself" (John 5:26). Life implied nature and essence, and Christ
taught that this had been given to Him to have as the Father has. Similarity of life thus contains similarity of might and similarity of essence follows on similarity of might.

7(12). Anyone who professes that there is a Father and a Son and maintains that the Father is Father of an essence unlike Himself, but of a similar
activity, thus nullifying the Son's true Sonship, is anathematized. Hilary
reiterated his view that the names Father and Son are not titular bu

[29] *De Syn.* 17–18 (PL 10.493B–495A).
[30] Cf. *de Trin.* XII 45 (p. 95 n. 181).
[31] Smulders, *op. cit.*, p. 195.

express a real relationship, for the name of Father is attributed to God the Father because of the nature of His Offspring, because He begot a nature which was not unlike or alien to Himself. Nothing other than God is born of God.

8(13). If it is understood that the Son is like in essence to the Father, it does not follow that the Son is the same as the Father or part of the Father, or that it is through an emanation or any such passion as is necessary for the procreation of corporeal children that the incorporeal Son subsists from the incorporeal Father. According to Hilary many heretics said that the Son is like the Father in divinity, in order to confirm their view that because of this similarity, the Son is the same Person as the Father. The birth of the Son excluded any such view. Although the One differs in no respect from the Other through mutual likeness, yet this very likeness which does not admit to a bare union (unio), confesses both the Father and the Son because the Son is the changeless likeness of the Father.

9(14). If someone, concerned about the distinct personal qualities of the Father and the Son, fears that the Son and the Father may sometimes be admitted to be the same Person and therefore denies that the Son is like in essence to the Father, he is declared anathema. While the previous anathema, according to Hilary, guarded against the teaching of a unity of Person (personalis unio) under the cloak of an essential likeness, this anathema prevented a repudiation of the unity of Persons leading to the preaching of the dissimilarity of their natures. In Father and in Son is preserved the likeness of an identical nature through an essential birth.

10(15). God did not become Father of the Only-begotten Son at any point in time, and the Only-begotten Son came into existence without passion, beyond all times and beyond all human calculation. Hilary stated that the eternal and infinite God cannot be understood as having become a Father in time. In the Gospel it is recognized that even in the beginning, the Only-begotten God, the Word, was with God, rather than being born.

11(16). The Father is not older in time than His Only-begotten Son, nor is the Son younger than the Father. Hilary maintained that if the Son was held to be younger in time, He would no longer be a true image and likeness of the Father, for that which is found to be dissimilar in time is no longer a true likeness. The fact that God is Father prevents there being any time in which He was not Father and consequently there can be no time in the Son's existence in which He was not Son.

12(17). The timeless substance of the Only-begotten Son is not to be attributed to the unborn essence of God for this would lead to calling the

Father Son. Hilary emphasized that the exclusion of time from the Son's birth should not lead to the assumption that there was no birth, thus reintroducing the heresy of the unity of Persons (haeresis unionis). Being outside time is something different from being unborn, because in the former case a birth (though outside time) is not excluded, while in the latter case it is.

It is worth noting that Hilary did not comment on the last statement which anathematized those who called the Son ὁμοούσιον δὲ ἢ ταυτοούσιον τῷ πατρί. Later on in his work he dealt with these terms fully and it therefore probably did not suit his purpose to discuss this anathema at this stage. Hilary stated that he had reviewed all the definitions of faith which the Eastern bishops had published against the recently emerging heresy,[32] but as we have seen above he actually discussed only twelve.

Hilary next discussed the Second Creed of the synod held on the occasion of the dedication of the church at Antioch (341). According to Athanasius the bishops at the synod were dissatisfied with the first definition of their faith and therefore composed another.[33] Hilary stated that the creed was drafted because of suspicions about the orthodoxy of one of the bishops.[34] If this is correct, the guilty man may well have been Theophronius of Tyana,[35] whose own confession of faith was the so-called Third Creed of Antioch.

Hilary's first criticism of this Second Creed was that it did not speak explicitly enough about the identical similarity of the Father and the Son, while it clearly taught that the Father, the Son and the Holy Spirit are three Persons but in agreement one.[36] According to Hilary, however, the bishops at Antioch did not oppose the heresy which declared that the Father and the Son were unlike in substance, but rather that heresy which attributed the three names to the Father, so that the Father could also be

---

[32] De Syn. 27 (PL 10.500B). According to a footnote by the Benedictines (PL 10.499 n. f) this "all" referred to what the synod of Sirmium had published, but this is impossible because the synod was referred to as the "recent heresy." These twelve anathemas were included in the statement published at Sirmium (June 358). Hilary elsewhere (de Syn. 90 PL 10.542A–B) hinted that the others were omitted, because it was thought that they might offend some bishops. Hilary also said that if they had been omitted because Basil and his friends had changed their view about these anathemas, then they had to be wary of the anathemas being repeated in the future. For this reason Hilary might have decided not to comment on them.

[33] Athanasius, de Synodis 23 (PG 26.722B; Opitz II 1 p. 249). For the creed cf. Hahn § 154.

[34] Hilary, de Syn. 28 (PL 10.502A).

[35] Kelly, Creeds, p. 268.

[36] In the creed it was said that: Ut sint quidem per substantiam tria, per consonantiam vero unum (de Syn. 29 PL 10.503B). The Greek text reads: ὡς εἶναι τῇ μὲν ὑποστάσει τρία, τῇ δὲ συμφωνίᾳ ἕν (Athanasius, de Syn. 23 PG 26.724B; Opitz II 1 p. 249,33).

called Son and Holy Spirit. The creed therefore declared that there were three subsistent Persons, but it did not separate the substance of Father and Son by introducing a dissimilarity of essence. Hilary did not object to the words: "They are three in substance but in agreement one," since the Spirit, the Paraclete, was also mentioned. Therefore it was more fitting that a unity of agreement should be asserted than a unity of essence based on likeness of substance.[37]

Hilary also remarked that the creed made no distinction whatever between the essence and nature of the Father and the Son. *Whole God* was born *from whole God* and the Son is thus in all in which the Father is. *One of One* excludes the passions of a human birth and teaches that the Son comes from no other source than God, nor is He different or alien to God. He Who was born does not differ from the Unborn except in having a cause of His origin, since the perfection of Both is the same. *King of King* allows no dissimilarity of power and *Lord of Lord* confesses that the lordship is equal, but the plainest statement of all was *unalterable and unchangeable, the unvarying image of the Godhead, essence, power and glory*. The Son derives the fact that He is unchangeable from the Father's substance. In His birth, that nature from which He is born, is not changed. When it is said that He was the *first-born of all creation, Who was in the beginning with God as God the Word*, it meant that He was born and the fact that He always was, shows that He is not separated from the Father by time. Hilary therefore concluded that by dividing the three substances (to exclude a monad God), the synod did not introduce any separation of substance between the Father and the Son. No distinction was made between the Father and the Son, the Unborn and the Only-begotten, in time or name or essence or dignity or domination.[38]

Hilary could interpret this creed in an orthodox way because Arianism proper is excluded. It is anti-Sabellian, anti-Marcellan and it has an Origenist flavour, with its guiding conception being the confession of three separate hypostases.[39] Hilary called this assembly a synod of saints.[40]

The next creed discussed by Hilary was the one traditionally known as the profession of faith of Philippopolis. Hilary however, referred to it as the creed of the bishops of the East gathered at Sardica.[41] One may assume that the bishops who took no part in the proceedings of the synod

[37] *De Syn.* 31–32 (PL 10.504A–505A.)
[38] *Ibid.* 33 (PL 10.505A–506B).
[39] Cf. Harnack, *op. cit.*, p. 244 n. 1; Kelly, *Creeds*, pp. 270–1.
[40] *De Syn.* 32 (PL 10.504B).
[41] Cf. their encyclical letter, *Coll. ant. Par.* Ser. A IV (*fragm.* III); *de Syn.* 33 (PL 10.506B); *contra Const.* 23 (PL 10.599A), 25 (PL 10.600B).

at Sardica, wanted to convey the impression that their creed was the creed of the official synod, in order to deceive those who were ignorant of what had really happened. But if the creed had not been drawn up at Sardica but at Philippopolis, it does seem strange that Hilary always referred to it as the creed of the Eastern bishops at Sardica. Feder thought that they might have met in Philippopolis before they went to Sardica.[42] When they arrived at Sardica they refused to meet the other (orthodox) group, but held a separate meeting. Then they sent their letter which contained this creed to the bishops in Africa and returned to the East via Philippopolis.[43]

The creed which was appended to the encyclical letter which was published, is the so-called Fourth Creed of Antioch. There were a few additional anathemas at the end.[44]

Hilary thought that in this creed concise but clear definitions had been used. It condemned those who maintained that the Son comes from things non-existent and those who said that the Son was born of some other substance and not of God. Hilary concluded that it was without doubt that He was born with those qualities which are God's, for the Son was generated from no other substance than the birthless and eternal substance of the Father. Furthermore any interval of times or ages was rejected because He Who does not differ in nature cannot be separated by time.

Hilary also remarked that the creed deprived the heretics of the opportunity to declare that there is any different nature in the Son. Those who say that there are three Gods, are anathematized. Men are sometimes called gods in recognition of their merit, but the substance of their nature and that of God is different. In the nature of God, God is one but in such a way that the Son is also God because He does not have a nature different from God the Father. Both are God for He is God from God. The similarity of the nature of the Begotten and the Begetter is thus safeguarded by the creed and confirmed by the application of one name. The creed also condemned those who contended that God is a solitary monad and that because God is one, He has in Himself the name of Father and of Son. The faith of the saints knows nothing of the Son being incapable of being born. His birth however, was so perfect, that He Who was born

[42] Cf. *Coll. ant. Par.* Ser. B II 1,7 (CV 65.120,4–5; *fragm.* II 7 PL 10.637B): Uenientes etenim Serdicam per singula loca synodos faciebant inter se et pactiones cum interminationibus.
[43] Feder, "Studien I," p. 68. According to Hefele–Leclercq, *op. cit.*, Vol. I.2 pp. 818–819, they sent their letter from Philippopolis, but because they considered themselves to have been the true council of Sardica, they said that it had been written at Sardica.
[44] Gwatkin's statement, *op. cit.*, p. 128 n. 4, that Hilary thought that the so-called fourth Creed of Antioch was only compiled at Philippopolis, is unfounded.

of the substance of God, was also born of His purpose and will.[45]

This creed which was sent to Emperor Constans at Trèves, as the Fourth Creed of Antioch, was an attempt at rapprochement between East and West. The condemnation of Arianism was more outspoken here than in any other creed published since the synod at Antioch. This creed also condemns the teachings of Marcellus and the additional anathemas were mainly directed against him. Hilary could therefore find many commendable things in this creed.

Hilary finally quoted the creed of the synod held at Sirmium (351) but he only commented on the anathemas which they had promulgated. He stated that a wider and broader exposition of the faith was necessary to oppose the subtle heresy which was revived by Photinus.[46] The creed, known as the First Creed of Sirmium, was none other than the Fourth Creed of Antioch with twenty-six additional anathemas (the first anathema was a repetition of all the anathemas appended to Antioch IV), which might have been a reproduction of the points debated between Photinus and Basil of Ancyra.[47]

1. The Son is not from things non-existent or from another substance but from God, and there was no time or age when He was not. This anathema was aimed at the Arians. Hilary remarked that because the Son is from no other substance but that of God, nothing else can therefore be born in Him, but all that is in God. The Unborn Father and Only-begotten Son share all qualities.

2-3. The Father and the Son are not two Gods, but the confession that God is one does not lead to the denial that Christ is God and before the ages Son of God, obedient to the Father in the creation of all things.[48] According to Hilary the very profession of the name gives us a clear insight into this fact. God the Son of God, was born from no other essence but that of God the Father. Because of Their identity of nature and name They must be one in the kind of Their essence, if the name of Their essence is necessarily one.

4. He who says that the Unborn God or part of Him was born of Mary, is condemned. Hilary said that this article maintained that the

---

[45] *De Syn.* 35–37 (PL 10.507C–509A).
[46] *Ibid.* 39 (PL 10.512C–513A).
[47] Kelly, *Creeds*, p. 281.
[48] Hilary's translation of no. 3 differs from the Greek. Cf. Athanasius, *de Syn.* 27 (PG 26 736C; Opitz II 1 p. 254,35–36): Καὶ εἴ τις λέγων θεὸν τὸν Χριστὸν πρὸ αἰώνων υἱὸν τοῦ θεοῦ ὑπουργηκότα τῷ πατρὶ εἰς τὴν τῶν ὅλων δημιουργίαν μὴ ὁμολογοίη, ἀνάθεμα ἔστω. Hilary, *de Syn.* 38 (PL 10.510A): Et si quis, unum dicens Deum, Christum autem Deum ante saecula filium Dei obsecutum Patri in creatione omnium non confitetur: anathema sit.

confession of a unity of name, did not repudiate the Person of the begotten essence, as if the substance of God was singular and undifferentiated.

5. The Son was born of the Father before the ages, and all things were
made through Him, and He did really exist before Mary and not only
according to foreknowledge or predestination. Thus was condemned the
view that the Son, before He was born in bodily form, did not exist
according to the essence of a personally subsistent nature.

6-7. The view that the substance of God was expanded and contracted,
and that the expanded substance of God constituted the Son or was called
the Son, is condemned. Hilary commented that contraction and expansion
are bodily affections, and that God Who is a Spirit, does not expand or
contract Himself through any change of substance. A denial of the im-
mutability of the Father and of the birth of the Son is to be condemned.

8. The Son is not the internal or uttered Word of God. According to
this heretical view, God the Father has as Son a word resembling any
word a human being utters, and Hilary thought that this view is justly
condemned, for God the Word was in the beginning with God.

9-10. The Son born of Mary is not man only, but in declaring that
God and man was born of Mary one should not conclude that the Unborn
God was born. Hilary stated that the Son born of Mary was God and
man, and God made man is not denied to be God but denied to be the
Unborn God. The Father was distinguished from the Son not in nature
or by diversity of substance, but only by the pre-eminence of His birth-
lessness.

11(12). When it is said: "The Word was made flesh," it does not mean
that the Word was transformed into flesh, or that He suffered change in
assuming flesh. Hilary said that the Word in becoming flesh, did not lose
what constituted the Word, nor did it become transformed into flesh so
that it ceased to be the Word. The Word was made flesh, so that the flesh
might begin to be what the Word is, and this was seen in His miraculous
power, glory on the mountain, knowledge of the thoughts of human
hearts, calmness in passion and life in death.

12(13). Anyone contending that because the Son of God was crucified,
His divinity suffered corruption or pain or change or diminution or
destruction, is condemned. Hilary declared that God the Word made
flesh, could not change under suffering. Suffering causes all flesh to change
through feeling pain. The Word made flesh was unchanged by the liabil-
ity to suffer, although He made Himself subject to suffering. He was able
to suffer and yet He was not passible because passibility denotes a nature
that is weak. The Godhead is immutable and yet the Word was made

flesh. The pains inflicted upon Him found in Him a material which they
could affect although the Word did not have the infirmity of passibility.
When He suffered His nature remained immutable.[49] This is the same
view which Hilary represented in his *De Trinitate*.

13–16(14–17). God the Father spoke to the Son when He said: "Let us
make man" and the Son and not the Unborn God appeared to Abraham,
wrestled with Jacob and the Lord, the Son, rained from the Lord, the
Father (Gen. 19:24). Hilary explained that these points had to be inserted
in the creed because Photinus denied them. These instances did not refer
to the Unborn God, but to the Son of God. Photinus had asserted that
the Son of God did not exist before He was born from the virgin.

17(18). When one hears of the Lord the Father and the Lord the Son it
does not mean that there are two Gods, nor that the Son is made equal to
the Father but that what He performed, was by the Father's authority.
Hilary even favourably interpreted this statement on the subordination
of the Son to the Father. God is One because of the character of His
natural essence and because the Only-begotten Son was born from the
Unborn God the Father, and drew His divine Being only from God.
Because of Their similar essence, They have one name for the similar
nature. The Son was subjected to render obedience, but the subjection
of filial love is no diminution of essence nor does pious duty cause a de-
generation of nature. The subjection and dignity of the Son are both
taught, for in calling Him Son, He is not only made subject to God the
Father, but His nature is also denoted. Elsewhere in his work Hilary
insisted that the subjection of the Son is different from the subjection of
creatures to God, for the subjection of the Son to the Father is due to
filial love and not to weakness.[50]

18–22(19–23). The Father and the Son[51] are not one Person. The Holy
Spirit, the Paraclete, is not the Unborn God and is different from the Son,
but is not a part of the Father or of the Son. The Father and the Son and
the Holy Spirit are not three Gods. Hilary remarked that the Son frequently declared that His works were the works of the Father and when
He intended to send the Paraclete, He sometimes said that He was to be

---

[49] *De Syn.* 49 (PL 10.516B–C): Verbum autem, quod caro factum est, licet se pas-
sioni subdiderit; non tamen demutatum est passibilitate patiendi. Nam pati potuit,
et passibile esse non potuit: quia passibilitas naturae infirmis significatio est; passio
autem est eorum quae sint illata perpessio: quae quia indemutabilis Deus est, cum
tamen Verbum caro factum sit, habuerunt in eo passionis materiam sine passibilitatis
infirmitate.

[50] Cf. *de Syn.* 79 (PL 10.532B).

[51] The Greek text added: "and the Holy Spirit." Athanasius, *de Syn.* 27 (PG 26.740A;
Opitz II 1 p. 255).

sent from the Father, piously referring all that He did to the Father. The heretics took this to mean that the Son Himself is the Paraclete. The Lord however prayed that another Comforter should be sent from the Father, and thus showed the difference between Him Who was sent, and Him Who asked that One be sent. One cannot assert that the Holy Spirit is a part of either the Father or of the Son, for the name of Holy Spirit has its own signification, and the Holy Spirit has the office and rank peculiar to His Person and the Father and the Son are known to be immutable. Finally, there is only one God, and it is contrary to religion to say that there are two Gods. Thus we should condemn even more the statement that Father, Son and Holy Spirit are three Gods.

23(11). The words in Isaiah 44:6 were aimed at the destruction of idols and those who are not gods and it must not be interpreted, as the Jews do, to mean the denial of the Eternal Only-begotten God. Hilary stated that the words: "Beside Me there is no God" cannot rob the Son of His divinity because beside Him Who is of God, there is no other God. The Jews being ignorant of the Only-begotten God, saw in this text proof of the bare unity of God. In confessing that God is one and that the Son is God, by using the same name one affirms that there is no difference of substance between the two Persons.

24-25. The Son was not made by the will of God like any created object, nor was the Son born against the will of the Father as if the Father was forced by a necessity of nature to beget His Son, but when He willed, before time and without passion, He begat Him of Himself. Hilary explained that to all creatures, the will of God has given substance, but through the perfect birth, the Son received a nature from a substance which is impassible and unborn. This did not mean that God the Father begot the Son out of necessity, imposed on Him by a law of nature. Before all time, with a will which was not subject to passion, out of the essence of His nature He gave to the Son a birth which conveyed the essence of His nature.

26. There are not Two Who are incapable of birth and unborn and without beginning. The Son is the beginning of all things, but God is the beginning of Christ and thus there is only One Who is without beginning. Hilary declared that God is one, and there cannot thus be two incapable of birth, for incapability of birth is the only quality that can belong to one person only. The Son is God because He derived His essence through birth from that essence which cannot be born.

27. Finally it was reiterated that Christ is God, Son of God before the ages, and that He aided the Father to perfect all things, and that He is

therefore Christ from all the ages and not only from the time He was born of Mary.

The majority of these statements condemned the views which were associated with Marcellus and Photinus. As a whole the declaration by the synod at Sirmium was moderate and Hilary was therefore able to interpret it favourably. His attempt to interpret all the creeds he treated as favourably as possible, was determined by the task he set himself in writing this work. It is unlikely however, that his interpretation of some of the creeds and anathemas was accepted and shared by all the bishops who subscribed to them.

Hilary justified the compilation of all these creeds and statements because of the frenzy of the heretics. The infinite and the boundless God cannot be made comprehensible by a few words of human speech, and brevity misleads those who listen and those who teach. The bishops who realize this, therefore employ many definitions and a flow of words, so that people might be imbued with the truth so often so differently expressed. Hilary describes the danger which threatens the Church in the East, for with the exception of Eleusius (of Cyzicus) and a few other bishops, the major part of the ten provinces of Asia did not know God and did not confess the true faith. The orthodox bishops were sent into exile not by laymen but by bishops of the Church. Hilary praises the West because they had no need to express their faith in writing, but abounding in the Spirit they held the true faith in their hearts.[52]

Hilary's own belief concerning the Father and the Son is that there is one God but this does not deny the divinity of the Son. Only the Father is incapable of birth. There are not two subsistent Persons but a similar substance in both Persons. The Father is greater than the Son because He is Father, but the Son is not less because He is Son. The difference is one in name only and not in nature. The Father is unaffected by time and the Son is equally eternal. The Son is in the Father because the existence of the Son is from no other source. They are one through the similarity of an identical nature, but They are not one Person. Hilary adds that if he said too little it is not belief but words which are lacking.[53]

Hilary again requests his readers not to judge his view until they have read his whole exposition[54] and then proceeds to discuss the interpretation of *homoousios*. He tells his brethren[55] that it is possible to confess that

---

[52] *De Syn.* 62–63 (PL 10.522A-523C).
[53] *Ibid.* 64–65 (PL 10.523C–524B).
[54] *Ibid.* 66 (PL 10.525A).
[55] The scholars Loofs, "Hilarius," p. 62 and Bardenhewer, *op. cit.*, p. 380, thought that from ch. 66 Hilary addressed the Eastern bishops, but that is incorrect. The

the Father and the Son are one in substance, and yet to use the expression in a wrong way. The word "one substance" is correctly used if it is understood to mean; in the natural qualities and likeness, and in a likeness which includes not only the species but genus, and also provided that the one substance signifies such a similitude of qualities that the unity is not a unity of a monad but of equals. Equality is an exact similarity, so that the likeness may be called an equality, provided that the equality implies unity, because it implies an equal pair, and that the unity which implies an equal pair does not mean a single Person. The expression "one substance" is therefore correctly used if the subsistent personality is not abolished and the one substance is not divided into two, because Their substance is so free from difference by the character of the Son's birth and by Their natural likeness, that it is called one.[56]

Hilary then enumerates three ways in which it is wrongly used: 1) if "one substance" teaches one solitary personal existence denoted by two titles; 2) if it is thought that the Father is divided and that He cut off a part of Himself to be His Son; 3) if in confessing that the Father and the Son are of one substance it is thought to imply a prior substance which the two equal Persons Both possess. Hilary concludes that if the word is used in any of these three senses, the Son's birth is excluded.[57] In the beginning of his refutation of the heretics, Hilary had enumerated these points as the objections which the Arians had raised to *homoousios*.[58] These objections were probably shared by many of the Eastern bishops. Only the first point however, could have been misused by the protagonists of the extreme Nicene view, who were inclined to neglect the personal distinction within the Godhead.

Hilary therefore thinks that one should not use *homoousios* alone, but that one should qualify it and state exactly what is meant in using it. This word should also not be held as all important as though true faith did not exist if it was not used. This was a very delicate point and it may be assumed that some bishops in the West were shocked when they read this. For many years most of the bishops who had only gradually come to

chapters 67–77 were in the first place addressed to the Western bishops and from ch. 78 he directly appealed to the Eastern bishops.
[56] *De Syn.* 67 (PL 10.525A–B): Nam si secundum naturae proprietatem ac similitudinem, ut similitudo non speciem solam afferat, sed genus teneat; religiose unam substantiam praedicamus, dummodo unam substantiam proprietatis similitudinem intelligamus, ut quod unum sunt, non singularem significet, sed aequales. Aequalitatem dico, id est, indifferentiam similitudinis, ut similitudo habeatur aequalitas; aequalitas vero unum idcirco dicatur esse, quia par sit; unum autem, in quo par significatur, non ad unicum vendicetur.
[57] *Ibid.* 68 (PL 10.525B–526A).
[58] *De Trin.* IV 4 (PL 10.98B–99A).

know the finer points in the doctrinal dispute, had raised the homoousion as their banner and thought this confession to be the only touch-stone of orthodoxy. Hilary also thinks it inadvisable for anyone who wanted to state that the substance of the Father and the Son is one, to begin here. It would be better to say that the Father is unbegotten, that the Son was born and that He drew His personal subsistence from the Father, being like the Father in might, honour and nature. He is subject to the Father as Author of His being. The Son is not incapable of being born, but equally eternal with the Father. It is not true that He came from nothing but was born being God and not a creature. God is not one in Person but in nature. After a declaration of all this, according to Hilary, one would not err in declaring that the Father and the Son are of one sub-stance.[59] It must not be denied that the Father and the Son are of one substance but reasons must be given for declaring this. It must be said that there was a birth and that there is a likeness between Father and Son.[60]

Hilary then examines the word *homoeousios* to ascertain whether similar-ity is fully appropriate for a description of the relation between the Father and the Son. The word similarity expresses the equality of one Person with the other, because things which are like one another are equal. Equality does not exist between things unlike, nor does similarity exist in only one thing. Hilary therefore maintains that the declaration that the Son is like in all things to the Father, means nothing else than that He is equal. Likeness means perfect equality and this fact is gathered from the Holy Scriptures: "And Adam ... begat a son according to his own image and according to his own likeness" (Gen. 5:3). By his birth Seth had the natural essence of Adam. He had a likeness to Adam for his nature was not different. Therefore a likeness of nature renders things equal, because of the likeness of a similar essence. Thus every son, by virtue of his natural birth is the equal of his father, because there is a likeness of nature. John taught the equality of nature of the Father and the Son: "The Jews sought ... to kill Him because ... He also said that God was His Father, making Himself equal with God" (John 5:18). The Son is like the Father, He is the Son of the Father and He is born of Him.[61]

Hilary states that he cannot understand why some bishops confess that there is a likeness between the Father and the Son, but deny that They

---

[59] *De Syn.* 69 (PL 10.526A–C).
[60] *Ibid.* 71 (PL 10.527B).
[61] *Ibid.* 72–73 (PL 10.527B–528C).

are equal. He reminds them that an anathema was pronounced on anyone who says that the Father was Father of an essence unlike Himself. The Father could not have given Him any other than His own essence. Likeness is then the sharing of one's own; the sharing of one's own is equality; and equality admits no difference. Things which do not differ at all are one, and the Father and the Son are one, not by unity of Person but by equality of nature.[62] The Lord taught that He was equal with God: "The Son can do nothing of Himself but what He seeth the Father do. Whatever He doeth, these also doeth the Son likewise" (John 5:19). There is no difference of natural power in Father and Son, for the Son's equality of power with the Father is not due to an increase and advance of the Son's nature, but to the Father's example. Things "done likewise" are the same and "the same things" prove equality.[63]

Hilary therefore concludes that the confession of a likeness of substance between the Father and the Son does not have to be viewed with suspicion. There is no real likeness if there is not an equality of nature, and an equality of nature cannot exist unless it implies a unity—a unity not of person but of kind. Thus the substance of the Father and the Son is one because it is similar, and it is similar because They are one.[64]

Hilary then addresses the Homoeousian bishops of the East. He says that they have inspired him with hope in the restoration of true faith, for they had consistently checked the attack of infidelity. What the heretics had formerly muttered in silence, had lately been boasted of in open triumph, for the heresy was now backed by civil authority. They had beguiled the emperor so successfully, that he expounded their infidel creed. He had however, successfully freed himself from any reproach by receiving an embassy from the Homoeousian bishops.[65]

According to Hilary, the bishops who had subscribed to the creed known as the Second Sirmian (357), are deceivers and hypocrites. They desired that no mention be made of ὁμοούσιος or ὁμοιούσιος on the ground that the meaning of the words was identical. Hilary exclaims that they must have been rustic bishops to be ignorant of the meaning of ὁμοούσιος, as if there had been no council and no dispute about the matter. If they were ignorant of the meaning of these words, why did they wish to be ignorant of the generation of the Son? If we cannot know how He was

---

[62] *Ibid.* 74 (PL 10.529 A): Ita similitudo proprietas est, proprietas aequalitas est, et aequalitas nihil differt. Quae autem nihil differunt, unum sunt; non unione personae, sed aequalitate naturae.
[63] *Ibid.* 75 (PL 10.529 A–530 A).
[64] *Ibid.* 76 (PL 10.530 A–B).
[65] *Ibid.* 78 (PL 10.530 C–531 B).

born, we nevertheless cannot be ignorant about the fact that the Son of God was born of no other substance but of God. Another point which Hilary attacks is their subordination of the Son to the Father. The Son is subjected to the Father like all other things but there is a difference, because the subjection of the Son is filial love, while all other things are subordinate because of their weakness. Hilary also wonders how it could be known that Christ had jointly suffered.[66] The confession seems to convey the impression that there were two Persons who suffered. What of the words: "Jesus Christ the Son of God"?[67] Jesus Christ is not one and the Son of God another; Hilary does not complain that the Homoeousians pardoned the subscribers to the Sirmium II, but neither does he believe that Ursacius and Valens, at their age and with their experience of these matters, were ignorant of the meaning of ὁμοούσιος. It seems to him that they must be lying. Yet he would rather be mistaken than assume that they really knew the meaning of this word, for that would mean that the Homoeousians had contaminated their faith by communion with heretics.[68]

Hilary then deals with the reasons why the Homoeousians thought ὁμοούσιος should be rejected, namely 1) the word led to the idea that there was a prior substance which two persons had divided between themselves. Hilary thought that no sane man would declare that there is a third substance which is common to Both the Father and the Son; 2) they raised the objection that the fathers, when Paul of Samosata had been pronounced a heretic, had rejected the word ὁμοούσιος on the ground that Paul had used this word in teaching that God was single and undifferentiated, thus at once being Father and Son to Himself. Hilary's reply is that no man who has been reborn in Christ and confessed both the Son and the Father, will share Paul's heretical view; 3) they disapproved of ὁμοούσιος because in the Nicene Council, the fathers were compelled to adopt this word to refute those who said that the Son was a creature. Furthermore it should not be accepted because it is not found in Scripture. To this Hilary expressed his astonishment, for on this assumption the word ὁμοιούσιος should be rejected too.[69]

Hilary fully discusses the third objection. The Arians rejected the word

---

[66] In Sirmium II it was said: Ut autem Scripturae omnes docent, et praecipue ipse magister gentium Apostolus, hominem suscepisse de Maria Virgine, per quem compassus est (de Syn. 11 PL 10.489B). The Greek translation reads: ἄνθρωπον ἀνέλαβεν ὁ Χριστὸς ἀπὸ Μαρίας τῆς παρθένου, δι' οὗ πέπονθε (Athanasius, de Syn. 28 PG 26.744A; Opitz II 1 p. 257,22).
[67] It is not clear which sentence in the creed of Sirmium II Hilary refers to.
[68] De Syn. 79 (PL 10.531B–533B).
[69] Ibid. 81–82 (PL 10.534A–535A).

in order to deny that God the Son was born of the substance of God the Father. By rightly adopting the word, the council caused the word which had been used as an instrument of evil, to become an instrument of good. The council at Nicaea certainly did not use the word in the sense that the Father and the Son divided and shared a substance anterior to Them. The council clearly stated that the Son was born from the substance of the Father. He was born and not made. The concept "of one substance" taught that there is not one solitary Person, but that the Son born of the substance of God, does not subsist from any other source nor in any diversity of a different substance. The meaning of ὁμοούσιος is therefore that the Son has the same nature as the Father.[70]

It could be said that the term should be disapproved of because it is usually wrongly interpreted. If this however was a valid objection, then Hilary thought that quite a number of texts should not be read because they were quoted by different heretics to support their views, e.g. John 10:30: "I and the Father are one" should not be read because Sabellius misused this text. All the Gospels would then have to be abolished, lest they were misinterpreted, or their statements were found to be inconsistent. The Christians should not glory in the cross of Christ because it is a stumbling-block to the world. Similarly it should not be preached that Christ died, thus denying the godless the argument that God is dead.[71]

Hilary maintains that because some misunderstand ὁμοούσιος it does not prevent him from interpreting it correctly. Furthermore, the fact that Paul of Samosata used it wrongly, does not prove the Arians correct in denying it. Eighty bishops[72] once rejected it, but three hundred and eighteen had accepted it at Nicaea. Both groups, in approving and disapproving of the word, opposed heretics, and their correct decisions should not be carped at. Another objection could be that some of those who had been present at Nicaea, have now decreed that the word ὁμοούσιος should not be used. Hilary's reply is that these same men also ruled the same about ὁμοιούσιος. There was the danger that if both these words were not accepted, neither of the two would be retained.[73]

By ὁμοούσιος Hilary understands God of God, not of an essence which is unlike, not divided but born, and that the Son is of the substance of the unborn God. Hilary had believed this before he had heard the word ὁμοούσιος, but the word did confirm his belief. Why is his faith then

[70] *Ibid.* 83–84 (PL 10.535B–536C).
[71] *Ibid.* 85 (PL 10.536C–538B).
[72] According to Athanasius seventy bishops were present when Paul of Samosata was deposed, *de Syn.* 43 (PG 26.769A; Opitz II 1 p. 268,28).
[73] *De Syn.* 86–87 (PL 10.538B–540A).

condemned when expressed by ὁμοούσιος, while it cannot be disproved
when expressed by ὁμοιούσιος? The Homoeousians condemn not only
his faith but their own, in condemning its verbal equivalent. If they think
that one must subscribe to the Samosatene Council to prevent anyone
from using ὁμοούσιος in the sense which Paul of Samosata had used it,
then one should also subscribe to the Nicene Council so that the Arians
may not impugn the word. Hilary appeals to his friends in the East to
decree that there is no difference between being of one or of similar
substance. The word ὁμοούσιος can be understood in a wrong sense, but
let it be proved how it can be understood in the correct sense. They hold
the same truth as the bishops in the West. The Homoeousians are not Arians
and why should they be thought to be Arians by denying ὁμοούσιος?[74]

The Homoeousians complain about the ambiguity of ὁμοούσιος,[75] while
Hilary finds ὁμοιούσιος inadequate. He states that many deceptions come
from similarity, e.g. gold plating may conceal another metal, sheep's milk
looks like cow's milk. Hilary therefore maintains that a true likeness
belongs to a true natural connection, but when this exists, ὁμοούσιος cannot be denied. It is a likeness according to essence if one thing is like
another; nothing can be like gold but gold.[76] In a final appeal to his
friends in the East, Hilary says that to approve ὁμοιούσιος one need not
disapprove of ὁμοούσιος. What about all the holy prelates now at rest,
who are now declared anathema? What the Homoeousians are attempting
to do is an impious act and Hilary cannot bear to hear one who uses
ὁμοούσιος in a right sense, being anathematized. Hilary understands the
word ὁμοιούσιος only if it is meant as a similarity of essence. Before even
hearing these two words he would have interpreted ὁμοιούσιος by ὁμοούσιος, i.e. that nothing could be similar according to nature unless it was
of the same nature. After the Nicene Council the fathers interpreted
ὁμοούσιος with care, but if anything has to be added to the interpretation,
Hilary wanted them all to consult together, so that what has been rightly
established be left undisturbed and what has been misunderstood, may
be removed.[77]

Hilary thus truly tried to promote the unity[78] between those who he
felt really confessed the same things, but he enumerates frankly the
obstacles which stood in the way of unity. As a scholar quite rightly put

[74] Ibid. 88 (PL 10.540A–541A).
[75] The text "homoeusii ambiguitas" (de Syn. 89 PL 10.541A), is clearly a spelling
mistake and should read "homousii," as in the Verona edition of 1730.
[76] De Syn. 89 (PL 10.541A–542A).
[77] Ibid. 91 (PL 10.543A–545B).
[78] Ibid. 83 (PL 10.535B).

it: "Die Schrift des Hilarius ist ein Friedenswerk auf ganz anderer Basis als das der Hofbischöfe: kein Totschweigen der Kontroverspunkte, kein Zurückschrauben der Entwickelung auf den Standpunkt der früheren Unbestimmtheit, sondern wirkliche Verständigung und positive Lehre. Er zeigt ein für jene Zeit seltenes Maass von Unbefangenheit und liebevollem Eingehen auf fremde Gedanken, aber trotz aller Moderation auch grosse Festigkeit."[79]

It is obvious that the *De Synodis* of Athanasius, written by the end of 359,[80] should be compared with that of Hilary. Athanasius exposes and refutes the Arians, but is conciliatory towards the Homoeousians and appeals to them to accept the word ὁμοούσιος.

After quoting most of the Arian formulas of faith, Athanasius refutes the Arians. They complained that the phrases ἐκ τῆς οὐσίας and ὁμοούσιος are an offence to some and a stumbling-block to many, but Athanasius replies that most men are well content with these words, e.g. the 400 bishops at Rimini. The terms are not at fault, but those who misinterpret them. Many people read the Scriptures wrongly, but the Scriptures are not the cause of this. Those who are offended by these terms are Arians. Athanasius states that he cannot understand their displeasure with the phrase ἐκ τῆς οὐσίας, because they have confessed that the Son was generated from the Father. If the names "Father" and "Son" are not only used as mere titles but truly mean what they express, then essence is signified. Athanasius dwells at length on the difference between creatures who are the works of God, the handywork of His will, and the Son Who is the Offspring of God, the Offspring of His essence. The objection by the Arians that these phrases are not Scriptural, is dismissed by Athanasius with the remark that the Arians also invented many phrases which are not from Scripture, e.g. "out of nothing, once He was not, He is alterable, Unoriginate and three hypostases." They had accepted essence as suitable once before (Dedication Creed at Antioch), but now they suddenly decided that essence should be abolished. If the Son is not like the Father in essence, something is wanting to the Image, and it would not be a complete Image.[81] The objection by the Arians that the sense of these expressions is obscure to them, and that they cannot master their meaning, is met by Athanasius with the simple answer that they should ask instruction from the well-informed; for otherwise every-

[79] J. Gummerus, *Die homöusianische Partei bis zum Tode des Konstantius*, Helsingfors, 1900, p. 114.
[80] J. Quasten, *Patrology*, Vol. III, Utrecht/Antwerp, 1960, p. 62.
[81] Athanasius, *de Syn.* 33–38 (PG 26.749D–761A; Opitz II 1 pp. 260–5).

thing in Scripture which is not understood should also be rejected.[82]

The Homoeousians are addressed quite cordially, as "brothers"[83] and "beloved ones."[84] They think the same as Athanasius does, but they only dispute the word. In confessing that the Son is from the essence of the Father and that He is not a creature or work of God, but His genuine and natural Offspring, and that He is eternally with the Father as being His Word and Wisdom, Athanasius concludes that they are not far from even accepting the word ὁμοούσιος. To say that the Son is "like according to essence" is inadequate, because one could say that a wolf is like to a dog but a wolf cannot be accounted the offspring of a dog. But since they say that the Son is "of the essence" (ἐκ τῆς οὐσίας) and "like-in-essence" (ὁμοιούσιος) to the Father, they signify nothing else but "coessential" (ὁμοούσιος).[85]

The Homoeousians alleged that the bishops who had condemned Paul of Samosata, had declared that the Son is not coessential with the Father. Athanasius knew that he would have to argue cautiously with them on this point. Prior to this council which condemned Paul of Samosata, Dionysius of Alexandria had been accused of denying that the Son was coessential with the Father. Athanasius, however, adduces the example of the Apostle Paul who had written about the law in different ways (cf. Rom. 7:12,14; 1 Tim. 1:8 and Gal. 3:11). In the same way a council had condemned the Samosatene for using ὁμοούσιος, while at Nicaea the council used this word in condemning the Arians. According to Athanasius, those who condemned the Samosatene took coessential in a bodily sense, for Paul had said that this phrase implied a prior essence from which two essences are derived. The Nicene fathers recognized that this word does not have this meaning when used of things immaterial and especially of God, and thereby acknowledging that the Word was not a creature but an Offspring of the essence of the Father, they used this term. Thus the Nicenes used ὁμοούσιος to establish the true genuineness of the Son and so that things which have an origin, have nothing in common with Him.[86]

---

[82] *Ibid.* 40 (PG 26.764A–B; Opitz II 1 p. 266).
[83] *Ibid.* 41 (PG 26.765A; Opitz II 1 p. 266).
[84] *Ibid.* 43 (PG 26.768C; Opitz II 1 p. 268).
[85] *Ibid.* 41 (PG 26.764D–768A; Opitz II 1 pp. 266–7).
[86] *Ibid.* 43–45 (PG 26.768C–776A; Opitz II 1 pp. 268–271). Various explanations have been given to the different reports by Hilary and Athanasius of the use of ὁμοούσιος in the synod which condemned Paul of Samosata. G. L. Prestige, *God in Patristic thought*, London, 1952², pp. 201–209, thought that Athanasius had given the correct report. F. Loofs, *Paulus von Samosata*, Leipzig, 1924, pp. 148–53; G. Bardy, *Paul de Samosate*, Louvain, 1929², pp. 336–49; Smulders, *op. cit.*, p. 92 n. 3 and Kelly, *Creeds*, pp. 247–8, believed that Hilary's account of the sense in which the word was used, was more reliable than that of Athanasius.

Athanasius states that if it is confessed that the Word is a genuine Offspring of the Father's essence and not a work, it should follow that He is inseparable from the Father, being connatural (ὁμοφυής) because He is born from Him and being such He should be called coessential. He is the Father's Word and Wisdom not from participation, but in essence. The text John 10:30 cannot mean that the Father and the Son are one only in agreement, for then saints and angels who are also in agreement with God would also be able to say: "I and the Father are one." This being absurd, it necessary follows that the oneness of the Father and the Son must be in essence. Athanasius also mentions that all the qualities which are attributed to God, e.g. almighty, light, eternity, Lord etc., are also attributed to the Son, except that He is called Father. An essence foreign to that of the Father does not admit to such attributes. The Son is therefore coessential with the Father, for what the Father has is the Son's by nature and He is Himself from the Father. Because of this one-ness of Godhead and of nature, He and the Father are one.[87]

Athanasius refuted the objection that "coessential" implies a prior essence from which two coessential substances were generated, and that it would be better not to speak of Father and of Son but brothers. He argues that there need only be the prior substance and one generated essence, for the generated essence and the original would be coessential. The oneness of the Father with the Son is not in the likeness of their teaching, but according to essence and in truth. Athanasius' objection to "like" is, that it is not used in connection with essence, but with habits and qualities, and in the case of essences, "identity" should be used and not "likeness." If by speaking of like according to essence, is meant like by participation, then ὁμοιούσιος may be used. But the Son is not by participation, but in nature and truth Son, Light, Wisdom, God, and therefore should be called not ὁμοιούσιος but ὁμοούσιος. The Nicene Council was correct in declaring that it is right to say that the Son, begotten from the Father's essence, is coessential with Him.[88]

There are many resemblances to be found in the work of Hilary and Athanasius. Hilary treated the objections to ὁμοούσιος more fully than Athanasius but it was due to the fact that he addressed his colleagues in the West and attempted to let them understand why this term was viewed with suspicion in the East. Hilary and Athanasius both pointed out that ὁμοιούσιος was inadequate. Hilary showed that similarity in essence means equality and Athanasius said that in the case of essence, identity of essence

[87] Ibid. 48–50 (PG 26.777B–784A; Opitz II 1 pp. 272–4).
[88] Ibid. 51–54 (PG 26.784A–789C; Opitz II 1 pp. 274–7).

is more fitting to be used than likeness. Hilary was perhaps more lenient towards the use of ὁμοιούσιος because he said that it could be used, although when correctly used it led to ὁμοούσιος. Athanasius was less compromising for he thought that where essence was concerned, similarity was inadequate and identity should be used. It must be borne in mind that Athanasius wrote after the councils of Rimini and Seleucia and this might have prompted him to this attitude.

The theory has been advanced that Hilary and Athanasius in thus interpreting *homoousios* did it in a homoeousian sense, i.e. that a generic unity rather than a numerical identity of substance was implied.[89] Before judging the merit of this view, it would have to be established in what sense ὁμοούσιος was used in the Nicene Creed.

It is probably due to the express wish of Emperor Constantine that the word ὁμοούσιος was inserted into the creed which was approved at Nicaea. Scholars also agree that the word was probably suggested to the emperor by his trusted counsellor, Ossius of Cordova. Some scholars find Western theological influences in the Nicene Creed,[90] but it has quite rightly been contended that ὁμοούσιος was not an accepted part of Western theological terminology, and that in its Latin translation it was never used as a theological key-word.[91] Much may therefore be said for the view that Ossius, while on his mission to the East to appease the different parties, came across the word ὁμοούσιος and finding it to be the rendering of the formula "unius substantiae," which was the accepted term in Western theology, thus suggested it to Constantine during the discussions at Nicaea.[92] It is not quite clear whether Ossius and Bishop Alexander of Alexandria had come to an agreement, as has been suggested,[93] nor what this consisted of. However it does seem unlikely that Alexander had suggested this term to Ossius.[94]

We do not know what had induced the emperor to demand the inclusion of this term in the creed, but one of its advantages was that it was ambiguous and could be interpreted in different ways by the respective theological groups.[95] This leads us to another problem, namely to

---

[89] Gummerus, *op. cit.*, p. 112; L. Coulange, "Métamorphose du Consubstantiel; Athanase et Hilaire," *Revue d'Histoire et de Littérature Religieuses*, Vol. 8 (1922), pp. 191–207.

[90] E.g. Harnack, *op. cit.*, p. 232 n. 4; H. Kraft, "'Ομοούσιος", *ZKG*, Vol. 66 (1954–55), p. 13.

[91] Lietzmann, *Geschichte der alten Kirche*, Vol. III p. 107; Kelly, *Creeds*, p. 251.

[92] Müller, *op. cit.*, p. 386; A. Gilg, *Weg und Bedeutung der altkirchlichen Christologie*, München, 1961², p. 64.

[93] Harnack, *op. cit.*, p. 195; Kelly, *Creeds*, p. 253.

[94] Clercq, *op. cit.*, p. 262.

[95] Berkhof, *Eusebius*, p. 183.

ascertain what interpretation the Nicene Council gave to this phrase.

The first occurrence of the word ὁμοούσιος[96] among Christian writers was in Gnostic circles. It had a generic sense, denoting things which belonged to the same class, made of the same stuff. Origen also had this generic sense in mind when he used the term in regard to the relations of the Persons of the Trinity. There was a community of substance between the Father and the Son, and the Son being an emanation from the Father, was ὁμοούσιος with the Father, because an emanation is of the same substance as the body from which it was an emanation or vapour. Paul of Samosata, according to Hilary, used ὁμοούσιος in the sense that the Father and the Son formed a single, undifferentiated being. Arius again, understood ὁμοούσιος in a materialistic sense, for he rejected the view that the Son was a μέρος ὁμοούσιον of the Father, thus implying a division of substance.

The word thus had a variety of meanings. Some scholars have asserted that when the word was used in the Nicene Creed, it meant to express the identity of substance between the Father and the Son.[97] In view of what has been said above however, it is doubtful whether the numerical identity of substance was the specific teaching of the Nicene fathers.[98] The question before the council was whether the Son was God in the true sense of the word. The problem of the Divine unity did not arise. Prior to Nicaea the word ὁμοούσιος had always conveyed, primarily at any rate, the generic sense, and it would be paradoxical to suppose that the Nicene fathers suddenly began employing a word which was familiar enough, in a novel sense. If Eusebius of Caesarea and his friends had had any suspicion that numerical identity of substance was being foisted on them, they would have objected to the word as Sabellian.

It may be concluded therefore, that every group was free to interpret the word as it wished. The Western bishops and a few in the East like Athanasius, Marcellus of Ancyra, Eustathius of Antioch and probably some Egyptian bishops, interpreted ὁμοούσιος in the sense of expressing a numerical identity of substance. But most of the Eastern bishops interpreted it in the "generic" sense in which the word had been previously used, e.g. by Origen. It was thus meant, as Eusebius of Caesarea explained it, to emphasize that the Son bore no resemblance to creatures, but that He was in every respect like the Father. A scholar has rightly asserted that ὁμοούσιος, as applied to the Godhead, requires the meaning of nu-

---

[96] For the following see Prestige, *op. cit.*, pp. 197ff.; Kelly, *Creeds*, pp. 243ff.; Kraft, *op. cit.*, pp. 3ff.

[97] E.g. Harnack, *op. cit.*, p. 217 n. 1; Seeberg, *op. cit.*, p. 42.

[98] For the following see Prestige, *op. cit.*, pp. 212–215; Kelly, *Doctrines*, pp. 234–7.

merical identity of substance, for since the divine nature is immaterial and indivisible, it follows that the Persons of the Godhead Who share it, must be one identical substance.[99] The majority of the Nicene Council however, did not interpret it in this way. A peculiar phenomenon is that Athanasius did not use it for a few decades after the council. A plausible reason was that he refrained from using the specific term, because he was conscious of the evil odour attached to the use of it. He did however, purposefully promote the doctrine for which it stood.[100]

In examining the theory of Gummerus, one must admit that Hilary did not mention identity of substance in his *De Synodis*. It is equally true that in his works written before and after this one, he did teach the numerical identity of substance in the Godhead.[101] In his *De Synodis*, which was written with a specific purpose, he wanted to allay the fear of the Homoe-ousians concerning the word ὁμοούσιος. That is why he wrote that when ὁμοούσιος was confessed, the "nativitas filii, subjectio, similitudo natu-rae"[102] was implied. It was to reject any suspicion of Sabellianism. It cannot be said, as Gummerus did,[103] that the correct interpretation of ὁμοούσιος was ὁμοιούσιος. There was no "correct" interpretation of ὁμοούσιος, as we have seen.

Hilary therefore writing to the Eastern bishops who were afraid that ὁμοούσιος was Sabellian, showed that it could be interpreted in a generic sense. But that does not imply that it should be interpreted only in a generic sense. In a work a few years later he insisted on the numerical identi-ty of substance. One must bear in mind that he was dealing with the Homoeousians who thought that ὁμοούσιος was Sabellian. Therefore he denies this, but says that it is to establish that the Son is God, born from the essence of God.

Hilary did explain ὁμοούσιος more fully than ὁμοιούσιος, as Gummerus said, but the reason was that it was still to be the basis of the union be-tween the Orthodox group and the Homoeousians. The ὁμοιούσιος was useful because it avoided any suspicion of Sabellianism, but it was in-adequate. Hilary emphasized that when a true likeness exists, then ὁμοούσιος is implied. A scholar has asserted that there is no real antithesis between generic and numerical oneness, if the Son's essential deity is acknowledged, for the Godhead is simple and indivisible.[104] Athanasius

[99] Kelly, *Doctrines*, p. 234.
[100] Gilg, *op. cit.*, p. 65; Kelly, *Creeds*, p. 260.
[101] Cf. *in Matt.* 8,8 (PL 9.961C); *Coll. ant. Par.* Ser. B II 11,5 (CV 65.153; *fragm.* II 32 PL 10.657A); *c. Aux.* 7 & 8 (PL 10.614A & B), 11 (PL 10.616A).
[102] *De Syn.* 70 (PL 10.527A).
[103] Gummerus, *op. cit.*, p. 112.
[104] Kelly, *Doctrines*, p. 254.

quite rightly insisted that "identity" is a more appropriate term than "likeness."

As was to be expected Hilary's work was criticized by the more radical bishops in the West, forcing him to write an *Apologetica ad reprehensores libri de Synodis responsa*.[105] Except for a few fragments, the work is lost.

The results of these attempts by Hilary and Athanasius to reconcile the Homoeousians and the West will be ascertained as the events which followed the publication of their works are treated.

5. HILARY AT SELEUCIA AND CONSTANTINOPLE

Before the bishops had assembled at Rimini and Seleucia, the bishops at the emperor's court at Sirmium decided to draft a formula which could be used at the respective councils as a basis for discussion. Among those present at the court at the time were Basil of Ancyra, Mark of Arethusa, Valens, Ursacius and Georg of Alexandria. This creed, the fourth formulated at Sirmium, became known as the Dated Creed because of the elaborate dating prefixed to it: "The Catholic Faith was published in the presence of our Master the most religious and gloriously victorious Emperor, Constantius, the eternal and august, and in the consulate of the most illustrious Flavians, Eusebius and Hypatius, in Sirmium on the eleventh day before the calends of June"[1] (May 22, 359). Mark of Arethusa is said to have been responsible for the final drafting of the creed,[2] which according to an ancient historian was originally written in Latin.[3] Athanasius remarked that this was the first time a creed had been dated and that this showed that this faith only dated from the reign of Constantius and not from of old.[1]

In this creed the Son was called ὅμοιον τῷ γεννήσαντι αὐτὸν πατρὶ κατὰ τὰς γραφάς. Further it was said that as the term "substance" was unknown to the people it gives offence and as the Scriptures do not contain it, it was removed and no further mention should be made of substance in regard to God. Finally the creed again described the Son as ὅμοιον τῷ

---

[105] PL 10.545C–548B.

[1] Athanasius, *de Syn.* 8 (PG 26.692B; Opitz II 1 p. 235,21–3).

[2] Hilary, *Coll. ant. Par.* Ser. B VI 3 (CV 65.163; *fragm.* XV 3 PL 10.721A–722A).

[3] Socrates, *h.e.* II 37 (PG 67.304C). Gummerus, *op. cit.*, p. 118 n. 2, thought this report not very trustworthy, and thought that in view of the bishops who were present, it was more likely that it was originally written in Greek. The report by Socrates is generally accepted by modern scholars. The original Latin version has been lost.

[4] Athanasius, *de Syn.* 3 (PG 26.685A; Opitz II 1 p. 232,29).

πατρὶ κατὰ πάντα as the Holy Scriptures themselves declare and teach.[5] As a whole "it was a mediating manifesto, designed as far as possible to please everybody,"[6] but in the end it pleased no one. This is illustrated by the disagreement which occured when the bishops had to sign the document. Valens only wrote "like" and only at the bidding of Constantius did he add "in all things." Basil who had to see his ὁμοιούσιος rejected, added that the Son was like the Father in all things, not just in will, but κατὰ τὴν ὑπόστασιν καὶ κατὰ τὴν ὕπαρξιν καὶ κατὰ τὸ εἶναι.[7]

This formula was essentially the creed which was signed by the delegates of Rimini at Nicé (Oct. 359). There were a few significant differences. It stated that the Son is like the Father but "in all things" was omitted and not only was the use of the word "substance" prohibited but also the use of the phrase "one hypostasis" in regard to the Trinity.[8]

The bishops in the East assembled at Seleucia by the end of September, 359. Hilary attended this council and he was the only bishop of the West to be present. Scholars have found it difficult to explain this fact. It is generally assumed however, that Basil of Ancyra and his friends were in some way responsible.[9] We do not, however, find anything in our sources to substantiate this assumption. Sulpicius Severus said that like all the other bishops, Hilary was summoned by the civil authority to attend the council because the emperor had given no special command about Hilary. Sulpicius said that he thought it was due to the providence of God that a man like Hilary who was instructed in divine doctrine, should be present when matters of faith was being discussed.[10]

It has been assumed that Hilary took no part in the discussions during the council.[11] According to an ancient historian he was questioned about the faith of the bishops in Gaul because the East suspected the West of believing in a union of a solitary God as Sabellius had done. After Hilary had reassured the Eastern bishops of his orthodoxy by giving an exposition of his faith, he was accepted in their communion.[12] Whether this was in the course of public or private discussions we do not know. Even if Hilary took no part in the official discussions, he did meet different bishops privately.

---

[5] For the creed cf. Athanasius, de Syn. 8 (PG 26.692B–693B; Opitz II 1 p. 235, 29–236,15).
[6] Kelly, Creeds, p. 290.
[7] Epiphanius, Haer. 73,22 (GCS 37.295).
[8] For the creed cf. Athanasius, de Syn. 30 (PG 26.745C–748C; Opitz II 1 pp. 258–9).
[9] Viehhauser, op. cit., p. 29; Reinkens, op. cit., p. 189; Feder, "Studien III," p. 15.
[10] Sulpicius Severus, Chron. II 42,2–3 (CV 1.95).
[11] Feder, "Studien III," p. 16.
[12] Sulpicius Severus, Chron. II 42,4–5 (CV 1.95–96).

Hilary wrote of the godlessness of those who said that Christ is unlike God, because He was not born from the substance of God and that He was a creature.[13] Hilary asked one of the bishops why they denied that the Father and the Son was of one substance or like in substance and why they condemned even those who said that the Son is unlike the Father. This bishop replied that Christ was not like God but like the Father. Hilary, who pretended to know nothing about the dispute, said that he found this answer even more obscure. The bishop then explained that the Father willed to create a creature who would will the same things as He and therefore Christ is like the Father because He is a Son of His will rather than of His divinity. Christ is unlike God because He is neither God nor from God, i.e. born from the substance of God. Hilary declared that he was astonished to hear this and could not believe it until he heard that this was the general opinion of this group of bishops.[14]

Just as at Rimini the two groups could not reach any agreement. The majority (Homoeousians) reverted to the creed of the Dedication Council (Antioch II), while the Acacians, condemning ὁμοούσιος, ὁμοιούσιος and ἀνόμοιος, accepted the Dated Creed (Sirmium IV) with the omission of "in all things" after "like." Both groups sent a delegation of ten men to the emperor at Constantinople and Hilary joined the delegates. The imperial officials apparently did not object to this. On 31 December 359 the Homoeousians finally submitted to the emperor's wish and the Homoean draft was signed. In January 360 a synod, dominated by the Homoeans, was held in Constantinople, and henceforth the official creed of the Church was that the Son was "like" the Father, without any qualification or addition.

It is very probable that while in Constantinople, Hilary wrote the second book of his *Adversus Valentem et Ursacium*, possibly with the intention of obtaining an annulment of the decisions of the council of Rimini. It seems likely, that his work was published before the Homoeousian delegates of Seleucia signed the Homoean creed on the last day of 359, and therefore sometime in December.[15] Of the fragments which were handed down to us the letters of Liberius and the documents of the councils of Rimini and Seleucia probably come from the work published at the end of 359.[16]

In the letter known as "Studens paci," Liberius declared that he no longer accepted Athanasius in his church communion. In the narrative

---

[13] *Contra Const.* 12 (PL 10.591A).
[14] *Ibid.* 14 (PL 10.592A–593A).
[15] Feder, "Studien I," pp. 122–3.
[16] For the so-called exile-letters of Liberius, see Feder, "Studien I," pp. 153–183,

text the reader is reminded that Liberius contradicted himself by excluding Athanasius from his communion and yet accepting the decrees of
Sardica which were favourable to Athanasius.[17] After the synod at Arles
(353) Liberius wrote a letter to Constantius, known as "Obsecro." Hilary
did not comment upon this letter in which Liberius requested that a new
council be held and which resulted in the synod at Milan (355).[18]

Other letters written by Liberius are one addressed to Eusebius (of
Vercelli), Dionysius (of Milan) and Lucifer, who were sent into exile by
the council of Milan (355)[19]; a fragment of a letter to Caecilianus, bishop
of Spolitinum[20]; a letter to Ossius of Cordova on the fall of Vincentius
of Capua (Arles 353)[21] with a comment by Hilary that Liberius himself
had been sent into exile and had changed his earlier attitude towards
Athanasius.[22] The work by Hilary also includes the letters written by
Liberius in his exile, namely the letter to the Eastern bishops and presby-
ters, known as "pro deifico," in which he said that he was no longer in
communion with Athanasius and that he had signed the creed of Sirmium.[23] In an explanatory paragraph we find the names of those who had
signed this creed which was probably the Sirmium I (351).[24] Finally we
find the letters of Liberius to Ursacius, Valens and Germinius, known as
"Quia scio" and to Vincentius, known as "Non doceo," without any
commentary by Hilary.[25]

We also find the letter which Constantius sent to the bishops who had
assembled at Rimini.[26] The bishops at Rimini decided that nothing new
should be added to the Nicene Creed and that "substantia" was to be
retained as the Church had always taught it.[27] Hilary wrote of this council
that the bishops had decided that those who were opposed to this reten-
tion of the traditional faith, should be condemned. There follows the
condemnation of the heretics which was proclaimed by this council.[28]
In the letter of the council of Rimini to Constantius the bishops declare

who proves their authenticity.
[17] *Coll. ant. Par.* Ser. B III 1–2 (CV 65.155–156; *fragm.* IV PL 10.678C–681B).
[18] For the letter cf. *Coll. ant. Par.* Ser. A VII (CV 65.89–93; *fragm.* V PL 10.681B–686B).
[19] *Coll. ant. Par.* Ser. B VII 2 (CV 65.164–166; *fragm.* VI 1–2 PL 10.686B–688A).
[20] *Ibid.* Ser. B VII 4 (CV 65.166; *fragm.* VI 3 PL 10.688A).
[21] *Ibid.* Ser. B VII 6 (CV 65.167; *fragm.* VI 3 PL 10.688B–C).
[22] *Ibid.* Ser. B VII 7 (CV 65.167–168; *fragm.* VI 4 PL 10.688C–689A).
[23] *Ibid.* Ser. B VII 8 (CV 65.168–170; *fragm.* VI 5–6 PL 10.689A–691A).
[24] *Ibid.* Ser. B VII 9 (CV 65.170; *fragm.* VI 7 PL 10.692A). Cf. Feder, "Studien I," p. 169.
[25] *Ibid.* Ser. B VII 10–11 (CV 65.170–173; *fragm.* VI 8–11 PL 10.693A–695D).
[26] *Ibid.* Ser. A VIII (CV 65.93–94; *fragm.* VII 1–2 PL 10.695C–696C).
[27] *Ibid.* Ser. A IX 1 (CV 65.95–96; *fragm.* VII 3 PL 10.697A–B).
[28] *Ibid.* Ser. A IX 2–3 (CV 65.96–97; *fragm.* VII 4 PL 10.697B–698A).

that they retain the Nicaenum and they request the emperor to allow them to return to their sees.[29] In the commentary we learn that the orthodox bishops sent ten delegates to the emperor but the heretics also sent delegates and they were received by the emperor while the orthodox bishops were not. Finally these ten orthodox bishops rejected the true faith and accepted the false faith which they had earlier condemned.[30]

In the next document it was said that the delegates in Nicé decided that Ursacius, Valens, Germinius and Gaius had been wrongly condemned by the council at Rimini. In the narrative text Hilary said that a copy of the confession which the delegates had signed would follow.[31] This might have been included in the original work of Hilary, or the promised document may merely be the next one in our collection, namely the letter of the council of Rimini to the Emperor Constantius, after they had subscribed to the formula of Nicé. In this letter they thanked the emperor for having permitted them to reject the words "ousia" and "homoousios" which were unknown and had caused all the trouble in the Church. They also requested to be allowed to return to their sees.[32]

Finally there is the letter of the delegates of Seleucia to the delegates of Rimini, informing them that Aetius was being condemned, but not his teaching and warning them to notice this distinction.[33] The delegates of Seleucia were apparently unaware of the complete submission of the Western delegates to the emperor's wishes. This document was written before their own submission on 31 December 359. In the commentary on this letter Hilary stated that the delegates of Seleucia, on arrival at Constantinople, had informed the delegates of the West about all that had happened. Hilary could not understand why the Western bishops did not change their view. He also refutes some of the phrases which were subscribed to by the council of Rimini. They had agreed that the Son "was not created like other creatures." This meant that they did not deny that the Son was a creature. He pointed out that creatures also differ from one another; for example an angel is not like a human being; man is unlike a bird; and a bird is not like a sheep. The second phrase to be considered was that the Son is not from the non-existent but "from God." This could mean that the Son was only from God through His will, for it was not said that He was from the substance of God. It was said that the Son was "eternally with the Father." To exclude any possibility of ascribing any

---

[29] *Ibid.* Ser. A V 1 (CV 65.78–85; *fragm.* VIII 1–3 PL 10.699A–701C).
[30] *Ibid.* Ser. A V 2 (CV 65.85; *fragm.* VIII 4 PL 10.701C–702A).
[31] *Ibid.* Ser. A V 3–4 (CV 65.85–86; *fragm.* VIII 5–7 PL 10.702A–C).
[32] *Ibid.* Ser. A VI (CV 65.87–88; *fragm.* IX PL 10.703A–705A).
[33] *Ibid.* Ser. B VIII 1 (CV 65.174–175; *fragm.* X 1 PL 10.705B–706B).

notion of time to the origin of the Son it should have been said that He
was before the eternal ages born from the true Father. Finally Hilary
refutes the phrase that the Son is "like the Father according to the
Scriptures." According to the Scriptures man is like God; and a mustard
seed, leaven and a fishing net are likened to the kingdom of heaven. The
commentary ends with a last warning that when they deny that Christ is
the true and Only-begotten Son of God, the bishops are fighting against
God.[34]

These warnings were all to no avail and the result of the discussions at
Constantinople are well-known.

6. HILARY AND THE EMPEROR CONSTANTIUS

While in Constantinople, Hilary wrote a letter to Constantius, known
as the *Ad Constantium Augustum liber secundus*. This title is not quite correct,
because we have seen that the *Ad Constantium liber primus* was not a
separate letter written by Hilary to the emperor, but part of his historical
work, *Adversus Valentem et Ursacium*. Hilary therefore wrote only one
letter *Ad Constantium*.

In the letter we find some evidence of the date when it was written.
Hilary was still in exile and Saturninus who was mainly responsible for
his banishment, was in the same city (Constantinople).[1] At that time a
synod was discussing matters of faith.[2] The problem is which synod
Hilary referred to. It was most probably the synod held in the beginning
of 360 (probably January) in Constantinople by the so-called Acacians.[3]
Feder however, doubted whether Hilary would have called this synod a
"synodus dissidens,"[4] and thought this could only refer to the meetings
of bishops which were held at the end of 359 when there was indeed a
difference of opinion. Feder also thought that the *Contra Constantium*,
which was written after the *Ad Constantium (II)*, must have been written
before January 360. According to him a description in a certain passage[5]
of Hilary's book conveyed the impression that it was written before

[34] *Ibid.* Ser. B VIII 2 (CV 65.175–177; *fragm.* X 2–4 PL 10.706B–710A).
[1] *Ad Const.* (II) 2.
[2] *Ibid.* 8 (CV 65.203,7–9; PL 10.569B): rogo, ut praesente synodo, quae nunc de
fide litigat, pauca me de scripturis euangelicis digneris audire.
[3] Loofs, "Hilarius," pp. 62–3; Bardenhewer, *op. cit.*, p. 385; Schanz, *op. cit.*, p. 290.
[4] *Ad Const.* (II) 10. Cf. Feder, "Studien III," p. 14. This phrase does not have to be
interpreted thus. "Dissidens" can mean "heretical" (cf. A. Blaise, *Dictionnaire Latin-
Français*, s.v. *dissidens* and *dissideo*; *Thesaurus Linguae Latinae*, Vol. V, col. 1468). Hilary
might also have meant: "a synod which differs (from me)."
[5] *Contra Const.* 7.

January 360. On the other hand this description of the way in which Constantius terrorized the Church can refer to conditions in January 360, for after what had been said it was not necessary for Hilary to mention explicitly the final submission of the Church to the will of the emperor (31 December 359).

Hilary thus addressed this letter to Constantius early in 360, requesting an opportunity to be heard by the emperor. Hilary wished to be allowed to prove his innocence of the charges for which he was banished and he wanted to make Saturninus confess his guilt.[6] Hilary also asked the emperor to allow him to say something about the matters of faith being discussed in the synod at the time. He wanted to instruct the emperor about the true faith as it is found in the Holy Scriptures and not in newly drawn up documents.[7] The question of the faith and Christian hope was very much in his mind.[8]

Sulpicius Severus said that Hilary had written three letters to Constantius to request an audience.[9] We only have one letter which fits this description. Whether Hilary really wrote three letters of which only one was handed down to us, or whether Sulpicius Severus referred to the three so-called letters to Constantius (so-called *ad Const.* (*I*); *ad Const.* (*II*) and *c. Const.*), we do not know.

The letter to Constantius reveals "a proper respect for the emperor."[10] The emperor is addressed as "piissime imperator (1), pietas uestra (2), dignantissime imperator (3), optime ac religiosissime imperator (4), dignatio tua (8)." Hilary describes Constantius as "bonus ac religiosus (1), imperator pius (2)," and Constantius is referred to as "beatae religiosaeque uoluntatis uirum (8)."

Hilary declares that he was banished as a result of false reports, that he has an important witness, the Caesar Julian, and that he had done nothing which was unworthy even of a layman (2). Hilary is afraid of the danger which is threatening the world and even the emperor (3). The emperor is desirous of hearing the word of God (8) but the bishops, from whom he wishes to hear the true faith, compose their own creeds instead of preaching about God (4).

Hilary asks why they search for a creed, as if there was none; and why must a creed be drawn up, as if people do not have it in their hearts (6).

---

[6] *Ad Const.* (II) 2–3.
[7] *Ibid.* 8.
[8] Cf. *ibid.* 3.
[9] Sulpicius Severus, *Chron.* II 45,3 (CV 1.98): tribus libellis publice datis audientiam regis (Hilarius) poposcit.
[10] K. M. Setton, *Christian attitude towards the Emperor in the Fourth Century especially as shown in addresses to the Emperor*, New York, 1941, p. 100.

In composing new creeds the old confessions were rejected but the new creed was never confirmed and as many creeds were written as there were differences of opinion (4). Annually or even monthly, new creeds were decided on and by always condemning a previous creed, people in the end condemn themselves (5). One emendation follows the other (7) and while one person is condemning another, almost no one is a Christian any more (5). That which the fathers decreed (Hilary is probably referring to Nicaea) is not wrong but because of human indiscretion it led to contradictions (7). In the last year four confessions[11] had been drawn up to no avail (5).

Hilary's solution to this problem is that the baptismal confession, namely faith "in the name of the Father and the Son and the Holy Spirit," should not be doubted or changed (4). The sailors fearing shipwreck because of a threatening storm, think it safer to return to the harbour. Facing a shipwreck of the faith, the Christians should return to their first and only evangelical faith which they confessed at their baptism (7). A creed is unnecessary. "Regenerated through faith we are being instructed in the faith as if it was possible to be regenerated without the faith. After our baptism we learn about Christ as if baptism can be of any value without faith in Christ."[12] All the heretics claim to preach according to the Scriptures but they do not have the sense of the Scriptures (9). Hilary will however, instruct the emperor about Christ (10). Finally he submits a short proof of what he intended to tell the emperor. It consisted of a number of texts from the Scriptures in the form of a creed, mainly concerning the Lord Jesus Christ (11).

From the above summary of the contents it is clear that the question of faith was foremost in his mind,[13] although he naturally would have also welcomed the opportunity to discuss the reasons for his banishment personally with Constantius. The letter has aptly been described by a scholar as polite and guarded, as it should be, yet firm and urgent, almost menacing in the pride of its orthodoxy.[14]

---

[11] The "proximi anni fides" were 1) *homoousion* was not to be used; 2) *homoousion* was to be preached; 3) *ousiam* was not used; 4) *ousiam* was condemned. It is difficult to ascertain which four statements were meant. The Benedictines (PL 10.567 n. b) thought Sirmium II (357), Ancyra, Rimini-Nicé, Seleucia (Acacians). To reach this conclusion a) *proximi anni* was not taken in a strict sense; b) *homoeousion* had to be substituted for *homoousion* in the second statement of faith. Loofs, "Hilarius," p. 63, thought that Sirmium IV (Dated Creed); the definition of the Western bishops at Rimini; Acacians at Seleucia; Constantinopolitan on 31 Dec. 359, were referred to. Feder, "Studien III," p. 13, suggested Sirmium II (357), Ancyra, Rimini (359) and Nicé. Hilary probably referred to Sirmium II (357); the Western bishops at Rimini; Sirmium IV (= Nicé); the Acacian formula at Seleucia.
[12] *Ad Const.* (II) 6 (CV 65.201,14–16; PL 10.567C–568A).
[13] Cf. Galtier, *op. cit.*, p. 64.
[14] Wilmart, *RB*, Vol. 24 (1907), p. 151.

A remarkable feature in this letter is Hilary's proposal to revert to the baptismal formula. A scholar found this an interesting aspect because the withdrawal of the Nicene Creed was hereby proposed by a leading combatant of the orthodox group in the Church.[15] As we saw above, Hilary did not think the declarations of the Nicene Council had been wrong, but rather that the Nicaenum had been misused by the heretics.[16] It is difficult to ascertain why Hilary proposed a reversal to the baptismal formula. It has been suggested that he wanted to save his Homoeousian friends who were faced with the prospect of exile, if they did not subscribe to the Homocan formula. If this formula was substituted by the baptismal formula, Hilary's friends in the East could have signed the creed without scruples and thus be spared the exile.[17] Hilary must have realized that the baptismal creed was open to even more abuse than the other creeds which had been drawn up after the Nicene Creed, for it was open to many interpretations. Hilary could not have made this proposal with the intention of excluding the heretics because they could have subscribed to the baptismal formula. As a scholar remarked, this was a concession which only a sense of extreme urgency could have induced Hilary to make,[18] but we will probably never know the precise reason for this proposal.

Constantius did not grant Hilary's request to be heard but sent him back to Gaul instead. According to Sulpicius Severus this was done because Hilary was regarded as the "discordiae seminarium et perturbator Orientis."[19] A modern scholar claims to have found some evidence in Hilary's work which may indicate that his return to Gaul was due to his own independent action rather than an imperial command.[20] This conjecture is apparently accepted by Wilmart,[21] but Le Bachelet rightly considered that the word "fugere" was interpreted in a too strict sense.[22] The meaning of this phrase however is obscure. Watson thought that, in accordance with the policy of the Homoeans, because the orthodoxy of the West was an influence which could not be ignored and because the Nicenes in the East were a power worth conciliating, Hilary was permitted to return. "Reasons of state as well as of ecclesiastical interest favoured

[15] Watson, *op. cit.*, pp. xxiii–xxiv.
[16] *Ad Const.* (II) 7 (CV 65.202,15–18; PL 10.568B–569A).
[17] Watson, *op. cit.*, p. xxiv.
[18] Watson, *loc. cit.*
[19] *Chron.* II 45,4 (CV 1.98).
[20] In *contra Const.* Hilary called himself an exile (2), he said that he was persecuted (9), and elsewhere we find the puzzling phrase "fugere mihi sub Nerone licuit" (11). Cf. Loofs, "Hilarius," p. 63.
[21] Wilmart, *RB*, Vol. 24 (1907), p. 150: à moitié renvoyé de Constantinople, à moitié fugitif volontaire.
[22] Le Bachelet, *art. cit.*, col. 2393.

his restoration."[23] It is difficult to find a reasonable answer to the question as to why Constantius ordered Hilary to return to Gaul when he knew that Hilary was bound to stir up trouble in the West. It is also unlikely that Hilary returned of his own accord because although he might have expected unrest in the West because of the troups which Constantius had demanded from Julian, Hilary could not foresee that the West would revolt against Constantius. If he had fled from Constantinople, as has been suggested, he could have expected arrest by imperial officials in the West.

It may be assumed that in the first half of 360 Hilary returned to Gaul. If the emperor had thought that Hilary would be grateful that he was ordered back to the West, he was mistaken. Hilary, who had not been given the opportunity to put his own case of unjust banishment personally to Constantius and who had not been allowed to take part in the discussions concerning the faith, reacted by writing his violent *Contra Constantium Imperatorem*.

According to Jerome Hilary wrote this work after Constantius' death.[24] In this work Hilary says that it is the fifth year after the council was held in Milan (355) and he and other bishops in Gaul had separated themselves from communion with Saturninus, Ursacius and Valens.[25] Hilary also mentions the final subjection of the Homoeousians and their banishment[26] by the synod of Constantinople (360). It is therefore likely that Hilary wrote this work just before he left Constantinople, or during his journey to Gaul. Some scholars considered that Jerome's report could indicate that the work was published after Constantius' death. Hilary however, could have published his book after arriving in Gaul. A fact which lends support to this view is that he addresses his fellow-bishops.[27] The work might even be seen to some extent as a means of informing his Western friends of the general situation. A scholar has suggested that this work was probably used by Julian as propaganda and that he might even have inspired Hilary to write it.[28] It is unlikely that Hilary would have written it only to serve Julian's propaganda. Hilary wanted to vent his feelings and denounce the way in which Constantius subjected the Church to his own wishes.

According to Setton, Hilary was more courageous behind the emperor's back than in his presence. In his *Ad Constantium* (*II*) he had addressed

[23] Watson, *op. cit.*, p. xxv.
[24] *De viris ill.* c. 100 (PL 23.738C–739A): et alius in Constantium, quem post mortem ejus scripsit.
[25] *Contra Const.* 2 (PL 10.578D–579A).
[26] *Ibid.* 15; 25 (PL 10.593B; 600B).
[27] *Ibid.* 2.
[28] A. Piganiol, *Histoire Romaine*, Vol. IV.2, Paris, 1947, p. 107 n. 94.

the emperor only in terms of respect while in his *Contra Constantium* he declared that he had known for a long time that Constantius was a peril to the faith. Drawing a parallel between Hilary's *Contra Constantium* and Athanasius' *Historia Arianorum*, Setton concluded that neither of them were cowards but they were not excessively brave men, for it was one thing to think ill of the emperor, but another to speak ill of the emperor in his presence.[29] One must however bear in mind the different background of Hilary's two works to Constantius. In *Ad Constantium (II)* Hilary still thought that he could achieve some results if he was given the opportunity to confront the emperor personally. In his other work he realized that all was lost and that the Church was a slave to Constantius and his court bishops.

In *Contra Constantium* the emperor is referred to as "omnium crudelium crudelissime (8), scelestissime mortalium (8), lupe rapax (10,11), sceleste (11,25), diabolicum ingenium (17), fallax blandimentum (20)."

Hilary begins by saying that it is time to speak out, for the time to remain silent has passed (1). After the events at Milan he had foreseen the danger threatening the Church. After his own banishment he had decided to take every honest and acceptable opportunity which occurred to unite with fellow-orthodox bishops. At the moment the Church is a "antichristi synagoga" (2). He had long been silent but for the sake of Christ he now had to speak (3). He did not fear to do so, trusting in God Who had in the past aided the Jewish youths in the oven, as well as Jona and Paul (4).

The struggle was against a deceitful persecutor, an enemy who flatters people, against Constantius the antichrist[30]: Constantius who does not scourge one's back but flatters the stomach; who does not imprison one to be free in spirit, but honours one in the palace to servitude; who does not behead people but kills their soul with gold, who procures unity (in the Church) so that there may be no peace; who erects churches to destroy the faith (5). It was not audacious of Hilary to call Constantius the antichrist for John the Baptist had told Herod that he could not marry his brother's wife (Mark 6:18) (6). Constantius is fighting against God; he is pretending to be a Christian but is really a new enemy of Christ; he draws up confessions of faith but lives in opposition to the true faith (7). Nero and other persecuters of the Christians gave martyrs to the Church and through the relics of these martyrs many miracles are performed. Under

---

[29] Setton, *op. cit.*, pp. 99–103.
[30] Elsewhere Hilary again calls Constantius the antichrist (c. 6), but also the precursor of the antichrist (c. 7). Athanasius, *Historia Arianorum* 74–77 (PG 25.781C–788A) also called Constantius the precursor of the antichrist. Cf. Lucifer, *De sancto Athanasio* II 11 (CV 14.168,13–6).

the guise of a Christian, Constantius extinguishes the Christian faith (8). The other persecutors of Christians were hostile to Christ alone but Constantius struggles against God the Father, because he thought that God had falsely stated that He was Father (9). The emperor is a wolf dressed up as a sheep. He bows his head to be blessed but with his feet tramples upon the true faith (10).

Hilary then describes how Constantius had terrorized the Church since 353 (11) and describes his own experience at the council of Seleucia (12–15). Constantius did not want words to be used which were not found in Scripture. To this Hilary replied: "Who commands bishops? And who forbids the form of the apostolic preaching?"[31] Hilary refutes in detail the view that the Son is like the Father. Constantius decreed that it be taught that the Son is like the Father but he did not mention that it was written that the Son is equal to the Father. The Jews wanted to kill Jesus because He had made Himself equal to God (John 5:18), and said that He did the same works as the Father. It was said that the Son is like the Father according to the Scriptures, but man was also created after the image and likeness of God. Hilary again declares that to employ "likeness" in connection with the Son and the Father is correct if a union (unio) was excluded by the use of the word "likeness." But first Hilary wants the word "equal" to be used before he concedes "likeness" being used. Constantius denies the birth of the Son by using the word "likeness" (17–22).

According to Hilary, Constantius is like an unskilled builder because he is displeased by the creeds which he has drawn up and thus always emends what he has previously done (23). All the creeds which the Church had drawn up were to be condemned because *homoousios*, *homoeousios* and even the use of *substantia* were rejected. The Church was ridiculed because bishops were forced to accept what they had previously rejected (25). Constantius confesses to be a Christian but his deeds testify to the contrary (26). People usually fight with living people but Constantius torments even those who had gone to their eternal rest. There is nobody, dead or alive, whose words have not been recalled by Constantius, even the creed of the bishops who had assembled at Nicaea. Hilary concludes his work with the words: "Know that you are an enemy of the divine religion, hostile to the memory of the saints and a rebellious heir of your pious father."[32]

It has been said that Hilary was one of the bishops who contributed

[31] *Contra Const.* 16 (PL 10.594A): Nolo, inquit, verba quae non scripta sunt dici. Hoc tandem rogo quis episcopis jubeat? et quis apostolicae praedicationis vetet formam?
[32] *Ibid.* 27 (PL 10.603A).

towards the solution of the growing problem of the relation between the Church and State.[33] On the other hand a scholar has asserted that Lucifer, Ossius and Hilary opposed Constantius only because they thought that he had endangered the true faith.[34]

From Hilary's two works to Constantius it is clear that Hilary was primarily concerned with the fact that the emperor was an Arian. There is only one sentence[35] which might in any way suggest that Hilary was thinking of the relation between the emperor and the Church. Hilary does not however, elaborate on this theme and it is not known what precisely he meant with these words. In Hilary's commentary on the Synodal letter of Sardica he wrote that the bishops would not want the emperor to force people to confess the true faith, for God, the Lord of the universe, does not require a forced confession.[36] Hilary here only develops the general principle of liberty in religion[37] and does not say anything of the relation between Church and State.

Berkhof quite rightly said that in his *Contra Constantium* Hilary was so preoccupied with the theological problem that he did not formulate any theory about the relation between Church and State.[38] The statement by the same scholar that it was only accidental that Hilary did not formulate the demand for the freedom of the Church,[39] is questionable. If Hilary ever thought about the problem of the relation between the Church and the State, then he would have surely referred to the problem in his letters to Constantius. Ossius for instance, although only late in his life, realized what limit there must be to the imperial power. In his letter to Constantius he clearly formulated that the emperor had to rule the Empire but that he was not to intrude into ecclesiastical matters, for those affairs were entrusted by God to His Church.[40] Hilary thus did not clearly define the different limits of imperial and church powers but his importance may be seen, as Berkhof justly put it, in the boldness and frankness with which he opposed the emperor.[41]

[33] Harnack, *op. cit.*, p. 252 n. 1; Jullian, *op. cit.*, p. 216; H. von Campenhausen, *Lateinische Kirchenväter*, Stuttgart, 1960, p. 78.
[34] K. Aland, "Kaiser und Kirche von Konstantin bis Byzanz," *Kirchengeschichtliche Entwürfe*, Gütersloh, 1960, p. 278.
[35] Cf. note 31 above.
[36] *Textus narrat.* 1 (CV 65.185,6–9; *ad Const.* (I) 6 PL 10.561A): Si ad fidem ueram istiusmodi uis adhiberetur, episcopalis doctrina obuiam pergeret diceretque: deus uniuersitatis est dominus, obsequio non eget necessario, non requirit coactam confessionem.
[37] S. L. Greenslade, *Church and State from Constantine to Theodosius*, London, 1954, pp. 41–2.
[38] H. Berkhof, *De Kerk en de Keizer*, p. 130.
[39] *Ibid.*, p. 101.
[40] Athanasius, *Historia Arianorum* 44 (PG 25.745C–D).
[41] Berkhof, *op. cit.*, p. 130.

CHAPTER IV

HILARY'S RETURN TO GAUL

1. THE SYNOD OF PARIS

Most scholars assume that Hilary returned to Gaul in the course of 360. Some think that he had reached Gaul by summer of that year[1] but other scholars put it at the end of 360 or the beginning of 361.[2] He was enthusiastically welcomed by his congregation.[3]

According to an ancient historian synods were held in many places.[4] Information about these synods is very vague and it cannot be established how many synods were held, nor when exactly they took place. This is also true of the synod held in Paris. Scholars differ in their estimates of when it took place. Some think it was held before the end of 360,[5] others put it somewhat later at the end of 360 or beginning of 361,[6] while some think it was only held in 361.[7] It is likely that Hilary was the force behind this synod. One scholar rightly said that the description in the encyclical letter of the events in the East was so lively that this synod probably assembled soon after Hilary's return to the West.[8]

The letter from this synod to the bishops in the East is found in one of Hilary's works.[9] Hilary had brought a letter with him from the bishops in the East (Homoeousians). In their encyclical letter the Western bishops thank God that they are free from the doctrinal error. From the letter which they had received they learnt what had happened in the East and how their delegates were misled at Nicé (1). They accept the word *homoousios* but reject the Sabellian blasphemy that the Father and the Son are a union. The Son is not a part of the Father, but whole and perfect Only-begotten God, born from the whole and perfect unborn God. He is one *ousia* or substance with the Father and not a creature or an adoptive

---

[1] Feder, "Studien I," p. 63; Smulders, *op. cit.*, p. 68; Griffe, *op. cit.*, p. 190.
[2] Loofs, "Hilarius," p. 64; Le Bachelet, *art. cit.*, col. 2394.
[3] Venantius Fortunatus, *Vita S. Hil.* I 11(PL 88.445C).
[4] Sulpicius Severus, *Chron.* II 45,5 (CV 1.98).
[5] Bardy, "Humaniste," p. 20; Galtier, *op. cit.*, p. 71; Kidd, *op. cit.*, p. 176; Holmes, *op. cit.*, p. 179; Goemans, *op. cit.*, p. 162; Jullian, *op. cit.*, p. 218 n. 4.
[6] Hefele–Leclercq, *op. cit.*, p. 960; Dormagen, *op. cit.*, p. 59.
[7] Loofs, "Hilarius," p. 64; Reinkens, *op. cit.*, p. 250; Le Bachelet, *art. cit.*, col. 2394.
[8] Feder, "Studien I," p. 63.
[9] *Coll. ant. Par.* Ser. A I (CV 65.43–46; *fragm.* XI 1–4 PL 10.710A–713A).

or nominal Son of God. They do not reject the idea of likeness between the Father and the Son but they understand this in the sense that the true God is like the true God. They confess that there is a unity of the God-head and not a union. The unity between Father and Son is not only in charity but also in divinity (2).

They absolutely reject the view of those who say that the Son did not exist before He was born. They never said that the Only-begotten was unborn, but they said that it was impious to think that there was any extent of time before God. The Son was obedient to the Father in accordance with the weakness of the flesh which He had assumed (3). From the letter of the Eastern bishops and from Hilary's reports, they realized that they had been deceived at Constantinople. They also condemn Auxentius, Ursacius, Valens, Gaius, Megasius and Justinus who were condemned by the Eastern bishops. Saturninus who had been excommunicated before is again condemned (4).

The doctrinal points which were emphasized in the letter were all made by Hilary in previous works of his and although he was not the only bishop of those who attended this synod, who knew all the finer points in the dispute, it seems likely that he had a hand in drawing up this document.

It may be assumed that after the synod Hilary would have continued to rally the West to the orthodox doctrine. Jerome[10] mentions a book of his *Ad praefectum Sallustium sive contra Dioscorum*. The book is lost but it must have been written during the reign of Julian, between 361–362, when Sallustius was head of the prefecture in Gaul.[11] The doctor Dioscorus probably opposed the Christians in some way and Hilary reacted with the above-mentioned work.

2. HIS OPPOSITION TO AUXENTIUS

We may assume that Hilary continued his task of inducing the bishops in Gaul and Italy to renounce their submission to the wishes of Constantius at Rimini and Nicé. Hilary was later joined by Eusebius of Vercelli who had returned to the West after attending the synod at Alexandria (362). According to ancient historians, Hilary and Eusebius were responsible for driving away the clouds of heresy from Italy and Gaul.[12]

[10] *De viris ill.* c. 100 (PL 23.739A); cf. *Ep.* 70,5 (CV 54.707,19).
[11] Bardenhewer, *op. cit.*, p. 386; Le Bachelet, *art. cit.*, col. 2394.
[12] Socrates, *h.e.* III 10 (PG 67.405B); Rufinus, *h.e.* X 32 (GCS 9,2 p. 994).

An important see, however, remained in the hands of one of the leaders of the anti-orthodox group at the council of Rimini. Auxentius of Milan who had succeeded Dionysius, who was banished by the council of Milan (355), remained in office despite the condemnation by the synod of Paris. When Emperor Valentinian went to Milan, Hilary and Eusebius decided to bring about the deposition of Auxentius. A scholar has rightly asserted that it would be unjust to accuse Hilary of being a mere busy-body, for although he did interfere outside his own province, it was a serious crisis.[13] He realized that if Auxentius was allowed to retain his see, it might imperil the Church in the West.

Valentinian arrived at Milan in November 364 and left again in the following autumn.[14] The action by Hilary and Eusebius of Vercelli against Auxentius thus probably took place by the end of 364 or early 365. What measures Hilary and Eusebius took we do not know. It is generally believed that they tried to stir up the members of the congregation against Auxentius.[15] Hilary says that Valentinian issued a grave edict that the peace in the church of Milan was being disturbed. Hilary maintained that Auxentius was a blasphemer and an enemy of Christ and that he did not hold the same faith as the emperor and all the other bishops. The emperor ordered two imperial officials and ten bishops to hear the case. Auxentius stated that his two accusers had once been condemned by Saturninus and therefore ought not to be heard as bishops. The objection was rejected and it was decided that the matters of faith were to be discussed. Auxentius said that he believed that Christ was true God and of one divinity and substance with God the Father. It was decided that Auxentius had to write it down so that everybody would remember what he had said. The copy of Auxentius' creed which was added to Hilary's work,[16] is lost.

Auxentius testified that he stood by the resolutions of Nicé. He could do this because this was still the official creed in the Empire. Auxentius also denied that he had known Arius. Auxentius described Christ as "ante omnia tempora natum Deum verum filium." Hilary immediately saw that in accordance with Arian doctrine, "true" could be applied to the Son and not to God. The rumour was spread among the populace that Auxentius was orthodox and that his belief was the same as that of Hilary. The emperor accepted the report by Auxentius but Hilary was not satis-

---

[13] Watson, op. cit., p. xlix.
[14] Ammianus Marcellinus, Res Gestae XXVI 5,4–8.
[15] J. Zeiller, "Auxence," Dictionnaire d'histoire et de géographie ecclésiastiques, Paris, 1931, Vol. V, col. 935. This view is probably derived from Auxentius' words: aliqui ex plebe ... excitati ab Hilario et Eusebio, contra Aux. 13 (PL 10.617B).
[16] Contra Auxentium 7 (PL 10.613B–614B).

fied and maintained that Auxentius really denied the true faith. Hilary and Eusebius thereupon were commanded by the emperor to leave Milan.[17]

It has been said that Hilary's view of the events at Milan was a rather one-sided one.[18] On the other hand, the letter which Auxentius wrote to the emperor naturally gave Auxentius' view of the events, and it is not inconsistent with Hilary's report. Hilary's action in Milan might be justified because he considered it an important see and also because having learnt the finer points of the heresy, he might have detected them in the views of Auxentius while the other bishops might not have grasped it. Hilary thus lost his struggle with Auxentius but he may have gained the advantage that Auxentius would henceforth have to be careful in what he taught.

Hilary left Milan but addressed a book to his fellow-bishops which was described by Jerome as "elegans libellus contra Auxentium."[19] It must have been written by the end of 364 or in the course of 365.

Hilary praises peace and unity but maintains that the only unity of the Church and the Gospel is the peace of Christ (1). This book was written so that nobody might unjustly accuse him. There are many antichrists, for everyone who denies Christ as He was preached by the apostles is antichrist (2). The Church had never sought secular power to promote the faith and Nero, Vespasianus and Decius were no patrons of the Church (3), but now the Church did seek secular support and it was she who threatened with exile and imprisonment (4). The time of the antichrist has arrived and his ministers are transformed into angels of light (5).

Hilary enumerates the heretical views about Christ: He is not of the divinity of the Father but He is mightier and more excellent than all other creatures; through the will of God He subsisted from nothing; before all time He was born God from God, but He is not from the substance of God; the unity between the Father and the Son is one of will and not of divinity; the name God is attributed to Him but also to men; He is said to be Son of God but through baptism everyone becomes a son of God; He is before the ages and time but the angels and the devil are also before time. Hilary concludes that the same things are attributed to Christ which are also attributed to angels and human beings (6).

After describing the events at Milan (7–9), Hilary refutes some of the views of Auxentius. Christ is said to be the image of God, but man was also created as the image of God. Christ is called God, but Moses was also

[17] *Ibid.* 8–9 (PL 10.614B–615B).
[18] Cazenove, *art. cit.*, p. 477.
[19] Jerome, *de viris ill.* c. 100 (PL 23.739A).

called god to Pharaoh (Ex. 7:1). Christ is Son and first-born of God, but Israel is also named the first-born son to God. Hilary maintains that to him anyone who denies that the Son is of one divinity with the Father, is antichrist (11). Finally Hilary warns his readers to beware of the antichrist and to shun Auxentius as an angel of satan and an enemy of Christ. Hilary desires peace only with those who, like the Nicene fathers, declare the Arians anathema and proclaim that Christ is truly God (12).

A copy of the letter which Auxentius sent to the Emperors Valentinian and Valens follows. Auxentius declares that he never knew Arius nor had he ever known his doctrine. What he believes he has been taught from the Holy Scriptures from his infancy. He confesses that the Son was born "ante omnia saecula et ante omne principium natum ex Patre Deum verum filium ex vero Deo patre." Finally Auxentius declares that he adheres to the declaration of faith by the council of Rimini (13–15).

From the above we may see why Hilary was not satisfied with Auxentius' exposition of faith. The phrase quoted above about the Son could be interpreted in different ways. It may be assumed that Hilary wanted Auxentius to confess that Christ was from the substance of God. This is what Auxentius had declared when pressed by Hilary, but when he wrote it down, it was omitted.

It has been said that this work of Hilary is a manifestation of his courage in demanding the spiritual independence of the Church.[20] Hilary did accuse the Church of using the methods which civil authorities employed and he warned that what is loved by the world is not of Christ because the world hates Christ,[21] but he did not develop a clear theory of the difference between the Church and State. It seems as if he objected to the forceful methods used by the Church more than anything else

3. HIS LAST YEARS

Hilary's action against Auxentius was his last known action against the Arians. As far as we know he spent his last years quietly in Poitiers. During this time he probably wrote the other works which are ascribed to him.

He wrote a *Tractatus in Psalmos* which according to Jerome was an imitation of the work of Origen.[22] Bardy however, thinks that Hilary's

[20] Galtier, *op. cit.*, p. 167.
[21] *Contra Aux.* 3–4.
[22] Jerome, *de viris ill.* c. 100 (PL 23.738B–C); *Ep.* 61,2 (CV 54.577).

work is original in so far as a work which uses material from previous writers can be considered original.[23] In this work Hilary alluded to the doctrinal questions without being polemical. Some of the views expressed in his earlier works are more clearly expressed in this commentary. The original work probably contained a commentary on all the Psalms. Only fragments of the work have been discovered so far.

He also wrote a book on Job, some hymns, a *Liber mysteriorum* and some letters. Jerome knew of a book on Canticles but had not seen it himself. It was probably in these years that Hilary also published book III of his *Adversus Valentem et Ursacium*. The documents which came down to us contain no narrative text by Hilary. They are: the letter of the synod of Paris to the Eastern bishops[24]; a letter of Eusebius of Vercelli to Gregory of Elvira[25]; a letter of Liberius to the bishops of Italy and of the bishops of Italy to those of Illyria[26]; a letter of Germinius of Sirmium to the Arian bishops[27]; a letter by Valens, Ursacius, Gaius and Paulus to Germinius,[28] and finally a letter of Germinius to Rufianus, Palladius and other bishops.[29]

These last documents were probably written in the winter of 366/367 and Hilary's work was thus written in this time. The precise date of Hilary's death is unknown. According to Jerome Hilary died in the fourth year of the reign of Valentinian and Valens.[30] Gregory of Tours who is probably dependent on Jerome's *Chronica*, also states that Hilary died in the fourth year of the reign of these two emperors.[31] Sulpicius Severus said that the bishop of Poitiers died in the sixth year after his return from exile.[32] Hilary probably returned in the summer of 360. It has been said that he died on 13 January,[33] but some old ritual books say that he died on 1 November.[34] Some modern scholars therefore accept 1 November 367[35] as corresponding best with the above reports, but other scholars think it was 13 January 368.[36]

[23] Bardy, "Traducteurs," p. 273.
[24] *Coll. ant. Par.* Ser. A I (CV 65.43–46; *fragm.* XI 1–4 PL 10.710A–713A).
[25] *Ibid.* Ser. A II (CV 65.46–47; *fragm.* XI 5 PL 10.713B–714B).
[26] *Ibid.* Ser. B. IV (CV 65.156–159; *fragm.* XII PL 10.714B–717A).
[27] *Ibid.* Ser. A III (CV 65.47–48; *fragm.* XIII PL 10.717B–C).
[28] *Ibid.* Ser. B V (CV 65.159–160; *fragm.* XIV PL 10.718A–719A).
[29] *Ibid.* Ser. B VI (CV 65.160–164; *fragm.* XV PL 10.719B–724A).
[30] *Chron.* (GCS 47.245). Cf. *de viris ill.* c. 100 (PL 23.739A), where it is only said that it was during the reign of these two emperors.
[31] *Historia Francorum* I 39 (Monumenta Germaniae Historica, Rer. Merov. 1 1 (1884) p. 51.
[32] *Chron.* II 45,9 (CV 1.99).
[33] *Acta Sanctorum*, s.v. XIII Ianuarii § III 31 (p. 786).
[34] Cf. Coustant, *Vita S. Hil.* c. XIV 113–5 (PL 9.177A–178D).
[35] Feder, "Studien I," p. 126; Labriolle, *op. cit.*, p. 361.
[36] Cazenove, *art. cit.*, p. 475; Holmes, *op. cit.*, p. 183. Giamberardini, *Ilario*, p. 18, thought it could have been on 13 January, 367.

CONCLUSION

Born 310–320 A.D. of rich parents, Hilary was converted to Christianity as an adult. Very little is known about his early life and he was probably elected as bishop of Poitiers a few years before 355. Before he took an active part in the Arian struggle he wrote a *Commentary on Matthew*. It is likely that he had acquired a reasonable knowledge of Greek before he went into exile. In his *Commentary on Matthew* some indications are found that he knew about the Arian doctrines, but his early work is not a positive refutation of the heretical views.

The majority of the bishops in the western part of the Church were only directly drawn into the Arian dispute when Emperor Constantius convened synods at Arles (353) and Milan (355). Hilary who had probably not attended these two synods, then came to the fore with a decree in which he severed communion with the Arian leaders in the West. We do not know in which way this decree was drawn up and whether Hilary found wide support among the other bishops in Gaul. The Arian leaders, however, responded by convening a synod in Béziers in the beginning of 356, and Hilary was banished. Hilary, who probably did not get the chance to fully state his case, wrote a work in which he indicated that the real reason for the drive to condemn Athanasius was the denial of the Nicene faith rather than the rejection of Athanasius. Before he went into exile he published this historical work *Adversus Valentem et Ursacium*.

Before September 356 Hilary arrived in the East and probably spent most of his exile in Phrygia. To some extent he was free to travel around and in the East he learnt the finer points of the Arian dispute. During his years of exile he wrote his main work, known today as *De Trinitate*. The first three books of this work were written some time before the rest, either in Gaul or during the first year of his exile. After a lapse of time he resumed this task and completed it.

Hilary wrote this work because he felt compelled to and he also thought he was under an obligation to undertake the task of expounding the orthodox faith. He also wanted to reply to the attacks on the true faith made by the heretics. Hilary held the faculty of reason in high esteem, because it is this faculty in man which desires to know more about God. Man must however, realize the limits of his faculty of reason because reason cannot lead to the knowledge of God. Furthermore, there should be an intimate relation between faith and reason for only a correct faith leads to a correct use of the faculty of reason and vice versa. To interpret the Scriptures correctly one must not read the Scriptures with pre-conceived ideas; the context in which a text is found should be carefully studied; the meaning of the words that are used should not be altered and one text should not be over-emphasized to the exclusion of other Scriptural evidence. A conclusion should be made only after all the textual evidence has been considered. The correct interpretation of the Scriptures is only found in the Church.

In *De Trinitate* Hilary made use of the work of other theologians before him and of those of his own time. He began his book by refuting the letter of Arius to Alexander, but he also treated many other heretical views. Hilary began by showing that in spite of Deut. 6:4 there is a distinction within the Godhead. God the Father spoke to God the Son in the creation of the universe and in that of man. In the dealings with the Patriarchs there is also a distinction within the Godhead, and Hilary's next point was to prove that this Other Person was also truly God. Hilary showed that this Other Person was God because of His power and nature. Hilary also pointed out the absurdity of the distinction which the Arians made between "true God" and "not true God." If the Son of God is God He is true God, for one does not speak of "fire" and "not true fire."

Hilary then proved that Christ was the true Son of God and not only Son of God by adoption. Hilary pointed to the use of the pronoun "My" by the Father and the Son when referring to one another. The fact that the Son alone knows the Father was due to His generation from the Father. The apostles confirmed the view that they knew that Christ was truly the Son of God by virtue of His birth. The sense in which man is called son of God is totally different from that in which Jesus Christ is called Son of God. God the Father did not give a mere adopted son on behalf of man-kind, but manifested His love of mankind by giving His Only-begotten Son.

The Arians used the fact that God is confessed to be immutable and incorporeal as an argument against confessing that the Son was born of God. Therefore Hilary showed that the Son was Son of God by nature. The origin of a person determined his nature and Hilary showed that the Son of God has God as His only Source of origin. The birth did not introduce any new element into the nature of the Son to make Him not God, but birth bestows an equality of nature. If it was conceded that Christ was born from God, then it would follow that He has the same nature as God and thus is God, and Hilary accordingly proves that the Son was born from God.

The Arians contended that if it was said that the Son was born, then He could not be eternal. Hilary therefore pointed out the difference between being born of one who previously did not exist (as in the case of human beings) and being born of the eternal God. Time is within the sphere of human knowledge but the Son was born before times eternal and His birth does not fall within the range of human thought. God the Father is always Father and the Son is therefore always Son.

According to the Arians, the words in John 10:30 only referred to a unity of will between the Father and the Son and not to a unity of nature. Hilary did not deny that there was unanimity between God and Christ, but said that this was not the only basis of Their unity, for They are one in nature, glory and power.

Hilary discussed different texts which were cited by the Arians to deny the Divinity of the Son. Hilary explained that Christ did not want to be called "good" if He was not acknowledged as Lord and Christ as well. The text John 17:3 did not mean that there is only one true God in the sense that Christ was not God, for only the belief in God and in Him, Jesus Christ, Who was sent by God, gives eternal life. The text that the Son can do nothing of Himself did not imply a lack of strenght, but only indicated the source of His authority. The Father is also greater than the Son because He is Father, but the Son, because He is the Son of God, is not of a lesser nature than the Father. The Son said that He did not know the hour of His coming, not because He was subject to ignorance, but for the sake of mankind.

The Arians maintained that because of His fear during the Passion and His weakness in suffering, Christ could not have had the nature of God. Hilary's teaching on the passibility of Christ has been differently interpreted. Hilary apparently made contradictory statements on this subject. He maintained that Christ was truly man, but His origin was different from that of ordinary man, for He was conceived by the Holy Spirit. Christ thus had a body to suffer, but not the nature to suffer. Christ did suffer but in His own way, in accordance with His body which was conceived by the Holy Spirit. There is a Docetic strain in Hilary's thought.

Finally Hilary refuted the allegation that Christ was not equal to God the Father. The subjection of the Son to the Father as described in 1 Cor.

15:27–28 is not an end but a perfection and no loss of the kingdom. His subjection is only explained if it is referred to the temporal dispensation. In the end the believers will be renewed and brought unto the knowledge of God and created again in the image of the Creator. Through true worship of God man advances to eternity and will remain in the image of the Creator.

This work of Hilary was the first systematic refutation of Arianism by a Western theologian and its value can hardly be over-estimated. With this book Hilary introduced speculative theology into the West and although his book was to be surpassed by later Western theologians, they are indebted to Hilary for the foundation which he had laid. With this work Hilary also brought the main arguments of the Arians to the knowledge of all his Western colleagues and the theology of the East which had for a long time been unknown to the great majority of bishops in the West, was introduced to them. The Church in the West was fortunate that a man of the ability of Hilary could step in at this stage and produce a book of the merit of his *De Trinitate*.

But his greatest merit was probably his attempt to reconcile the East and the West by writing his *De Synodis*. He was perhaps the only person fully qualified for this task because he knew the theology of the East just as well as that of his own West.

The great value of Hilary's viewpoint expressed in this work was that he maintained that the interpretation of a formula was of importance and he pointed out the danger of blindly clinging to a formula (homoousios) as the banner of orthodoxy. This was especially of importance to the bishops in the West. He discussed the objections which the Homoeousians raised against *homoousios* and also appealed to his Western colleagues not to condemn *homoeousios* before it was ascertained what was meant by this word. Hilary admitted that in the latter term the personal distinction within the Trinity was safeguarded, and this was a disadvantage of *homoousios*. But if *homoeousios* was correctly used it would lead to *homoousios*. His whole exposition in *De Synodis* meant much to his Western colleagues. His work must have enlightened many of them and his suggestions of a less condemnatory and rigid attitude towards the Homoeousians must have made an impression on them because his orthodoxy was well-known in the West. On the other hand he could successfully allay the fears and objections of the Homoeousians to *homoousios*.

The fact that Hilary adopted this conciliatory attitude must be regarded as the chief merit of his work. Athanasius also adopted this attitude but although his work was published after that of Hilary it cannot be definitely proved that he was influenced by Hilary. Hilary's *De Synodis* has quite rightly been described as one of the greatest efforts of conciliation attempted in this struggle.[1]

Hilary's appeal did not lead to any immediate results because the emperor subjected the Church to his own will. It is difficult to determine whether Hilary's work had any influence on the bishops who attended the synod at Alexandria (362). This applies to a Western bishop like Eusebius of Vercelli, who a few years later closely worked with Hilary in the West. A scholar has asserted that it was due to Hilary that the Homoeousians joined the Homoousians at the synod of Alexandria (362) against the renewed Arianism.[2]

Another scholar has rightly pointed out that in spite of his ouvertures to the East, Hilary remained in fact a Western theologian with the Western emphasis of the unity of God. The East laid more emphasis on the fact that the Son was seen as a separate Person alongside the Father.[3] The final solution to this doctrinal problem was achieved by the Cappadocians who approached the Trinitarian problem from the Eastern pluralistic point of view.

Hilary played no positive part in the deliberations at Seleucia. At Constantinople he requested an audience with the emperor, but it was refused him and he was sent back to Gaul. In his two works to Constantius he did not formulate a theory on the difference between Church and State, but he did contribute towards this by the boldness with which he opposed the emperor.

In Gaul Hilary set about the task of inducing the bishops who had succumbed to the emperor at Rimini and Nicé to retract, and he was successful to a large extent. He did not, however, succeed in his attempt to have Auxentius of Milan deposed from his see. As far as we know he spent his last years quietly in Gaul.

Hilary was the greatest Western bishop in the Arian struggle and he truly merited the honour of being the first doctor of the Western Church, the title being bestowed on him by Pope Pius IX in 1851.

---

[1] Dormagen, *op. cit.*, p. 47.
[2] W. Pannenberg, "Christologie," *RGG*, Tübingen, 1957³, Vol. I, col. 1767.
[3] Löffler, *art. cit.*, p. 35.

BIBLIOGRAPHY

Aland, K., "Kaiser und Kirche von Konstantin biz Byzanz," *Kirchengeschichtliche Entwürfe*, Gütersloh, 1960, pp. 257-279.

Antweiler, A., "Des heiligen Bischofs Hilarius von Poitiers zwölf Bücher über die Dreieinigkeit, aus dem lateinischen übersetzt und mit Einleitung versehen," *Bibliothek der Kirchenväter*, Zweite Reihe, Vol. V-VI, München, 1933-4.

Bakhuizen van den Brink, J. N., "Traditie," *Pro Regno Pro Sanctuario. Een bundel studies en bijdragen van vrienden en vereerders bij de zestigste verjaardag van Prof. Dr. G. van der Leeuw*, Nijkerk, 1950, pp. 1-17.

— "Traditio," *Nederlands Theologisch Tijdschrift*, Vol. 2 (1947-8), pp. 321-340.

— "Traditio im theologische Sinne," *Vigiliae Christianae*, Vol. 13 (1959), pp. 65-86.

Baltzer, J. P., *Die Theologie des h. Hilarius von Poitiers*, Rottweil, 1879.

— *Die Christologie des hl. Hilarius von Poitiers*, Rottweil, 1889.

Bardenhewer, O., *Geschichte der altkirchlichen Literatur*, Vol. III, Freiburg im Breisgau, 1912.

— Sonderdruck der Nachträge und Ergänzungen aus der zweiten Auflage des 3. Bandes, Freiburg im Breisgau, 1923.

Bardy, G., "L'Occident en face de la crise arienne," *Irénikon*, Vol. 16 (1939), pp. 385-424.

— "Traducteurs et adaptateurs au IVe siècle," *Recherches de Science Religieuse*, Vol. 30 (1940), pp. 257-306.

— "Un humaniste chrétien: saint Hilaire de Poitiers," *Revue d'histoire de l'église de France*, Vol. 27 (1941), pp. 5-25.

Beck, A., "Die Lehre des hl. Hilarius von Poitiers über die Leidensfähigkeit des Leibes Christi," *Kirchliche Studien und Quellen*, Amberg, 1903, pp. 82-102.

— "Die Lehre des hl. Hilarius von Poitiers über die Leidensfähigkeit Christi," *Zeitschrift für katholische Theologie*, Vol. 30 (1906), pp. 108-122, 305-310.

Berkhof, H., *Die Theologie des Eusebius von Caesarea*, Diss. Leiden, Amsterdam, 1939.

— *De Kerk en de Keizer*, Amsterdam, 1946.

Beumer S.J., J., "Hilarius von Poitiers, ein Vertreter der christlichen Gnosis," *Theologische Quartalschrift*, Vol. 132 (1952), pp. 170-192.

Bidez, J., *La Vie de l'Empereur Julien*, Paris, 1930.

Brisson, J.-P., *Hilaire de Poitiers, Traité des Mystères* (Sources Chrétiennes 19), Paris, 1947.

Cazenove, J. G., "Hilarius Pictaviensis," *A Dictionary of Christian Biography and Literature*, ed. by H. Wace and W. C. Piercy, London, 1911, pp. 473-8.

Chadwick, H., "Hilarius von Poitiers," *Die Religion in Geschichte und Gegenwart*, Vol. III, 3rd ed., Tübingen, 1959.

Clercq, V. C. de, *Ossius of Cordova*, Diss. Catholic Univ. of America, Washington, 1954.

Coulange, L., "Métamorphose du Consubstantiel; Athanase et Hilaire," *Revue d'Histoire et de Littérature Religieuses*, Vol. 8 (1922), pp. 169-214.

Coustant, P., *Vita Sancti Hilarii* (PL 9.125-184), Paris, 1844.

Dormagen, Abbé E., *Saint Hilaire de Poitiers et l'Arianisme*, Saint-Cloud, 1864.
Dorner, J. A., *Entwicklungsgeschichte der Lehre von der Person Christi*, Vol. I, 2nd ed., Berlin, 1851.
Douais, Abbé C., *L'Église des Gaules et le conciliabule de Béziers*, Poitiers-Paris-Montpellier, 1875.
Duchesne, Abbé L., *Fastes épiscopaux de l'ancienne Gaule*, Vol. II, Paris, 1900.
Emmenegger, J. E., *The Functions of Faith and Reason in the Theology of Saint Hilary of Poitiers*, Diss. Catholic Univ. of America, Washington, 1947.
Evans, E., *Tertullian's Treatise against Praxeas*, London, 1948.
Feder S.J., A. L., "Studien zu Hilarius von Poitiers I. Die sogenannten *Fragmenta historica* und der sogenannte *Liber I ad Constantium imperatorem* nach ihrer Überlieferung, inhaltlichen Bedeutung und Entstehung," *SbW*, Vol. 162,4, Wien, 1910.
—   "Studien zu Hilarius von Poitiers II. Bischofsnamen und Bischofssitze bei Hilarius," *SbW*, Vol. 166,5, Wien, 1911.
—   "Studien zu Hilarius von Poitiers III. Überlieferungsgeschichte und Echtheitskritik des sogenannten *Liber II ad Constantium*, des *Tractatus mysteriorum*, der *Epistula ad Abram filiam*, der Hymnen. Kleinere Fragmente und Spuria," *SbW*, Vol. 169,5, Wien, 1912.
—   "Kulturgeschichtliches in den Werken des hl. Hilarius von Poitiers," *Stimmen aus Maria-Laach*, Vol. 81 (1911), pp. 30–45.
—   "Epilegomena zu Hilarius Pictaviensis I & II," *Wiener Studien*, Vol. 41 (1919), pp. 51–60, 167–181.
Förster, Th., "Zur Theologie des Hilarius," *Theologische Studien und Kritiken*, Vol. 61 (1888), pp. 645–686.
Galtier S.J., P., *Saint Hilaire de Poitiers le premier docteur de l'église latine*, Paris, 1960.
Giamberardini O.F.M., G., "De incarnatione Verbi secundum S. Hilarium Pictaviensem," *Divus Thomas*, Vol. 50 (1947), pp. 35–56, 194–205; Vol. 51 (1948), pp. 3–18.
—   *De Divinitate Verbi, Doctrina S. Hilarii Pictaviensis*, Cairo, 1951.
—   *S. Ilario di Poitiers e la sua attività apostolica e letteraria*, Cairo, 1956.
Gibbon, E., *The History of the decline and fall of the Roman Empire*, edited by J. B. Bury, Vol. II, London, 1909.
Gilg, A., *Weg und Bedeutung der altkirchlichen Christologie* (Theologische Bücherei Vol. IV), 2nd ed., München, 1961.
Goemans O.F.M., M., *Het Algemeen Concilie in de Vierde Eeuw*, Diss. Nijmegen, Nijmegen-Utrecht, 1945.
Greenslade, S. L., *Church and State from Constantine to Theodosius*, London, 1954.
Griffe, E., *La Gaule chrétienne à l'époque romaine*, Vol. I, *Des origines chrétiennes à la fin du IVe siècle*, Paris-Toulouse, 1947.
Gummerus, J., *Die homöusianische Partei bis zum Tode des Konstantius*, Helsingfors, 1900.
Gwatkin, H. M., *Studies of Arianism*, 2nd ed., Cambridge, 1900.
Haarhoff, T., *Schools of Gaul. A study of Pagan and Christian education in the last century of the Western Empire*, Oxford, 1920.
Haarlem, A. van, *Incarnatie en verlossing bij Athanasius*, Diss. Leiden, Wageningen, 1961.
Hahn, A., *Bibliothek der Symbole und Glaubensregeln der alten Kirche*, 3rd ed., revised by G. L. Hahn, Breslau, 1897.
Harnack, A. von, *Lehrbuch der Dogmengeschichte*, Vol. II, 4th ed., Tübingen, 1909.
Harvey, W. Wigan, *Sancti Irenaei Libros quinque adversus Haereses*, Vol. I–II, Cambridge, 1857.
Hefele, C. J. – Leclercq, H., *Histoire des Conciles*, Vol. I.2, Paris, 1907.
Holmes, T. Scott, *The Origin and Development of the Christian Church in Gaul during the First Six Centuries of the Christian Era*, London, 1911.

Jullian, C., *Histoire de la Gaule*, Vol. VII, Paris, 1926.

Kelly, J. N. D., *Early Christian Creeds*, London, 1950.

— *Early Christian Doctrines*, London, 1958.

Kidd, B. J., *A History of the Church to A.D. 461*, Vol. II, *A.D. 313–408*, Oxford, 1922.

Kraft, H., "'Ομοούσιος", *Zeitschrift für Kirchengeschichte*, Vol. 66 (1954–5), pp. 1–24.

Labriolle, P. de, *Histoire de la littérature latine chrétienne*, 3e éd. rev. et augm. par G. Bardy, Paris, 1947.

Le Bachelet, X., "Hilaire," *Dictionnaire de Théologie catholique*, Vol. VI.2, Paris, 1947, col. 2388–2462.

Leclercq, H., "Poitiers," *Dictionnaire d'archéologie chrétienne et de liturgie*, Vol. XIV.1, Paris, 1939, col. 1252–1340.

Lietzmann, H., "Hilarius, Bischof von Poitiers," *Paulys Real-encyclopädie der classischen Altertumswissenschaft*, Vol. VIII, Stuttgart, 1913, col. 1601–04.

— "Das Problem Staat und Kirche im weströmischen Reich," *AbhB*, Berlin, 1940.

— *Geschichte der alten Kirche*, Vol. III, *Die Reichskirche bis zum Tode Julians*, 2nd ed., Berlin, 1953.

Löffler, P., "Die Trinitätslehre des Bischofs Hilarius von Poitiers zwischen Ost und West," *Zeitschrift für Kirchengeschichte*, Vol. 71 (1960), pp. 26–36.

Loofs, F., "Hilarius von Poitiers," *Realencyklopädie fur protestantische Theologie und Kirche*, Vol. VIII, 3rd ed., Leipzig, 1900, pp. 57–67.

— Vol. XXIII, Ergänzungen und Nachträge A–K, Leipzig, 1913.

— *Leitfaden zum Studium der Dogmengeschichte*, 6th ed. by K. Aland, Pt. 1 & 2, Tübingen, 1959.

McHugh, J. F., *The Exaltation of Christ in the Arian Controversy*, Shrewsbury, 1959.

McKenna C.SS.R., S., "Saint Hilary of Poitiers—The Trinity," *The Fathers of the Church*, Vol. XXV, New York, 1954.

McMahon, J. J., *De Christo Mediatore Doctrina Sancti Hilarii Pictavensis*, Diss. Mundelein, Mundelein, 1947.

Müller, K., *Kirchengeschichte*, Vol. I.1, 2nd ed., Tübingen, 1929.

Opitz, H.-G., *Athanasius Werke*, Vol. II.1, Berlin, 1940–1.

Pannenberg, W., "Christologie," *Die Religion in Geschichte und Gegenwart*, Vol. I, 3rd ed., Tübingen, 1957.

Piganiol, A., *Histoire Romaine*, Vol. IV.2, *L'Empire Chrétien (325–395)*, Paris, 1947.

Prestige, G. L., *God in Patristic Thought*, 2nd ed., London, 1952.

Rasneur, G., "L'Homoiousianisme dans ses rapports avec l'orthodoxie," *Revue d'histoire ecclésiastique*, Vol. 4 (1903), pp. 189–206, 411–431.

Rauschen, G., "Die Lehre des hl. Hilarius von Poitiers über die Leidensfähigkeit Christi," *Theologische Quartalschrift*, Vol. 87 (1905), pp. 424–439.

— "Die Lehre des hl. Hilarius von Poitiers über die Leidensfähigkeit Christi," *Zeitschrift für katholische Theologie*, Vol. 30 (1906), pp. 295–305.

Reinkens, J. H., *Hilarius von Poitiers*, Schaffhausen, 1864.

Schanz, M., *Geschichte der römischen Litteratur bis zum Gesetzgebungswerk des Kaisers Justinian*, Vol. IV.1, 2nd ed., München, 1914.

Seeberg, R., *Lehrbuch der Dogmengeschichte*, Vol. II, Darmstadt, 1959 (Unveränderter photomechanischer Nachdruck der 3. Aufl., Leipzig, 1923).

Setton, K. M., *Christian attitude towards the Emperor in the Fourth Century especially as shown in addresses to the Emperor*, Diss. Columbia Univ., New York, 1941.

Smulders S.J., P., *La doctrine trinitaire de S. Hilaire de Poitiers* (Analecta Gregoriana Vol. XXXII), Rome, 1944.

Tillemont, M. Lenain de, *Mémoires pour servir à l'histoire ecclésiastique des six premiers siècles*, Vol. VII, 2nd ed., Bruxelles, 1732.

Viehhauser O.S.B., A., *Hilarius Pictaviensis geschildert in seinem Kampfe gegen den Arianismus*, Klagenfurt, 1860.

Watson, E. W., L. Pullan and others, "St. Hilary of Poitiers – Select Works," *A Select Library of Nicene and Post-Nicene Fathers of the Christian Church*, Second Series, Vol. IX, Grand Rapids-Michigan, 1955 (photolithoprinted = New York, 1908).
Weyer, H., *Novatianus, De Trinitate*, Darmstadt, 1962.
Wild, P. T., *The Divinization of Man according to Saint Hilary of Poitiers*, Diss. Mundelein, Mundelein, 1950.
Wilmart, Dom A., "L'Ad Constantium liber primus de Saint Hilaire de Poitiers et les Fragments historiques," *Revue Bénédictine*, Vol. 24 (1907), pp. 149–79, 291–317.
— "Les Fragments historiques et le Synode de Béziers en 356," *Revue Bénédictine*, Vol. 25 (1908), pp. 225–9.

INDEX

1. SCRIPTURE REFERENCES

Genesis
1:6,7   56
1:14   92
1:26   56, 60
5:3   154
15:6   114
16:9,10,13   57
17:20   57
18:10,17 ff   58
18:20–1   114
18:25   62
19:24   58, 61–2, 150
22:12   114
28:13   62
32:44f   62
35:1   58, 62

Exodus
3:2,4,6   58
3:14   62, 89–90
4:22   70
7:1   73, 137, 182

Deuteronomy
6:4   50, 51, 55, 59, 74

Psalms
15(16):10   118
21:32LXX   70
32:6LXX   93
44(45):8   58, 131, 132, 136
71:5LXX   92
71:17LXX   92
81(82):6   64, 73, 83
109:3LXX   72, 77–8
148:5LXX   56

Proverbs
8:21LXX   95
8:22LXX   92–5, 137
8:24,25LXX   93

8:26–30LXX   93
8:28–31LXX   57

Isaiah
1:2   64
1:14   127
9:5LXX   57
43:10   59
44:6   151
45:11LXX   93
45:11–16   59, 136
64:3LXX   63
65:1,2   63
65:13–16   63
65:16LXX   62

Hosea
1:7   59

2 Macc.
7:28   56

Matthew
3:17   64
5:17   132
7:2   35
7:23   115
9:4   115
10:22   132–3
10:38–9   118
11:27   62, 65, 67–8, 110, 137
12:18   59, 101
12:28   101
13:43   134
14:33   72
16:16   67
17:1–2   134
17:5   64, 70
23:10   107
25:12   115
25:34   134

Acts
1:7   117
2:16,17   101
4:32   97

Romans
5:10   69
8:3   69, 121
8:9–11   101
8:14,15   70
8:29   131
8:31–32   71
9:5   90, 103, 138
10:4   132
10:13ff   63
11:36   103, 135

1 Corinthians
1:9   69
1:23   127
2:7–8   128
3:8   97
8:6   55-6, 102, 108
12:5–6   102
12:28   102
13:13   34
15:3–4   128
15:24   134
15:26   134
15:27–8   132
15:28   134
15:47   119

2 Corinthians
13:4   106, 128

Galatians
3:27,28   98

Ephesians
1:19–22   133–4

2:3   70
4:4,5   98
4:5   130
4:11   102

Philippians
2:6   104
2:6–11   138
2:7   121
2:8   133
2:9   112
2:10   112
2:11   104
2:19,20   133
3:21   134

Colossians
1:15   36, 104, 130, 138
1:15–20   104
1:16   36, 60, 109
1:16,17   113
1:18   131
1:19–20   113
2:2–3   114
2:8   88
2:9   105
2:13–5   125
3:9,10   135

1 Thessalonians
5:2   113

Titus
1:2   90, 92

1 John
2:22   69
2:23   69
5:1   69, 73
5:20   69

2. REFERENCES TO ANCIENT WRITERS

Ammianus Marcellinus 29, 180
Athanasius 16, 23, 24, 31, 50, 53, 55, 56,
   58, 59, 61, 62, 64, 66, 70, 75, 76, 78, 79,
   82, 83, 84, 86, 87, 89, 94, 95, 96, 100,
   101, 102, 103, 104, 105, 107, 111, 113,
   114, 115, 123, 145, 148, 150, 156, 157,
   159, 160, 161, 165, 166, 175, 177
Augustine 4, 40
Ausonius 6

Cassian 40
Cassiodorus 40, 139
Epiphanius 141, 142, 166
Facundus 24
Gregory of Tours 183
Irenaeus 58, 59, 65, 74, 103, 113, 123
Jerome 1, 4, 6, 11, 12, 32, 38, 40, 139,
   174, 179, 181, 182, 183
Lucifer 175

3. REFERENCES TO MODERN AUTHORS

4. REFERENCES TO OTHER PROPER NAMES